Annual Review of Addictions and Offender Counseling II

Annual Review of Addictions and Offender Counseling II

Best Practices

Edited by
STEPHEN SOUTHERN
and KATHERINE L. HILTON

RESOURCE *Publications* • Eugene, Oregon

ANNUAL REVIEW OF ADDICTIONS AND OFFENDER COUNSELING II
Best Practices

Copyright © 2015 Wipf and Stock Publishers. All rights reserved. Except for brief quotations in critical publications or reviews, no part of this book may be reproduced in any manner without prior written permission from the publisher. Write: Permissions, Wipf and Stock Publishers, 199 W. 8th Ave., Suite 3, Eugene, OR 97401.

Resource Publications
An Imprint of Wipf and Stock Publishers
199 W. 8th Ave., Suite 3
Eugene, OR 97401

www.wipfandstock.com

ISBN 13: 978-1-4982-1713-2

Manufactured in the U.S.A. 04/09/2015

Contents

1. Editorial   1
2. Powerful Resolutions for Addictions with Mind-Body Counseling Techniques   6
   Jan C. Lemon and Buddy Wagner
3. Understanding Substance Abuse Through an Adlerian Theoretical Lens: An Exploration of Adler's Theory as Applied to Substance Abuse and Treatment   22
   Katie A. Wachtel, Todd F. Lewis, and Stephen P. Hebard
4. Addiction Training in Counselor Education: A Survey of the Current Status and Future Plans   41
   Tiffany K. Lee and Gary H. Bischof
5. Training Students in Counselor Education Programs in Process Addictions: A Pilot Study   66
   Judith A. Nelson, Angie D. Wilson, and Leigh F. Holman
6. Competency Based Alcohol and Drug Clinical Supervision Model   84
   Christine Chasek
7. Multiple Relationships with Clients: Applying the Concept of Potentially Beneficial Interactions to the Practice of Addiction Counseling   96
   Kevin Doyle

8   Brief Alcohol Counseling Interventions in a Trauma Setting with Latina/o Clients   108
    Nathaniel N. Ivers, Laura J. Veach, Regina R. Moro, Jennifer L. Rogers, and Mary Claire O'Brien

9   Incorporating Family Systems Models into Substance Abuse Interventions with Latino Adults   126
    Aaron S. Hymes

10 Providing Forensic Services in Community Mental Health Agencies: Ethical Considerations and Forensic Training Needs of Community Mental Health Counselors   141
    Courtney C. C. Heard

11 The MO(o)D PIRATE Malingering Mnemonic Risk Assessment: General Implications and Guidelines for Correctional Counselors   156
    Paul A. Carrola and Gerald A. Juhnke

12 Assessment of Treatment Fidelity to Moral Reconation Therapy: Are Treatment Providers Adrift?   177
    James S. Korcuska, David Hulac, and Irene Harper

1

Editorial

The *Annual Review of Addictions and Offender Counseling II: Best Practices* represents the desire of the editorial board of the *Journal of Addictions and Offender Counseling (JAOC)* to promote high quality literature focused on the practice of counseling in these fields. The first *Annual Review* began as a way to maintain publication of practice-focused literature while the scope of JAOC was refocused toward publication of primary research findings. The executive board of the International Association of Addictions and Offender Counselors (IAAOC), authorized the development of these publications for members and all counseling professionals.

This second volume continues the mission of the first. The content specifically targets issues pertinent to counseling practice with addictions and offender populations, including but not limited to ethics, theory, assessment, treatment techniques, clinical resources, education, and training and supervision. We have endeavored to secure manuscripts from addictions and offender counseling, although JAOC and the *Annual Review* tends to receive submissions addressing various aspects of substance use disorders. We included some training or professional issues manuscripts, as well as some research articles with clinical practice implications. It was especially important to include chapters addressing treatment needs of Latino/a populations. The following chapters are included in the second volume of the *Annual Review of Addictions and Offender Counseling*.

Powerful Resolutions for Addictions with Mind-Body Counseling Techniques

JAN C. LEMON AND BUDDY WAGNER

The authors provide current literature and techniques in Mind-Body Therapy for addictions counseling. In addition, the authors discuss the connection between neuroscience and addiction counseling and provide methods that work on subconscious emotional processes of the client.

Understanding Substance Abuse Through an Adlerian Theoretical Lens

KATIE A. WACHTEL, TODD F. LEWIS, AND STEPHEN P. HEBARD

Substance abuse and addiction exact an enormous toll on society. As such, it is important to identify positive and effective treatment models. Alfred Adler's theory of Individual Psychology is one such model that offers a compelling perspective of how substance abuse problems develop, as well as a variety of interventions.

Addiction Training In Counselor Education

TIFFANY K. LEE AND GARY H. BISCHOF

The authors examined the state of addiction instruction among CACREP programs and the methods used to integrate the 2009 CACREP addiction-related competencies. The study investigated if programs had plans to add addiction courses, faculty with expertise, and the Addiction Counseling option.

Training Students in Counselor Education Programs in Process Addictions: A Pilot Study

JUDITH A. NELSON, ANGIE D. WILSON, AND LEIGH F. HOLMAN

The addictions field continues to grow and is expanding beyond the area of substance use disorders. Process addictions are now an integral aspect of addictions treatment, diagnosis, and assessment. An initial study was conducted to initiate an understanding of levels of knowledge students in counselor education programs have in diagnosing, assessing and treating clients with process addictions, indicators of where and how they learned about process addictions, and of how students believe they will integrate their level of the treatment of process addictions into clinical practice. This article provides a brief overview of process addictions, a summary of original research, implications of this study, discussion, and recommendations for future research.

Competency Based Alcohol and Drug Clinical Supervision Model

CHRISTINE CHASEK

A competency based supervision model is proposed combining the framework developed by the Center for Substance Abuse Treatment, the Blended Model of Supervision, and the Integrated Developmental Model based on supervisee needs. The application and structure of the newly defined Competency Based Alcohol and Drug Clinical Supervision Model is presented.

Multiple Relationships with Clients: Applying the Concept of Potentially Beneficial Interactions to the Practice of Addiction Counseling

KEVIN DOYLE

Counselors who work with clients with substance use disorders face numerous possibilities for interactions with current and former clients. The current ACA Code of Ethics continues to permit potentially beneficial interactions, a concept introduced in the previous Code. An overview of these interactions is presented, along with proposed guidelines for counselors and supervisors to ensure ethical behavior.

Brief Alcohol Counseling Interventions in a Trauma Setting with Latino/a Clients

NATHANIEL N. IVERS, LAURA J. VEACH, REGINA R. MORO, JENNIFER L. ROGERS, AND MARY CLAIRE O'BRIEN

Alcohol screenings and brief counseling interventions (ASBCIs) administered at trauma centers can help reduce risky drinking behaviors. However, few guidelines exist for culturally modifying ASBCIs for Latinas/os. Utilizing the cultural concepts of locus of control, individualism-collectivism, and communication styles, we present guidelines to consider when providing ASBCI to Latina/o clients.

Incorporating Family Systems Models into Substance Abuse Interventions with Latino Adults

AARON S. HYMES

Substance abuse with Latino adults remains a problem in the United States of America. Family systems theory (Bowen, 1991) focuses on interdependence in the family leading to balance and decreased dysfunction. Family systems theory incorporated into substance abuse interventions with Latino adolescents shows positive outcomes yet has not been applied to interventions with Latino adults. This article seeks to describe the need to incorporate family systems theory into substance abuse interventions used with Latino adults.

Providing Forensic Services in Community Mental Health Agencies: Forensic Training Needs of Community Mental Health Counselors

COURTNEY C. C. HEARD

This article addressed the training needs of community mental health counselors providing forensic services. Disparities in forensic mental health counseling training are contextualized through a discussion of forensic programs in operation in community mental health agencies.

The MO(o)D PIRATES Malingering Mnemonic Risk Assessment: General Implications and Guidelines for Correctional Counselors

PAUL A. CARROLA AND GERALD A. JUHNKE

Corrections counselor frequently encounter inmates who report severe emotional and psychological symptoms and stressors. To date, no standardized, free, brief, face-to-face malingering risk assessment exists within the counseling literature and none has been published in the IAAOC's flagship journal, JAOC. To address this malingering risk assessment absence, the authors created the MO(o)D PIRATE Malingering Mnemonic Risk Assessment. The assessment is an evidenced informed instrument that considers 9 malingering risk factors identified within the literature or experienced by the author's combined span of 37 years counseling and consulting in corrections.

Assessment of Treatment Fidelity to Moral Reconation Therapy: Are Treatment Providers Adrift?

JAMES S. KORCUSKAK, DAVID HULAC, AND IRENE HARPER

Moral Reconation Therapy (MRT; Little & Robinson, 1988) is a widely used treatment program for offenders. Treatment effect size is small (Ferguson & Wormith, 2012) and fidelity of implementation (FOI) of MRT unclear (Wilson, Bouffard, & Mackenzie, 2005). We examined FOI for a statewide offender program. Providers trained in MRT delivered it to participants in a pretrial sentencing program. No previous studies of MRT have employed a fidelity of implementation measure. Since no known Provider Quality Assessment (PQA) tool for MRT existed, we developed one. Our results from the MRT Integrity Check (MICk) suggest that providers registered treatment with moderately high levels of fidelity, but that group facilitation skills as measured by the Group Psychotherapy Intervention Rating Scale (GPIRS; Burlingame, Fuhriman, & Johnson, 2002) were under-utilized

Stephen Southern and Kate Hilton
Department of Psychology & Counseling
Mississippi College
Clinton, Mississippi.

2

Powerful Resolutions for Addictions with Mind-Body Counseling Techniques

JAN C. LEMON AND BUDDY WAGNER[1]

The authors provide current literature and techniques in Mind-Body Therapy for addictions counseling. In addition, the authors discuss the connection between neuroscience and addiction counseling and provide methods that work on subconscious emotional processes of the client.

The field of addiction counseling has changed significantly over the last few years as a result of advances in neuroimaging, electrophysiology, and genetic analysis. Through the understanding of neuroscience and the brain, scientist, counselors, and psychologists have a greater awareness of addictive behaviors, tolerance, and withdrawal. Leshner (2001) stated, "We now know in great detail the brain mechanisms through which drugs acutely modify mood, memory, perception, and emotional states" (p. 75). As with many chronic brain diseases, current therapies for addiction are helpful to some, but far from adequate for others. Because we now know

---

1. Jan C. Lemon, Department of Counseling and Psychology, Mississippi College; Buddy Wagner, Department of Counseling and Psychology, Mississippi College. Correspondence concerning this article should be addressed to Jan C. Lemon, Department of Psychology and Counseling, Box 4013, Clinton, MS 39058. Email: lemon@mc.edu

so much about the neurotransmitter interactions in the brain, addiction treatment can be overly regarded as an abnormality of brain physiology that is resolved by the correct psychopharmacologic agent (Hyman & Malenka, 2001). This purely medical approach omits client behaviors, personal characteristics, and environmental factors and ignores the soul of the individual. The physiology of the brain can be changed by using techniques that transform thoughts, actions, and emotions and by training the client's brain for emotional and physical well-being. This article provides research and techniques concerning Mind-Body Therapy for addictions and suggests a "whole person" approach, which may include current medical therapeutic methods when needed with adjunct techniques that work on the subconscious emotional processes of the client and activate innate mental resources that are used to restore harmony and health (Lemon & Wagner, 2013).

Mind-Body techniques treat the entire person by helping the client improve his or her self-esteem, change unproductive thoughts, gain control over addictive patterns, and improve general health. Effective counseling, using these methods, not only changes the thoughts, emotions, and beliefs but actually changes the brain as well. Through the concepts of neuroplasticity and neurogenesis, Mind-Body Therapy transforms the brain and supports the building of new neurons (Ivey, Ivey, Zalaquett, & Quirk, 2009). Mental health professionals are now becoming enlightened about the relationship between therapy and neuroscience and are using mind/body techniques to override the brain and modify its function (Peres & Nasello, 2008). Mind-Body Therapy discovers the client's strengths and uses these strengths to help resolve the problem. In addition, this view of counseling recognizes that most problems are not solvable, but resolvable. The client does not need to spend a lifetime stuck in the problem when enough of the problem can be resolved so that life is improved for the client. This positive approach to recovery offers an alternative and complementary means to overcome addiction. Specifically, this article will discuss specific Mind-Body Therapies such as Mindfulness, hypnosis, and Neuro-linguistic Programing and will include current research and specific techniques to use in the treatment process.

Mindfulness

Related Literature

Jon Kabat-Zin (2005) defines mindfulness as "moment to moment non-judgmental awareness cultivated by paying attention in a specific way, that is, in the present moment, and as non-judgmentally and as openheartedly as possible" (p. 108). Brewer, Bowen, Smith, Marlatt, and Patenze (2009) stated, "A recent consensus definition of mindfulness emphasizes two complementary elements: (1) the placement of attention on the immediate experience; and (2) adopting an open curious, accepting attitude towards that experience" (p. 1699). Even though mindfulness practices are centuries old, they are just recently being used in the area of addictions. O'Connell (2009) stated that there is a growing body of evidence to show that mindfulness has a number of useful applications in clinical practice and serves as an adjunct to traditional regimes. The author further stated that mindfulness motivates patients to understand their feelings and provides the methodology to improve awareness of triggers that may cause relapse. In addition, the author found that mindfulness methods are well-received by both patients and staff, and mindfulness practices help individuals become aware of their compulsive thinking.

Brewer, et al (2009) stated that recent neurobiological and cognitive data support two specific components of mindfulness: (a) attention and (b) acceptance. These two areas target rumination and stress, which are important in the treatment of substance abuse disorders. The authors add that as patients practice mindfulness they have a greater ability to maintain focus and pay attention in the present moment. The study concluded that Mindfulness Training decreases avoidance, provides a greater tolerance to unpleasant systems and emotional states, and creates awareness of maladaptive behaviors.

Dakwar, Mariani, and Levin (2011) studied mindfulness impairments in individuals seeking treatment for substance abuse. The authors stated, "Mindfulness has become increasingly important in the fields of mental health, pain management, stress reduction, and most recently, substance use disorder treatment" (p. 165). The study examined mindfulness impairments in a substance-using population using the *Mindful Attention Awareness Scale* (MAAS). The subjects were 315 treatment-seeking individuals at a university-based clinical research site. The results indicated that mindfulness-related attentional impairments may be common in individuals seeking treatment for substance abuse disorders, and that treatment using Mindfulness practices provided positive results. The study further discussed the high comorbidity between ADHD and SUDs and stated that the impairments in attention may lead to increased vulnerability to substance abuse.

Because Mindfulness Training shifts attention from a passive state to an intentional state, the client is instructed to practice paying attention in the present moment, which may break the ruminative cycle and lead to less stress (Brewer, et al., 2009). Other studies have found that Mindfulness practice allows clients to become more aware of the compulsive nature of their thinking, to understanding thoughts and emotions as opposed to controlling them, and to decrease stress in the role of relapse prevention (O'Connell, 2009; Ostafin, Bauer, & Myxter, 2012; Vallejo & Amaro, 2009).

Techniques

Exercises in sensing. Kabat-Zin (1990) describes a technique called body scanning. These sessions last from ten to twenty minutes and are composed of the client deeply breathing while experiencing all of the sensations in the body. The client takes a slow journey through the body focusing attention on one area at a time. This is done through quietly meditating while focusing on one's breath. Beginning with the crown of the head, the client should focus on this area while continuing to breathe slowly. A simple affirmation may be added at each point while being totally aware of each area of the body. O'Connell (2009) adds to the body scanning discussion, "For those with high levels of agitation, a mindfulness activity such as walking or swimming is recommended instead. Exercises with breath awareness or breath counting are given to those with high levels of anxiety and those experiencing widespread physical pain" (p. 186). In addition to the scanning, the clients are asked to continue being mindful throughout the day of other activities using the same method of focusing intently.

Taking refuge. Jacobs-Stewart (2010) stated that there is a tradition in Buddhism of taking refuge through three specific practices. According to the author these practices are: (a) taking refuge in awakening, (b) taking refuge in the path of understanding and love, and (c) taking refuge in community. The author added that the practice of taking refuge in awakening is characterized by clients awakening to the spiritual essence within us and learning the concept of simply being. This practice is founded on the core belief that each individual has an essential essence that is beautiful, lovely, and true. The client is taught to appreciate who they really are and to experience the joy of total acceptance. In addition, the Jacobs-Stewart discusses taking refuge in the path of understanding and love. This technique requires sitting in meditation and welcoming all the different thoughts and allowing them to simply flow through the mind. It also involves embracing all the feelings and sensations that come with the thoughts and recognizing that thoughts do not have to be believed. Jacobs-Stewart concludes with discussing the concept of taking refuge in community. This involves having the wisdom and support an individual needs by drawing from the encouragement and teaching of significant others. Taking refuge with important individuals in one's life provides a validation of unconditional acceptance from kind and caring people.

Loving-kindness meditation. Leppma (2012) stated, "Loving-kindness meditation is a type of mindfulness-based meditation that emphasizes caring and connection with others" (p. 197). To heal into the depths of an addictive mind, clients admits their wrongs and receive the acceptance and kindness of another individual and follow with the practice of cultivating loving-kindness towards ourselves (Jacobs-Stewart, 2010). One particular technique is to have clients in a seated position with eyes closed while focusing on their breath. During meditation, the participants imagine a cherished loved one and allow tender, loving feelings to be generated toward that person. While enjoying these feelings of love, clients turn these feeling toward themselves and relax into warmth and acceptance (Leppma, 2012).

Coping with thinking. O'Connell (2009) discusses an exercise in which the client is taught to differentiate between compulsive thinking and mindfulness. The author adds that most addicts have problems with turning off constant thoughts, and that this technique is promoted as a way to reduce the inner mental noise. The client is asked to focus on a specific part of their body while calculating two double digit numbers. According to O'Connell, this simple exercise demonstrates that active feeling can override compulsive thinking and moves awareness away from resentment, injustice, loss, or anger. When clients shift their awareness to a body part, they can no longer focus on chaos and pain in their own lives.

Ericksonian Hypnosis

Related Literature

Bell-Gadsby (2001) pointed out that the traditional model of treating addictions is limiting, and that this traditional view point assumes that all addicts fit into one class with the one principle of treatment being abstinence. Ericksonian hypnosis, on the other hand, creates an environment of acceptance rather than judgment and of health rather than pathology. Manganiello (1984) found significant differences among methadone addicts who were treated with hypnosis compared to those who were treated by conventional means. In this study the group receiving hypnosis experienced less discomfort, less drug use, and a higher percentage of participants remained drug free at a six month follow-up (94%). In another study, Potter (2004) used hypnosis as a treatment means for 18 clients, which was composed of 15 alcoholics, 2 cocaine addicts, and a marijuana addict. After a one-year period, 14 of the participants were free of addiction. The hypnosis method used in this study was borrowed from an effective alcoholism treatment program, which used an intensive regime of 20 daily sessions.

Page and Handley (1993) reported that hypnosis was successfully used to help a female in her twenties overcome a $500 (five grams) per day cocaine addiction. Two amazing facts surrounded this report: (a) the client had been drug free for nine years when the article was written, and (b) hypnosis was the only intervention used. Another study by Pekala, et al. (2004) evaluated the effectiveness of a self-hypnosis protocol with chronic drug and alcohol patients in increasing self-esteem, improving affect, and preventing relapse. The study employed four experimental groups: (a) a control group, (b) a hypnosis treatment group, (c) a trans-theoretical cognitive-behavioral group (TCB), and (d) a stress management (attention-placebo) group. Participants consisted of 261 veterans admitted to a Substance Abuse Residential Rehabilitation Treatment Program (SARRTP). Participants were assessed using a pre- and post-intervention and again at a 7-week follow-up. The results indicated that hypnosis was not only effective in preventing relapse but also proved to be a useful adjunct in helping chronic substance abuse individuals with their reported self-esteem, serenity, and anger/impulsivity.

In Ericksonian hypnosis, the individual's unique personality, skills, and behaviors are used to facilitate change. Individuals are empowered to access previously undiscovered inner resources and abilities to resolve the addiction. Each individual works out his or her own plan for recovery. Rather than being powerless to deal with the addiction, this approach believes that each individual has the ability to take an active role in recovery. Most addicts are afraid to face many of the core issues that led them to abuse substances, and these issues often revolve around past traumas. These past traumas can be treated through reframing, indirect suggestion, and metaphors and may assist the client to self-soothe in healthy ways (Bell-Gadsby, 2001). Rossi (1993, 1996) stated that many addictions have their compulsion source in the prolonged stresses of everyday life. He indicated that these addictions can often be resolved through therapy that is oriented toward insight, attitude, and behavior change. Other authors noted that understanding hypnosis empowers the therapist to find client's strengths, use indirect suggestions, utilize what the client gives at the present moment, and assist the client in setting positive goals (Bell-Gadsby, 2001; O'Hanlon, 2011; Wagner, 2012; Zeig, 1990). Hypnosis is not a cure-all; however, it has been proven to be a viable tool to use in the treatment of addictions. It is respectful of the client and allows the client is become the expert in finding resolutions to the addiction.

Techniques

Task assignment. This technique is used as a counterintuitive procedure. Rather than suggesting the lessening or refraining from the addictive behavior, the suggestion is made to perform the addictive behavior in a different way. This is a very simple method to loosen a client's belief system and help the client solve his or her own problem. For example, the therapist might ask the compulsive eater to eat for fifteen minutes at the first of every hour for a specific time period. When the typical behavior pattern is changed, it loses it power and falls apart. For this technique to be successful, the therapist must be sincere and serious and be confident that the client will perform the assignment.

Turning the addictive behavior into an ordeal. This practice involves giving the client permission to continue with the addictive behavior but to make it such an ordeal that the substance is not worth what it takes to get it. For example, if an alcoholic stops at a particular bar on his way home from work, suggest that he can drink but only if he drives 20 miles out of his way to drink. Another alternative would be to suggest that the client stop at his favorite bar but can only have one drink every 20 minutes and between drinks must leave the bar and engage in a conversation with a stranger before having another drink.

Linking the destructive behavior to a healthy behavior. This practice suggests that the individual might continue with the addictive behavior but perform a healthy behavior as he is performing the addictive behavior. For example, a smoker might choose to smoke but must go outside and walk around the block while smoking. Linking the two behaviors allows the client to continue with the addictive behavior but moves the client toward a healthy behavior. Often the person will do more and more of the healthy behavior and less and less of the addictive behavior. The goals are to see the addictive behavior as no longer consequential, and eventually the client will stop the behavior altogether using the time for something more productive.

Utilization of client's motivation. In this practice, the client is not expected to do more or less than he or she is motivated to do. If the client's motivation is low then the client is asked to take a small, easy step. If the motivation is high, the client is asked to take larger steps. For example, if an alcoholic is not very motivated to quit, then the assignment might be that the individual wait 60 seconds before taking a drink when one is desired. With high motivation, the client may be asked to cut the number of drinks in half.

Reframing. Lankton and Lankton (1983) defined reframing as the process of helping the client to identify a different framework for understanding and resolving a problem. Related to addictions, the therapist would help the client restate the addiction in a way so that it is no longer a problem. The therapist would attempt to reframes the label of "addict" and asks the person, "What are the behaviors that cause you to be labeled an addict?" In revealing the behaviors, the client now has specific actions that can be discussed and changed. According to the authors, this new way of viewing the problem might eliminate resistance, lead to more effective means of satisfying the actual needs of the client, and create the possibility of new learning.

Posthypnotic suggestion. In this particularly technique, a suggestion is made during trance that will be performed at some later time. It is usually tied to a piece of behavior that causes the problem. For example, the suggestion might be made that every time you lift your hand to take a drink, you will be aware that you can lift yourself out of your addiction by making better choices. Alman and Lambrou (1992) stated that posthypnotic suggestions are a powerful extension of hypnosis. These suggestions can enhance one's ability to change or improve actions and feelings at will. Obviously a posthypnotic suggestion cannot be used if hypnosis is not used; however, the concept can be utilized in traditional talk therapy. For example, the client might repeat over and over throughout the day, "Every time I lift my hand to take a drink, I am aware of my personal power to lift myself out of my addiction by making better choices." Over time, the individual will be aware of the choice he or she has with each drink, rather than making an unconscious choice to drink.

Symptom prescription. According to Erickson (1985), this technique allows the therapists to participate in the symptomatology by first accepting it, which then opens the possibility of manipulating it out of existence. Erickson was creative in finding different ways to prescribe a symptom. His methods included symptom scheduling, symptom embellishment, symptom displace, and symptom substitution (Short, Erickson, and Klien, 2006). Symptom scheduling is setting times when the individual will actually perform the symptom. For example, the therapist might prescribe that the person drink alcohol only at scheduled times of the day. The individual would need to watch the clock to perform the activity at the exact time on the agreed schedule.

Symptom embellishment is increasing the number of times the behavior occurs. If the person normally drinks three times a day, the number of times might be increased to six. Symptom displacement is leaving the symptom in a specified place limiting where a person would be allowed to drink. Symptom substitution is experiencing the symptom in a different way. For example, if the addict drinks primarily beer, then the client might replace the beer with other drinks that he or she less prefers. Rather than trying to eliminate the symptom, the therapist prescribes the symptom as the cure, which gives the client control of the problem.

Neuro-linguistic Programming

Related Literature

Neuro-linguistic Programming (NLP) is an approach to communication, personal development, and psychotherapy created in the 1970s. The title refers to a stated connection between the neurological processes, language, and behavioral patterns that have been learned through experience, which can be utilized and organized to achieve specific goals in life (O'Connor & Seymour, 2011). In NLP, nominalizations are distortions of reality. A nominalization turns a set of actions or symptoms into a static label, thereby, missing the dynamic reality of the problem itself. Using the label "addiction" misses the underlying usefulness of the behavior and does not allow the client to understand how the behavior has served a practical use in his or her life (Gray, 2013). Bandler & Grinder (1982) described these behaviors as positive intentions. In the process of reframing the addictive behavior, the mind is asked: (a) "What is this behavior's function?" and (b) "What is the positive intention of this behavior?" The premise is that every behavior serves a purpose, and once the positive intent of the behavior is recognized, the individual can begin to find a healthy way to accomplish this purpose.

Gray (2013) suggested that we think of preferences and skills instead of diseases. When we think of an addiction as a set of preferences, then we may be able to find a more valuable set of preferences to replace the problem set. Finding the usefulness of the problem behavior makes it possible to find personal activities that lead to resolution. Bandler & Grinder

(1982) stated that the addict is a multiple personality in that he or she has two ways of operating in the world—a drugged state and a sober state. Treating an addict from a NLP standpoint is to set an anchor for each state and then collapse the anchors. The next step is to communicate with the part that makes the client abuse drugs and find out the secondary gain of the behavior. Finally, find alternative behaviors that get the secondary gains but do not produce the damage that the drug produces. Addictions are treated by providing the client with a response option that is more powerful, more accessible, and more immediate than the drug itself.

Gray (2013) suggested that we think of an addiction as a learned skill set that becomes preferred patterns of behavior. With this knowledge of personal behaviors, the client can find a pattern of behavior that is more effective and is able to embrace social integration, positive self-regard, and transcendence. When this occurs, the addictive behaviors cease. Andreas and Andreas (1989) suggested using the method of compulsion blow-out to solve the immediate problem of craving and to discover a more purposeful behavior. The authors stated that this technique allows an individual to eliminate even very intense, strong compulsions. After a compulsion is broken, the individual is still able to do the behavior without the compulsive desire.

A more elegant approach to the problem of addiction was provided by Andreas & Andreas (1994). The authors stated that many people use drugs to try to induce inner states similar to the states produced by the process of Core Transformation. While drugs might produce these states temporarily, this false sense of peace creates a variety of problems. The fact that so many in our culture rely on drugs indicates how strong the desire is to experience inner well-being. The approach of Core Transformation leads the individual to uncover a series of outcome sequiturs from the problem behavior that would eventually lead to deep, core-level values and experiences. These core values could be understood as the ultimate positive intent of the behavior. As these core values are revealed on a conscious level, the client is empowered to redirect organismic energies. Andreas & Andreas (1994) gave an example of working with an individual who had been addicted to alcohol for 20 years, which included drinking a 12-pack of beer every day. Earlier NLP work had brought some resolution to the problem, but the process of Core Transformation helped him resolve the issue more completely. Through this process, the individual made a significant shift in his response to alcohol.

Techniques

The Swish. This is a generative pattern that programs the brain to go in a new direction. To perform this technique, the individual uses imagery to see himself or herself as a sober individual. Through this imagery process, the client creates a personal picture, which embellishes the value of changing the addictive habit, includes the differences it would make to him or her as a person, and provides a new depth of meaning in life. In other words, the client creates a new self-picture without the habit. The client would then be asked to create a second personal portrait that portrays using the drug. This undesirable picture would be big and bright with the imagined sober picture placed in the lower right corner. This technique calls for the sober picture to be small and dark. The client would then perform the swish technique, which would include making the smaller, darker, sober picture become bigger and brighter until it covers the drug using picture, which simultaneously gets smaller and darker. The client would quickly complete this process five times while allowing a blank screen between each swish. (Bandler, 1985)

Six-Step Reframing. Changing the frame in which a person perceives events in order to change the meaning is called reframing. By changing the meaning, responses and behaviors also change. Bandler and Grinder (1982) developed a six-step process for reframing: (a) the pattern to be changed must be identified, (b) establish communication with the part responsible for the pattern, (c) separate the behavior from the positive intention of the part responsible for the behavior, (d) access a creative part and generate new behaviors to accomplish the positive function, (e) ask the part if it is willing to take responsibility for using the new alternatives in the appropriate context, and (f) do an ecological check to be sure that no part of the person objects to the new alternatives. An ecological check is simply asking if any part of the person has an objection to the new behaviors. If there is an objection, then the objection must be alleviated before the new behavior will be successful.

Core Transformation. Andreas and Andreas (1994) developed a ten-step process, which invites the client to identify the behaviors, feelings, and responses of the addiction. The therapist then uses these revelations to lead the person on a personal uplifting journey. The client experiences, receives, and welcomes the addictive part of self and discovers the purpose or first intended outcome of the addictive behavior. Working with this revealed addictive part, the individual discovers the outcome chain by working backwards to determine the deepest, most important outcome the part is seeking. This deep, desired outcome is called the core state. The client then assumes that he or she has the core state and imagines experiencing the changes that would occur as a result of achieving this state. Next, the individual notices the chronological age of this part and allows this aspect of self to mature to the present age of the person. The process then involves locating the mature part in the body and allowing it to permeate the entire being. Finally, the client asks all parts of self if there are any objections to this new way of being, and if so, works with this objecting part until it is satisfied with the new core state.

The Compulsion Blowout. This is a very powerful pattern that allows for the elimination of even very intense, strong compulsions such as addictions. Andreas & Andreas (1987) explain how to create and use this pattern. This technique involves finding the sub-modality of the object that drives the compulsion and increasing the sub-modality so that the object becomes more and more desirable until a qualitative shift takes place, and the object is no longer desirable. In the case of alcoholism, the client would be asked to explore the personal attraction of alcohol consumption. For example, it may be revealed that alcohol brings about a relaxed state for the client. The individual would then be instructed to become more and more relaxed until a qualitative shift takes place thus making the object no longer desirable.

Time Line Therapy. James and Woodsmall (1988) wrote about successful therapy done with a cocaine addict using Time Line Therapy. According to the authors, past experiences influence who one is and how one behaves; therefore, memories are not only recorded and stored but have more and more influence with age. The time line consists of how one encodes and stores these memories. With Time Line Therapy, the individual is able to change significant numbers of personal memories in a short time. By changing these memories, the core personality is affected, and access to past decisions is achieved. Through this process, values can be changed, and motivations and behaviors can be altered.

Conclusions

Growing numbers of psychologists, counselors, and neuroscientist are coming together to create a bridge between brain study and the practice of psychotherapy. In the area of addictions, the interaction between neural networks and individual behaviors is even more complex. Mind-Body techniques are certainly part of the foundation of that connecting bridge. These techniques can be a valuable asset to the psychotherapy community and can provide adjunct support or an alternative approach to a traditional medical regime for addictions. In addition, long-term recovery requires addressing the individual needs of the addict and applying a whole-person approach. Mind-Body Therapy is increasingly popular and affective in linking feelings, beliefs, attitudes, spiritual life, and physical well-being.

There is no doubt that addiction counseling is complex; however, recognizing the fact that new mental, emotional, and behavioral patterns create neuropathways in the brain is a step toward changing addictive patterns even down to the cellular level. Many addicts feel stranded and alone and need to experience acceptance, belonging, and awakening. Mind-Body techniques assist the client in developing self-knowledge, self-control, and personal honesty. Most important, Mind-Body Therapy promotes small changes in the behavioral actions of the client, which can produce a new found hope for enjoying a better and more authentic life. Evidenced-based research in this domain is providing practitioners with exciting new options in the treatment of a serious health problem.

References

Alman, B. M., & Lambrou, P. (1992). *Self-hypnosis: The complete manual for health and self change* (2nd ed.). New York, NY: Brunner-Routledge.

Andreas, C. & Andreas, S. (1989). *Heart of the mind*. Moab, UT: Real People Press.

Andreas, C. & Andreas, T. (1994). *Core transformation*. Boulder, CO: Real People Press.

Andreas, S. & Andreas, C. (1987). *Change your mind and keep the change*. Moab, UT: Real People Press.

Bandler, R. (1985). *Using your brain for a change*. Moab, UT: Real People Press.

Bandler, R. & Grinder, J. (1982). *Reframing*. Moab, UT: Real People Press.

Bell-Gadsby, C. (2001). *Addictions: The handbook of Ericksonian psychology*. Phoenix, AZ: The Milton H. Erickson Foundation Press.

Brewer, J. A., Bowen, S., Smith, J. T., Marlatt, G.A., & Patenze, M.N. (2009). Mindfulness-based treatments for co-occurring depression and substance use disorders: What can we learn from the brain? *Addiction, 105*(10), 1698–1706. doi10.1111/j.1360-0443

Dakwar, E., Mariani, J. P., & Levin, F. R. (2011). Mindfulness impairments in individuals seeking treatment for substance use disorders. *The American Journal of Drug and Alcohol Abuse, 37*, 165–169. doi: 10.3109/00952990.2011.553978

Erickson, M. H. (1985). *Life reframing in hypnosis*. New York, NY: Irvington Publishers.

Gray, R. (2013). *Thinking about drugs and addiction*. Retrieved from http://www.nlpco.com/library/therapy/addictions/

Hyman, S. E., & Malenka, R. C. (2001). Addiction and the brain: The neurobiology of compulsion and its persistence. *Neuroscience, 2*, 695–703.

Ivey, A., Ivey, M. B., Zalaquett, C., & Quirk, K. (2009, December 3). Counseling and neuroscience: The cutting edge of the coming decade. *Counseling Today*. Retrieved from http://ct.counseling.org/2009/12/reader-viewpoint-counseling-and-neuroscience-the-cutting-edge-of-the-coming-decade/

Jacobs-Stewart, T. (2010). *Mindfulness and the 12 steps*. Center City, MN: Hazelden.

James, T., & Woodsmall, W. (1988). *Time line therapy*. Capitola, CA: Meta Publications.

Kabat-Zinn, J. (1990). *Full catastrophe living*. New York: Hyperion.

Kabat-Zinn, J. (2005). *Coming to our senses*. New York: Hyperion.

Lankton, S. R., & Lankton, C. H. (1983). *The answer within: A clinical framework of Ericksonian hypnotherapy*. New York, NY: Brunner/Mazel.

Lemon, J. C., & Wagner, J. W. (2013). Exploring the mind-body connection: Therapeutic practices and techniques. *ACA VISTAS* 2013, Summer (3). Retrieved from http://www.counseling.org/docs/vistas/exploring-the-mind-body-connection-therapeutic.pdf

Leppma, M. (2012). Loving-kindness meditation and counseling. *Journal of Mental Health Counseling, 34*(3), 197–205.

Leshner, A. (2001). Addiction is a brain disease. *Issues in Science & Technology, 17*(3), 75–81.

Manganiello, A . J. (1984). A comparative study of hypnotherapy and psychotherapy in the treatment of methadone addicts. *American Journal of Clinical Hypnosis, 26*(4), 273–279.

O'Conell, O. (2009). Introducing mindfulness as an adjunct treatment in an established Residential drug and alcohol facility. *The Humanistic psychologist, 37*, 178–191.

O'Connor, J. & Seymour, J. (2011*). Introducing NLP*. San Francisco, CA: Conari Press.

O'Hanlon, B. (2011). *An uncommon casebook: The complete clinical work of Milton Erickson, M.D.* [E-reader version]. Retrieved from hppt://www.smashwords.com/extreader/read/100160/

Ostafin, B. D., Bauer, C., & Myxter, P. (2012). Mindfulness decouples the relation between automatic alcohol motivation and heavy drinking. *Journal of Social and Clinical Psychology, 31*(7), 729–745.

Page, R. A., & Handley, G. W. (1993). The use of hypnosis in cocaine addiction. *American Journal of Clinical Hypnosis, 36*(2), 120–123.

Pekala, R. J., Kumar, V. K., Elliott, N. C., Masten, E., Moon, E., & Salinger, M. (2004). Self-hypnosis relapse prevention training with chronic drug/alcohol users: Effects on self-esteem, affect, and relapse. *American Journal of Clinical Hypnosis, 46*(4), 281–297.

Peres, J., & Nasello, A.G. (2008). Psychotherapy and neuroscience: Towards closer integration. *International Journal of Psychology, 43*(6), 943–957. doi: 10.1080/00207590701248487

Potter, G. (2004). Intensive therapy: Utilizing hypnosis in the treatment of substance abuse disorders. *American Journal of Clinical Hypnosis, 47*(1), 21–28.

Rossi, E. L. (1993). *The psychobiology of mind-body healing.* New York, NY: W.W. Norton & Company, Inc.

Rossi, E. L. (1996). *The symptom path to enlightenment.* Pacific Palisades, CA: Palisades Gateway Publishing.

Short, D., Erickson, B. A., & Klein, R. E. (2006). *Hope & resiliency.* Norwalk, CT: Crown House.

Vallejo, Z., & Amaro, H. (2009). Adaptation of mindfulness-based stress reduction program for addiction relapse prevention. *The Humanistic Psychologist, 37,* 192–206. doi: 10.1080/08873260902892287

Wagner, B. (2012). *Brief and unusual therapies.* [E-reader version] Retrieved from http://www.smashwords.com/extreader/read/144672

Yapko, M.D. (2012). *Trancework: An introduction to the practice of clinical hypnosis.* New York, NY: Routledge, Taylor & Francis Group.

Zeig, J.K. (1990). Ericksonian psychotherapy. In W.M. Munion (Ed.), *What is psychotherapy? Contempory Perspectives* (pp. 371–377). San Francisco, CA: Josey-Bass.

3

Understanding Substance Abuse Through an Adlerian Theoretical Lens

An Exploration of Adler's Theory as Applied to Substance Abuse and Treatment

KATIE A. WACHTEL, TODD F. LEWIS, AND STEPHEN P. HEBARD[1]

Substance abuse and addiction exact an enormous toll on society. As such, it is important to identify positive and effective treatment models. Alfred Adler's theory of Individual Psychology is one such model that offers a compelling perspective of how substance abuse problems develop, as well as a variety of interventions.

According to the National Survey on Drug Use and Health (NSDUH), approximately 22.5 million Americans aged 12 or older engaged in illicit drug use in 2011 (Substance Abuse and Mental Health Services Administration [SAMHSA], 2012). In addition, 51.8% of Americans of the same ages reported being current alcohol drinkers, and there was an increase in illicit drug use in individuals aged 18 and older from 2002

---

1. Katie A. Wachtel, Department of Counseling & Educational Development, The University of North Carolina at Greensboro; Todd F. Lewis, Department of Counseling & Educational Development, The University of North Carolina at Greensboro; Stephen P. Hebard, Department of Counseling & Educational Development, The University of North Carolina at Greensboro. Correspondence concerning this article should be addressed to Katie A. Wachtel, 228 Curry Building, PO Box 26170, Greensboro, NC 27402–6170. Email: kawachte@uncg.edu

to 2011 (SAMHSA, 2012). In recent years, substance abuse among adolescents and young adults has received increased attention. According to Monitoring the Future (MTF), a yearly survey examining prevalence rates of substance abuse among adolescents, approximately 49.1% of high school seniors had experimented with illicit drugs in 2012 (National Institute on Drug Abuse [NIDA], 2012). Although alcohol and tobacco use among this population has decreased, abuse of marijuana and prescription medications continues to be a concern (NIDA, 2012). Similarly, abuse of prescription drugs appears to be most prevalent among young adults aged 18 to 25. In 2010, approximately 3,000 young adults died as a result of a prescription drug overdose (NIDA, 2013). These statistics verify that substance abuse remains a significant issue in American society, and these trends demonstrate the need for effective treatment strategies.

These alarming statistics beg the questions of what is the most effective way to treat substance abuse issues and what does this treatment look like? In today's mental health and substance abuse fields, increased emphasis has been placed on the use of Evidence-Based Treatments (EBTs) in practice because of the empirical support for their effectiveness (Jensen-Doss & Hawley, 2010). Indeed, EBTs have contributed extensively to our knowledge of effective interventions for substance abuse issues. However, critics of EBTs (Hubble, Duncan, Miller, & Wampold (2010) have suggested that client and contextual factors are of greater importance than the techniques upon which EBTs are often based. In addition, clinicians who must follow an EBT are precluded from the flexible use of theory and interventions, which may impact the therapeutic alliance, considered to be the most important common factor related to therapeutic effectiveness (Hubble et al., 2010). Whereas some theoretical approaches may not have amassed a significant amount of outcome research, this does not inherently render them ineffective with substance abuse problems.

Psychological and counseling theories have made a significant contribution to the psychological sciences, especially on a clinical level. Theories help clinicians conceptualize how problems develop and provide an organizing roadmap for how to proceed in counseling. All theories propose ideas for how to help people lead more productive lives (Sharf, 2004). Psychological theories can offer substance abuse clinicians an effective method for conceptualizing client problems and developing treatment plans. The flexible use of theory allows clinicians to be responsive to client feedback if a theory is not a good fit. One theory that than can provide an important contribution to substance abuse treatment approaches, yet which has received relatively little attention in this literature, is Adlerian theory.

Adlerian theory offers a comprehensive model for how substance abuse problems develop as well as several assessment and intervention techniques (Linkenbach, 1990). Carlson, Watts, and Maniacci (2006) noted that the characteristics of Adlerian theory—brief, present and forward looking, directive, and eclectic—make it suitable for clinicians in today's managed care world, whether in mental health or substance abuse treatment settings. The eclecticism of Adlerian theory (Carlson et al., 2006) allows for flexibility when combined with traditional, "disease model" based substance abuse interventions. We have found in our work with substance abuse clients that the Adlerian concepts of lifestyle, striving, and social interest, are exceptionally powerful ideas for those in recovery.

In this paper, we discuss substance abuse through the lens of Alfred Adler's theory of Individual Psychology and explore strategies to incorporate Adlerian theory into current substance abuse practice. We will begin by discussing the key tenets of Adlerian theory in order to develop a foundation from which to understand individual development. Enhanced understanding of Adler's concepts, such as life tasks, social interest, organ inferiority, lifestyle, and family constellation can provide the groundwork for conceptualizing the individual's relationships to self, others, and the world and the development of substance abuse problems. We then outline several techniques highlighted by Adler and his followers that may prove beneficial in addressing substance related issues. Finally, we discuss how incorporating Adlerian concepts when working with those suffering from substance-related issues provides insight into their unique experiences that play a role in the development of substance abuse. We argue that focusing on the unique experiences of an individual, rather than following a medical model protocol, can provide an alternative and effective treatment and may lead to more successful outcomes.

Key Tenets of Adlerian Theory

Adler's theory incorporates elements from a variety of influences and perspectives. The integration of components from psychoanalysis, cognitive, behavioral, and constructivist schools of thought leaves a complex set of ideas that may prove beneficial in the conceptualization and treatment of substance use disorders (Lewis, 2013). Basic understanding of each of the main tenets of the theory can provide a framework for conceptualizing substance abuse from an Adlerian perspective. These tenets are reviewed below.

Socio-Teleo-Analytic Theory

Adlerian theory is considered a socio-teleo-analytic theory (Mosak & Maniacci, 1999). Adler viewed individuals as social creatures, believing they have an innate propensity to interact with others. He also believed that human behavior is purposive and goal directed; all behavior can be explained as movement towards a goal. Adler believed much of human behavior is not fully understood by the individual (Sweeney, 2009). According to Adler, early development is essential in understanding the development of neuroses, including substance abuse (Dreikurs, 1990). Individuals begin to navigate their understanding of life from the moment they are born. In Adlerian theory, neuroses are thought to be a result of an individual's inability to successfully negotiate the life tasks (Adler, 2005).

Life Tasks

Adler described three main life tasks with which all humans are faced and must accomplish: work, love and friendship (Adler, 2005). Rudolf Dreikurs added the two additional tasks of spirituality and self (Sweeney, 2009). Successfully engaging in each life task is thought to be essential to the positive health and well-being of an individual. An inability to cope with one or more life tasks can lead to the development of mental health and behavioral problems, including substance abuse as an unhealthy coping mechanism (Dreikurs, 1990; Steffenhagen, 1974). Individuals use addictive substances to avoid dealing with life tasks or because they perceive them to aid in coping when problems arise. According to Adler, substance abuse is a prime example of shirking responsibility for life and thus hinders one's ability to effectively tackle the life tasks (Adler, 2005).

Is this to say that all who are unable to navigate the life tasks will develop a problem with substance abuse? Not necessarily. According to

Dreikurs (1990), being unsuccessful at the life tasks manifests itself in different ways depending upon an individual's environment. Certainly, failure to meet the life tasks successfully may be one reason why an individual turns to drugs. However, in order to fully understand the development of addiction through an Adlerian model, it is important to examine how the social environment and early family experiences contribute to an individual's approach to life (Adler, 2005). Because Adler believed that an individual's behavior is strongly influenced by and occurs within a social context, understanding the individual as a whole requires exploration of his or her social environment and level of social interest.

Social Interest

Social interest is one of the main tenets of Adler's theory. Social interest is described as the natural responsibility of all humans to be part of the whole group. Those with high social interest are thought to have deeper empathy and understanding of others (Adler, 2005). Social interest is thought to be a key to healthy human functioning. Its development begins in early childhood where humans experience a social environment that fosters feelings of empathy for others and a growing desire to belong (Mozdierz, Greenblatt, & Murphy, 2007). Individuals who do not develop this attraction to community have difficulty approaching the life tasks and consequently struggle with emotional and behavioral problems (Adler, 2005). It is easy to see the significance of belonging and community feeling in the three original Adlerian life tasks. Qualities such as cooperation and respect are developed and demanded when individuals are confronted by the life tasks of friendship and love, whereas work is a product of societal expectation and often requires individuals to interact to achieve. Those who become discouraged and lack perseverance in the face of imperfections in social realms may believe that they are inadequate, unable, or may become fearful when approaching life tasks (Sweeney, 2009).

A common characteristic of many who use substances is egocentricity, which suggests low social interest (Dreikurs, 1990). In a study by Mozdierz et al. (2007), the researchers attempted to correlate social interest and pathology in a sample of inpatient alcoholic veterans. The authors hypothesized that individuals struggling with alcoholism who had higher social interest would report less pathology than those with low social interest, suggesting validity in Alder's belief that social interest is a main factor in what he called "neuroses." The researchers used the Millon Mulitaxial Clinical Inventory (MCMI II) and the Sulliman Scale of Social Interest (SSSI) to test their hypothesis. Results supported the researchers' hypothesis, suggesting that those with lower social interest were more likely to experience depression, anxiety, and personality disorders, in addition to their heavy alcohol use, than individuals reporting higher levels of social interest (Mozdierz et al., 2007). Those who have lower levels of social interest appear to struggle with greater levels of psychopathology, which may lead to or exacerbate heavy alcohol use.

Individuals with low social interest also are thought to be more concerned with "How am I doing?" versus "What am I doing?" (Sweeney, 2009). This idea suggests a relationship between social interest and self-esteem. Those with low social interest are concerned with their success in relation to others or in relation to their perception of what excellence should look like. In comparison, those with high social interest demonstrate a sense of confidence in how they are doing by focusing instead on what they are doing. Those with high social interest are capable of more growth and are better equipped to manage life's adversities (Dreikurs, 1990). In this sense, symptoms of substance abuse may be explained as a defense against taking responsibility for the individual's perception of personal shortcomings. According to Steffenhagen (1974), Adler described feelings of shyness, isolation, oversensitivity, impatience, irritability, anxiety, and depression as possible common perceived deficiencies that may lead to the abuse of substances. Drugs and alcohol are often used as an attempt to avoid personal blame for these perceived deficiencies (Steffenhagen, 1974). Adler discussed low self-esteem as a reflection of feelings of inferiority. He uses the metaphor of physical inferiorities, which he called organ inferiority, to describe the ways in which personal flaws can lead individuals to feel a sense of inferiority in the social context. According to Adler, it is an individual's interpretation of these physical inferiorities, and the psychological impact these interpretations have that can influence feelings of psychological inferiority. If these feelings of inferiority become intense, they can lead to an inferiority complex.

Organ Inferiority and Inferiority Complex

Adler theorized that the characteristics of those who are not prepared to develop high social interest correlate with characteristics of those who use substances. He described these individuals as "he who thinks more of himself than others; he who takes and does not give; he who sees life as if its sole duty is to make him comfortable; and he who does not expect life's difficulties to concern him" (Adler, 2005). Adler purported that individuals whose lifestyles supported these characteristics may experience distress in the form of an inferiority complex and question their abilities and effectiveness (Dreikurs, 1990). Feelings of inferiority, by themselves, are normal experiences; however, the inferiority complex refers to feelings of low-self-esteem, self-doubt, and non-acceptance by society that become intense and overwhelming. Adler used the metaphor of organ inferiority to describe the inferiority complex. He stated that physical illness at an early age may result from inferior organs at birth. These children may experience certain situations as more difficult than their peers (Dreikurs, 1990). When individuals experience life tasks as more difficult than others, they may perceive the world as oppositional and develop feelings of hypersensitivity (Adler, 2005). According to Adler, hypersensitivity is a manifestation of improper development and an inability to feel a sense of belonging (i.e., lack of social interest). Similarly, when the personality is unprepared to tackle a life task, individuals may feel a sense of psychological hypersensitivity, which leads to the inferiority complex (Adler, 2005).

According to Adler, the inferiority complex can hinder an individual's sense of confidence, feelings of belongingness, and ability to successfully navigate the life tasks (Adler, 2005; Dreikurs, 1990). Adler explained the development of substance abuse as a response to the inferiority complex, where an individual essentially turns to substances as a method of coping (Adler, 2005). Because individuals exist within a social context, feelings of low self-esteem and inferiority may be heightened when individuals examine themselves as they relate to others (Steffenhagen, 1974). Substance abuse may be a strategy for individuals to isolate themselves from others, to avoid these uncomfortable feelings, and to deny personal shortcomings (Adler; 2005; Steffenhagen, 1974). As one can see, an inferiority complex can lead to a self-defeating lifestyle (Corsini & Wedding, 2008).

Lifestyle

The development of social interest and feelings of inferiority are thought to relate to one's lifestyle. An individual's lifestyle is described as the way in which he or she approaches or avoids life's tasks (Adler, 2005). The lifestyle is considered the unity between the individual's thoughts, feelings and behaviors that are thought to lead to a specific life goal and is analogous to personality (Sweeney, 2009). Adler described many who use alcohol and drugs to be characteristic of the pampered lifestyle (Dreikurs, 1990). Pampered children are raised in an environment in which they learn to think only of themselves. This pampering leads to a dependency on others that encourages greedy behavior and fosters exploitation of kindness and social interest demonstrated by others (Dreikurs, 1990). Pampered children also may have difficulty forming healthy attachments with others and as a result may resort to abusing substances to help ease anxiety in social situations (Steffenhagen, 1974).

Pampered children often acquire things easily and seldom are faced with the task of waiting for or working for what they desire. Adler suggested a relationship between pampered individuals and feelings of inferiority, in that individuals who feel inferior are impatient. Strength, on the other hand, is equated with self-confidence, and those who are confident are able to wait. Individuals who use substances often display impatience (Adler, 2005). Impatience, then, is a characteristic of the pampered lifestyle in that those who spent their early childhood in this environment expect to be indulged. They are products of the pleasure principle, demanding satisfaction and fearing failure when triumphs are not instantly obtained (Adler, 2005). The desire to achieve immediate pleasure, coupled with a low social interest and the qualities of impatience and hypersensitivity, leave the individual vulnerable to the use of alcohol or other drugs. The use of substances can be explained as an attempt to avoid undertaking the life tasks, as an avenue to gain pleasure, or both (Dreikurs, 1990). Children who do not feel strong often develop lifestyles where they retreat into daydreams in order to avoid reality and fantasize about how they wish their situation to be, demonstrating both avoidance and pleasure seeking tendencies. In this way, Adler (2005) described substance abuse as the daydreams of adults.

Family Constellation, Early Recollections, and Birth Order

Understanding family dynamics can offer significant insight into an individual's approach to life (Sweeney, 2009). Dreikurs (1990) pointed out that no two cases of individuals who abuse substances are completely alike. For this reason, Adler explained the importance of early development and family constellation. Adler believed that one's lifestyle is formed at an early age. During the first years of life, the family is the most influential environmental factor on development. Adler contended that the socio-psychological configuration of the family is important to understanding the experience of each individual and the interactions within the group (Sweeney, 2009). He observed that individuals who hold similar positions within families display similar characteristics; however, he also noted that factors such as sibling gender, number of siblings, number of years between siblings, miscarriages, and ideas about gender roles play an important role in the makeup of one's family constellation and how it impacts the individual (Sweeney, 2009). Family constellation refers to one's position in the family and how members of the family get along. Adler held that examining one's psychological position within the family was of key importance (Sweeney, 2009). For example, an individual who is the youngest, but whose siblings are significantly older, may feel more like an only child than a youngest child. One way to understand an individual's psychological position within the family is to examine his or her early recollections (Sweeney, 2009).

Adler described an early recollection as one's insight into a specific moment in time that holds the keys to how an individual perceives the world (Clark, 2002). By recalling this life event, the Adlerian practitioner may better understand a client's self-concept, self-ideal, context or world, and ethical convictions (Slavik, 1991). Eliciting multiple early recollections may give both the counselor and client insight into one's motivation for coping through the use of substances and a more holistic conceptualization of the client's clinical presentation.

Adler believed that early recollections provide a window into an individual's lifestyle. Examining early recollections in order to interpret substance abuse may be an effective technique in understanding, and thus more effectively treating, an individual. Colker and Slaymaker (1984) conducted a study assessing the reliability of interpreting early recollections in a sample of substance abusing individuals and found these interpretations to be an effective way to identify motives of behavior. Another study found positive results in using early recollections with adolescents who abused substances as a method to identify patterns that may have led to use (Mansager et al., 1995). Use of Adlerian sand tray therapy was also found to be an effective method in incorporating early recollections and patterns into treatment for substance abuse (Monakes, Garza, Weisner, & Watts, 2011). Other techniques, such as spitting in the soup, antisuggestion, and the push-button technique (defined below), may be helpful in assisting clients in identifying self-defeating behaviors related to their use (Sweeney, 2009).

Even within the same family, children of different birth order positions experience situations differently and these differences in perception affect development (Stein, De Miranda, & Stein, 1988). Because lifestyle is formed by approximately age six, Adler believed siblings no more than six years older or younger have the most significant impact on individual development. Adler reported that each birth order position is characteristic of certain qualities carried into adulthood (Sweeney, 2009). Past research suggests youngest children are more densely represented among substance abuse populations due to their inclination to manipulate, tendency to act impulsively, and spoiled upbringing (Conley, 1980). Conley (1980) sought to test these findings by studying substance dependency traits and ordinal position in an inpatient sample of patients suffering from alcoholism and a nonalcoholic sample. Although Conley found little relationship between alcoholism and birth order position, the researcher did find that alcoholism was closely related to a lifestyle pattern of over-dependency on others. These results suggest that while there may not be a strong relationship between alcohol dependency and birth order, heavy alcohol use does appear to relate to characteristics Adler believed correlate with substance abuse.

In contrast to Conley's (1980) study, Stein et al. (1988) hypothesized that first-born children would be less likely to engage in substance abuse and delinquent behavior because of their propensity toward high self-esteem and adherence to parental values. In contrast to their hypothesis, the researchers found a higher prevalence of first-born children in a sample of male inpatient substance abuse patients. The authors posited that the prevalence of substance abuse among first-born children may be related to first-borns feeling a higher frequency and intensity of family pressure, which they may cope with by abusing substances (Stein et al., 1988). Further research, however, is needed to substantiate these findings.

Each of the aforementioned Adlerian concepts provides a lens through which we can better comprehend how an individual developments substance abuse, and the function it plays in his or her life. These tenets are brought together and explored primarily through the lifestyle assessment (see below). Similarly, Adlerian techniques can provide a concrete set of strategies in working with these individuals to decrease substance abuse and maintain sobriety.

Specific Adlerian Techniques

Successful understanding of Adlerian concepts can provide a framework for understanding the development and descent into substance abuse; however, in order to provide effective treatment of substance-related issues, knowledge of specific techniques and strategies is essential. Adler provided a set of concrete strategies for working with a range of mental health and behavioral problems that may prove effective in the treatment of substance abuse.

The Lifestyle Assessment is an important tool for understanding the holistic nature of one's being (Sweeney, 2009). Indeed, all of the major tenets discussed above, the life tasks, social interest, inferiority complexes, lifestyle patterns, family constellation, early recollections, and psychological birth order can be assessed with a thorough lifestyle assessment. These assessment observations are used to investigate, to hypothesize, and to integrate responses into a complete understanding of the individual. The result is discovery of one's private logic, the justification upon which his or her lifestyle is based. Understanding one's private logic, lifestyle, and general "movement" in life can shed great insight into the "why" of substance abuse. A counselor may then challenge the automatic nature of the client's set of expectations and perceptions about life, others, and the self.

Spitting in the Soup refers to a counselor's attempt to diminish the "sweetness" associated with a behavior that is ultimately self-defeating (Sweeney, 2009). For example, exposing the hidden goals of an individual's substance abuse, such as to assuage loneliness, may lessen the satisfaction gained when using substances.

The response to the question, "How would life be different if you felt you did not need drugs and alcohol?" may lead to an opportunity for a counselor to suggest that a client *Act "As If"* he or she were not addicted to drugs. A client of an Adlerian substance abuse counselor may be invited to act *as if* he was excited to begin treatment or *as if* he had feelings of control when noticing triggers for alcohol or drug use.

The *Push-Button Technique* is an imagery-based intervention used to encourage an individual to experience both positive and negative emotions (Sweeney, 2009). By "pushing the button," clients imagine a situation in which they normally experience positive emotions or negative emotions and assess their physical experience in relation to their thoughts. This tactic may aid a substance abusing individual to become more aware of craving sensations as well as their power to evoke positive emotions unrelated to substance abuse.

Adlerians often use the technique of *Antisuggestion* with clients to encourage confidence in one's ability to control unwanted feelings. Antisuggestion involves exaggerating the symptom. For example, the individual who is anxious around others who use drugs or alcohol may find that when he attempts to become even more anxious, actually tries to exaggerate his anxiety, he is unable to do so. The strategy of *Catching Oneself*, or developing a mental stop sign to interrupt one's pattern of thinking or behaving, may work well when used alongside other behavioral techniques. Catching oneself in a pattern of worry may allow one to try Antisuggestion or other interventions to change current substance abuse patterns.

Application of Adlerian Theory to the Treatment of Substance Abuse

Popular treatments for substance abuse include medication management and cognitive-behavioral interventions because they address unhealthy thoughts and behaviors that exacerbate abuse of substances. Adlerian theory, regarded as one of the first cognitive-based theories, also uses cognitive and behavioral techniques. Indeed, Adler's theory and cognitive-behavioral therapy (CBT) have some overlapping views and techniques (Monakes et al., 2011). Both attempt to challenge cognitive distortions. Adlerians examine lifestyle to explore the ways in which thoughts, feelings and behaviors interact to affect one's approach to life, much as CBT therapists aim to help clients understand the interaction between thoughts, feelings and behaviors as a technique to overcome life's obstacles. These similarities demonstrate ways in which Adlerian concepts are already being utilized in substance abuse therapeutic settings.

However, Adlerian theory focuses more heavily on understanding and explaining substance abuse than many other counseling approaches. Indeed, the third stage of Adlerian therapy is "insight" (after building rapport [stage 1] and assessment [stage 2]) where the Adlerian clinician helps clients see thinking errors, basic mistakes and faulty goals that are contributing to their problems. By assessing the underlying causes for substance abuse as an avoidance or pleasure technique, Adlerian clinicians strive to enhance awareness and encourage clients to "reorient" (stage 4) based on this insight.

Adlerian terminology is used in many treatment settings for substance abuse, possibly in an unintended way. Adler discussed the "ah-ha" moment, which is common language in recovery settings. Crossroads Counseling, a treatment facility in Denver, Colorado, has purposefully implemented Adlerian concepts and techniques in their treatment with positive results (Prinz & Arkin, 1994). Crossroads does not emphasize "powerlessness over alcohol" in order to avoid perpetuation of excuse making. They use a group process in order to promote social interest (Prinz & Arkin, 1994). Group therapy is a common treatment avenue for substance abuse populations and the use of group coincides with Adler's belief that individuals who use substances have low social interest and could benefit from community engagement and feelings of belonging that groups provide.

As noted above, the general "flow" of Adlerian therapy is from building rapport to reorientation and behavior change. The lifestyle assessment is a critical process to help clinicians understand the family issues, early childhood experiences, early memories, and social feeling that all play a role in behavioral problems, including substance abuse. Appendix 1 includes a case study using Adlerian theory and techniques with a client struggling with multiple substance abuse problems.

Conclusion

Adler's theory provides important insights into the development of substance abuse as a coping mechanism for managing the life tasks. Some empirical research has supported elements of Adlerian theory, indicating its potential to be an effective lens from which to better understand and treat substance abuse problems. However, more research is needed that examines the effectiveness of Adlerian theory in the treatment of substance abuse issues; indeed, the potential usefulness of this approach in explaining and treating substance abuse issues warrants further study. Despite the limited empirical research, we believe that the substance abuse treatment field may benefit from approaching substance abuse from a new perspective and the variety of Adlerian techniques may prove applicable to this population.

References

Adler, A. (2005). Narcotic abuse and alcoholism. In Stein, H. T. (Ed.), *The Collected Clinical Works of Alfred Adler: Volume 7* (pp. 50–59). Bellingham, WA: The Classical Adlerian Translation Project.

Carlson, J., Watts, R. E., & Maniacci, M. (2006). *Adlerian therapy: Theory and practice.* Washington, DC: American Psychological Association.

Clark, A. J., (2002). *Early recollections: Theory and practice in counseling and psychotherapy.* New York, NY: Brunner-Routledge.

Colker, J. O., & Slaymaker, F. L. (1984). Reliability of idiographic interpretation of early recollections and their nomothetic validation with drug abusers. *Individual Psychology: the Journal of Adlerian Theory, Research & Practice, 40*(1), 36–44.

Conley, J. J. (1980). Family configuration as an etiological factor in alcoholism. *Journal of Abnormal Psychology, 89*(5), 670–673.

Corsini, R. J., & Wedding, D. (2008). *Current psychotherapies.* Belmont, CA: Thomson Brooks/Cole.

Dreikurs, R. (1990). Drug addiction and its individual psychological treatment. *Individual Psychology, 46*(2), 208–216.

Hubble, M. A., Duncan, B. L., Miller, S. D., & Wampold, B. E. (2010). Introduction. In B. L. Duncan, S. D. Miller, B. E. Wampold, M. A. Hubble (Eds.) , *The heart and soul of change: Delivering what works in therapy* (2nd ed.) (pp. 23–46). Washington, DC US: American Psychological Association.

Jenson-Doss, A. & Hawley, K. M. (2010). Understanding barriers to evidenced-based assessment: Clinician attitudes toward standardized assessment tools. *Journal of Child & Adolescent Psychology, 39*(6), 885–896.

Lewis, T. F. (2013). *Substance abuse and addiction treatment: Practical application of counseling theory.* Boston, MA: Pearson.

Linkenbach, J. (1990). An Adlerian technique for substance-abuse prevention and intervention. *Individual Psychology, 46,* 203–207.

Mansager, E., Barnes, M., Boyce, B., Brewster, J. D., Letora, H. J. III, Marais, F., ...Thompson, D. (1995). Interactive discussion of early recollections: A group technique with adolescent substance abusers. *Individual Psychology: the Journal of Adlerian Theory, Research & Practice, 51*(4), 413–421.

Monakes, S., Garza, Y., Wiesner III, V., & Watts, R. E. (2011). Implementing Adlerian sand tray therapy with adult male substance abuse offenders: A phenomenological inquiry. *Journal of Addictions and Offender Counseling, 31,* 94–107.

Mosak, H., & Maniacci, M. (1999). *A primer of Adlerian psychology: The analytic-behavioral-cognitive psychology of Alfred Adler.* Philadelphia, PA: Brunner/Mazel Taylor & Francis Group.

Mozdzierz, G., Greenblatt, R. L., & Murphy, T. J. (2007). The measurement and clinical use of social interest: Validation of the Sulliman scale of social interest on a sample of hospitalized substance abuse patients. *Journal of Individual Psychology, 63*(2), 225–234.

National Institute on Drug Abuse (NIDA). (2012). Monitoring the future study: Trends in prevalence of various drugs. Retrieved from http://www.drugabuse.gov/related-topics/trends-statistics/monitoring-future/trends-in-prevalence-various-drugs.

National Institute on Drug Abuse (NIDA). (2013). *Abuse of prescription (Rx) drugs affects young adults most*. Retrieved from http://www.drugabuse.gov/related-topics/trends-statistics/infographics/abuse-prescription-rx-drugs-affects-young-adults-most.

Prinz, J., & Arkin, S. (1994). Adlerian group therapy with substance abusers. *Individual Psychology: the Journal of Adlerian Theory, Research & Practice, 50*(3), 349–358.

Sharf, R. S. (2004). *Theories of psychotherapy and counseling: Concepts and cases (3rd ed.)*. Pacific Grove, CA: Thomson/Brooks/Cole Pub. Co.

Slavik, S. (1991). Early memories as a guide to client movement through life. *Canadian Journal Of Counselling And Psychotherapy, 25*(3), 331–337.

Steffenhagen, R. A. (1974). Drug abuse and related phenomena: An Adlerian approach. *Journal of Individual Psychology, 30*(2), 238–250.

Stein, S. M., De Miranda, S., & Stein, A. (1988). Birth order, substance abuse, and criminality. *Individual Psychology: the Journal of Adlerian Theory, Research & Practice, 44*(4), 500–506.

Substance Abuse and Mental Health Services Administration. (2012). Results from the 2011 National Survey on Drug Use and Health: Summary of national findings. *NSDUH Series, H-44*(12–4713). Retrieved from http://www.samhsa.gov/data/NSDUH/2k11Results/NSDUHresults2011.htm.

Sweeney, T. J. (2009). *Adlerian counseling and psychotherapy: A practitioner's approach*. New York, NY: Routledge Taylor & Francis Group.

Appendix 1: Case Study

Z is a 25 year-old Caucasian male court ordered for individual counseling due to a third charge for driving under the influence. Z is currently on probation from working as a truck driver and reports no history of long-term intimate relationships. He reported drinking approximately 10–20 beers per day. He stated he also smokes marijuana approximately 1–2x per week, and has used other illegal substances (prescription pain killers, LSD, and Benzodiazepines) on occasion, but stated his use of these substances is infrequent. At intake, counselor performed a lifestyle assessment to gain insight regarding the client's purpose for alcohol use, views of early experiences, and his perceived role within the social context of his family.

Z reported that he is the youngest of three children. Z has two older brothers who are 32 and 30 years old. He stated his brothers have always spent significant time together and continue to share similar interests into adulthood. Z describes himself as an outsider. Whereas his siblings were high-achieving and social, he shared that he has struggled with academics and has always preferred to spend his time by himself. According to Z, he has always felt difficulty connecting with his brothers and often felt like an annoyance to his parents. Z reported that both his parents worked full-time and value a strong work ethic and high achievement. For this reason, Z stated he feels like a disappointment to his parents and stated he believes they favor his elder brothers. Z stated the only attention he received from his parents was negative attention and despite his best efforts growing up, he always seemed to be in trouble.

Z's early memories portray themes related to feelings of inferiority in social contexts. For instance, he recalls his fifth birthday party that was overshadowed by his brother's baseball tournament victory. Specifically, he recalls the praise that his father gave his brother for his pitching performance and then being sent to his room for pushing this brother because he blew out the candles on his cake. Another of his early recollections was a description of a time that he played tee-ball at the age of 4 and was stung by multiple wasps. Z remembers running off the field to his mother and father, who he described as embarrassed and ashamed of his tearfulness.

Using Adlerian concepts and the information provided by the client, the counselor hypothesized that Z's substance abuse may function as an escape from feelings of inferiority when comparing himself to others, particularly his brothers, and his perceptions of disconnectedness with his family of origin. Z describes himself as preferring to spend time alone, suggesting low levels of social interest. Z's use of alcohol and other drugs may be a way to further isolate himself from activities and people in which he feels he will be unsuccessful and inferior. Z's assessment provided insight into his difficulty in achieving each of the life tasks, as evidenced by his current probation at work, his lack of intimate relationships, his report of having few meaningful friendships, his low self-esteem, and his difficulty connecting with others. It is possible that Z's use of alcohol provides him with a way to successfully avoid each of these life tasks and may allow him to avoid the potential failure he foresees in attempting to successfully navigate work, family, friendship, spirituality, and the self.

In the subsequent sessions following the lifestyle assessment, the counselor balanced challenge and support of the client. Z is adamant that using alcohol is a necessary part of his daily process in "winding down" from work. The process of spitting in the client's soup was performed by the shared hypothesis that his use of alcohol leads to poor decision-making (e.g., driving while under the influence) and perpetuated feelings of loneliness. Z shared that one of the most difficult challenges he faces is the craving for alcohol he experiences when he wakes in the morning. By applying the use of antisuggestion, Z has reported a decrease in this symptom when he invites cravings to be stronger. Furthermore, Z has been taught to catch himself when he has morning cravings through mental imagery, and then immediately do something to distract himself, like taking a walk. When he pictures himself as tired and angry later in the day because he cannot "continue his buzz" while on the road, he decides that he should refuse alcohol in early mornings. In session, use of the push-button technique has helped Z identify the link between his emotional experience and use of alcohol. When Z reminisces to times when he is sober and hiking in the woods with a friend from high school, he experiences happiness, freedom, and connection with another person. In contrast, by "pushing the button," he can readily access the feelings of loneliness and shame that are present when he imagines himself alone at home after drinking a case of beer. Z was encouraged to "push" the former button to improve his emotional state. A final technique that has been successful as an intervention with Z involves directing him to explore what it would be like to "act as if," especially when exploring his desire to become more social. Z has reported that when he acts as if he were excited for the opportunity to go on dates, he has generally felt able to be positive and sociable without the use of alcohol.

4

Addiction Training in Counselor Education
A Survey of the Current Status and Future Plans

TIFFANY K. LEE AND GARY H. BISCHOF[1]

The authors examined the state of addiction instruction among CACREP programs and the methods used to integrate the 2009 CACREP addiction-related competencies. The study investigated if programs had plans to add addiction courses, faculty with expertise, and the Addiction Counseling option.

Researchers strongly suggest counselor educators integrate addiction training into the curriculum for school counselors (Burrow-Sanchez, Lopez, & Slagle, 2008), marriage, couple and family counselors (Crespi & Rueckert, 2006), and rehabilitation counselors (Ong, Lee, Cha, & Arokiasamy, 2008). In fact, faculty from counselor education programs accredited by the Council for Accreditation of Counseling and Related Educational Programs (CACREP) propose addiction education is necessary for all counselors-in-training, regardless of their program specialty

---

1. Tiffany K. Lee, Specialty Program in Alcohol and Drug Abuse (SPADA), Western Michigan University and Gary H. Bischof, Department of Family and Consumer Sciences, Western Michigan University. Correspondence concerning this article should be addressed to Tiffany K. Lee, SPADA, Western Michigan University, 1903 W. Michigan Avenue, Kalamazoo, MI 49008 (E-mail: tiffany.k.lee@wmich.edu)

or area of concentration (Lee, 2011; Madson, Bethea, Daniel, & Necaise, 2008; Morgan, Toloczko, & Comly, 1997). Substantial scholarly attention has been dedicated to the lack of consistency in addictions training in the counseling profession. However, there is a dearth in the literature regarding the current status of addiction instruction in CACREP-accredited programs, addiction-related expertise among faculty, and the methods of implementing the 2009 CACREP standards that include addiction competencies.

The next section of this article outlines addiction training in counselor education programs. The authors present research related to: (a) the methods by which instruction is provided (e.g., requiring or offering a course), (b) the specific curricular components (e.g., screening and assessment) taught in courses, (c) counselor education graduates, (d) the 2009 CACREP program standards, and (e) faculty expertise.

Addiction Training

Over a decade ago, researchers found almost all counselor education faculty (97%) in their study reported the need for preparation in the area of addictions (Morgan et al., 1997). Others assert addiction instruction and training are inadequate (Morgan et al., 1997; Salyers, Ritchie, Luellen, & Roseman, 2005; Toloczko et al., 1998; Whittinghill, Carroll, & Morgan, 2004). Morgan et al. (1997) examined CACREP-accredited programs and determined 30% of the programs required a course in addiction and 77% offered an elective course. Thirty-one percent of the respondents stated faculty had plans at that time to provide systematic, substance abuse training to all students, regardless of specialty area. However, when the study was replicated seven years later, there was no increase in the percentage of counselor education programs requiring an addiction course (i.e., remained at 30%) and only 50% of programs offered an elective course, a 27% decrease from the previous study (Whittinghill et al., 2004). Four studies, conducted over a ten year period between 1997 and 2007, consistently found 30% of institutions offering counselor education programs *require* completion of an addiction course (Dawes-Diaz, 2007; Morgan et al., 1997; Salyers et. al., 2005; Whittinghill et al., 2004).

While research has consistently shown that 30% of CACREP-accredited counselor education programs require an addictions course, the students who complete the course may be enrolled in a particular specialization. A study completed by Salyers et al. (2005) revealed the inclusion of addiction training is more common in the curricula of two specializations, Mental Health Counseling and Community Counseling. More specifically, 92% of Mental Health Counseling programs and 83% of Community Counseling programs incorporated training either as a separate, required addiction course or the training was infused into other courses. This research does not necessarily indicate training is not occurring, just that there are inconsistencies in requirements among counselor education programs (e.g., required addiction course).

Curriculum Components

Addiction course designs and the addiction-related content have also varied among counseling programs. Morgan et al. (1997) found more than half (57%) of courses focus on counseling skills including assessment, diagnosis, case management, treatment, relapse prevention, and tools of recovery. The second highest percentage of courses (28%) focuses on a basic overview of substance abuse including types of drugs and pharmacology, models of addiction, etiology, epidemiology, community resources, and intervention.

Information related to addiction training in counselor education programs has largely been obtained from surveying faculty members and analyzing course syllabi (e.g., Morgan et al., 1997; Salyers et al., 2005). In 2007, however, one dissertation study surveyed graduates of counselor education programs and the author found graduates are not satisfied with the addiction training they received in their master's program (Dawes-Diaz, 2007).

Perceptions of Graduates

Dawes-Diaz (2007) determined almost 24% of graduates indicated their institution did not offer an addictions course and 14% noted addiction-related instruction was not addressed at all during their training. For example, between 23% and 31% of graduates specified they had no education in pharmacology (30.5%), etiologies (29.5%), criteria for referral (26.5%), screening (25.5%), and assessment and diagnosis (23.6%). Not only does research indicate students need more instruction in addictions while enrolled in counselor education programs, but 81% of these graduates highly recommend one or more required addiction courses (Dawes-Diaz, 2007).

If graduates are not satisfied with their training related to addiction, another option is to obtain education after the master's degree. Professional counselors who hold membership in various counseling organizations (e.g., American Counseling Association) were asked about their training during and after their graduate degree education (Harwood, Kowalski, & Ameen, 2004). Continuing education was shown to be the primary method by which these practitioners received substance abuse training. For example, in one year, 27% of professional counselors had 1–9 hours of continuing education/professional development in substance abuse, 23% had 10–29 hours, and 24% had 30 or more hours. In summary, three-fourths of respondents participated in seminars and workshops during the previous year, while 26% of professional counselors had no continuing education related to substance abuse. These numbers indicate an interest in post-master's addiction education and suggest possible deficiencies in addiction training in the past.

Council for Accreditation of Counseling and Related Educational Programs (CACREP) Standards and Addiction Competencies

CACREP released the new 2009 standards and there was a multitude of changes associated with substance abuse and addictive behavior training. For instance, the 2009 CACREP standards require *all* students, regardless of program option, to know the "theories and etiology of addictions and addictive behaviors, including strategies for prevention, intervention, and treatment" (CACREP, 2009, Standard G.3.g, p. 10).

The most substantial change in addiction training is the creation of accreditation standards for an Addiction Counseling program. In 2004, 25 out of 89 CACREP-accredited program liaisons indicated they offered a non-accredited substance abuse program (Whittinghill et al., 2004). When asked if their faculty would consider adding a substance abuse counseling program if CACREP created standards, the majority of those indicating interest in obtaining accreditation were participants from institutions that offered a master's degree in substance abuse counseling.

Another significant change is the program option called Clinical Mental Health Counseling (CMHC). This 60 credit-hour program option replaces the previously CACREP-accredited Community Counseling and Mental Health Counseling programs. The CMHC students have more expansive addiction training requirements than students enrolled in other CACREP program options, such as Career Counseling and School Counseling. For instance, CMHC students are to identify "standard screening and assessment instruments for substance use disorders and process addictions" (CACREP, 2009, Standard G.4., p. 32) and provide "appropriate counseling strategies when working with clients with addiction and co-occurring disorders" (CACREP, 2009, Standard D.8., p. 31).

Although the 2009 CACREP standards for the CMHC program option indicate an increase in addictions training requirements for these mental health counselors, there remains uncertainty regarding the non-prescriptive nature of these new competencies and how they may be implemented or integrated into existing curricula. In essence, accreditation standards are often descriptive enough to provide direction, but sufficiently vague to allow for creativity. The assumption is CMHC program faculty will have adequate expertise in a given area in order to integrate accreditation standards into curricula. Unfortunately, researchers have suggested in the past that many institutions offering counselor education programs have a limited number of full-time faculty with formal addiction training (Morgan et al., 1997; Toloczko, et al., 1998).

Faculty Expertise

In 1997, researchers studied CACREP-accredited programs and reported 58% of respondents have faculty with prior formal addiction education, and 11% of faculty have membership in addictions-affiliated organizations (Morgan et al., 1997). Over a decade later, if these numbers have not increased, integrating the 2009 competencies into a CMHC program could potentially be difficult for some CACREP counselor education programs.

In summary, there has been a lack of consistency pertaining to the methods by which addiction education has been delivered to counselors-in-training (Salyers et al., 2005). For instance, some institutions have required students to complete an addictions course, while other institutions have addressed substance abuse and addictive behaviors in the core counseling courses (e.g., Human Growth and Development) or during practicum or internship. Previous research has also shown through analyses of course syllabi that the addiction concepts being taught (e.g., assessment, intervention, pharmacology) varied greatly among CACREP-accredited counselor education programs (Morgan et al., 1997). Without faculty expertise, implementing the 2009 CACREP standards may be a challenge.

Examination of Addiction Training: A Survey

The current study examined the present status of addiction training among CACREP-accredited programs and how these programs plan on integrating the addiction-related competencies outlined in the 2009 CACREP standards. More specifically, the authors investigated whether programs are requiring completion of an addictions course or if the training is infused into one or more core courses. In addition, the instruction of specific addiction content (e.g., etiologies, pharmacology, prevention, treatment) and the perceived importance of this content were also studied. To update prior research (Morgan et al., 1997; Toloczko et al., 1998), the authors gathered data related to the number of counselor education faculty with addiction expertise. Lastly, the researchers inquired about future program plans for (1) adding new faculty with expertise in addictions and (2) offering the Addiction Counseling program. This investigation is the first to be identified that has ascertained the anticipated changes within CACREP-accredited programs as a response to the 2009 addiction-related standards.

Method

A 15-item, online questionnaire was developed by the authors based on a review of previous research on addictions-related training in counselor education (e.g., Dawes-Diaz, 2007; Morgan et al., 1997; Salyers et al., 2005; Whittinghill et al., 2004) and the 2009 CACREP standards (CACREP, 2009). There were no survey questions specifically asking participants for any personal identifying or demographic information.

Participants were chosen by criterion sampling. Respondents were to be the designated CACREP liaison at their institution. If an institution did not have a designated liaison, then the unit or training director was also an approved participant for the purposes of this study. In June 2010, a copy of the CACREP directory of accredited counselor education programs was obtained online through the CACREP website. Each program had information available including the mailing address, website link, and the CACREP liaison's name. According to the website, there were 518 CACREP-accredited counselor education program options available. Some institutions had more than one accredited program option. A total of 218 institutions were found to have accredited programs and the contact person at each institution was obtained by the researchers.

Approval was given by Western Michigan University's Human Subjects Institutional Review Board and in July 2010, the 218 CACREP liaisons were contacted by postcard for advanced notification. A week later, an invitation was sent by e-mail. Subsequently, three reminder e-mails were delivered to the liaisons that had not completed the survey. A total of 101 liaisons viewed the consent document page; 20 did not continue past the consent page and seven dropped out after starting the survey. Seventy-four participants ($N = 74$) completed the questionnaire, for a 33.9% response rate. The average time to complete the survey was nine minutes.

The liaisons reported a total of 443.5 full-time, counselor education faculty members at their institutions. The range was 2 to 12 faculty members and the mean was 6 faculty members per institution. A total of 154 program options were offered at the 74 institutions. The two most frequently offered program options were School Counseling ($n=55$; 74.3% of the sample) and Community Counseling ($n=34$; 45.9% of the sample). There were five institutions that offered a non-accredited, substance abuse counseling program option, or 6.7% of the sample. Refer to Figure 1 for all options offered.

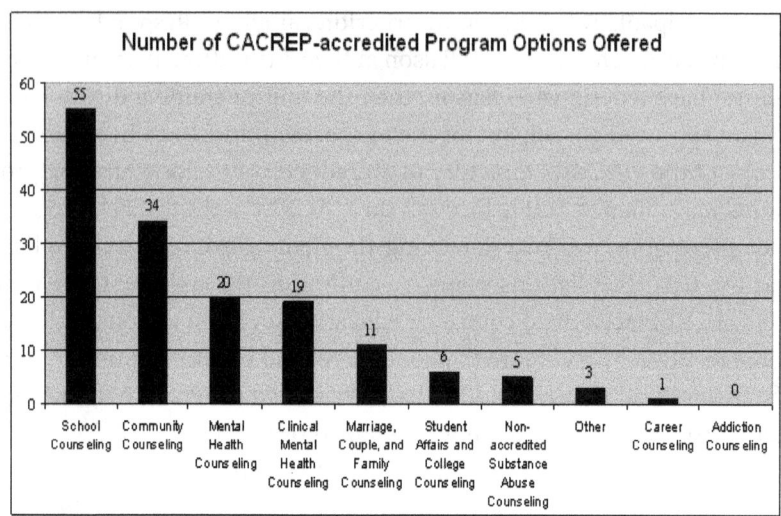

Figure 1. Number of CACREP-accredited program options offered. This figure illustrates the type of accredited counselor education program options available at the 74 liaisons' institutions.

Results

The authors will address the results as follows: (a) the current state of addiction training in CACREP-accredited, counselor education programs, (b) the future program plans resulting from the 2009 CACREP standards, and (c) the liaisons' opinions of addiction training.

The Current State of Addiction Training

This section covers the results of the survey that examined what type of addiction content is delivered to students, whether addiction courses are required and/or offered, faculty expertise, and whether the courses are taught by a counselor educator with expertise.

Content delivered to students. A list of 11 addiction-related criteria was created by the researchers (see Table 1). The listing was based on a review of prior research that investigated the importance of specific addiction-related curriculum components (Dawes-Diaz, 2007; Hosie et al., 1990; Morgan et al., 1997; Von Steen et al., 2002; Whittinghill,

2006; Whittinghill et al., 2004) and a review of the addiction training requirements in the 2009 CACREP standards (i.e., the Human Growth and Development competency and the CMHC competencies).

Participants were asked to indicate which of the 11 components were currently taught to all students at some point in the counselor education curricula. Fifty percent or more of the liaisons in the sample reported their institutions provided addiction-related instruction pertaining to each of the 11 components. The researchers found addiction screening was the most frequently covered content (by 78% of institutions) and the content least likely to be taught was process addictions (50%). Students in six of the institutions (8.1%) were not exposed to any of the 11 components (see Table 1).

Addiction courses. The CACREP liaisons were also asked how addiction training was currently implemented at their institutions, specific to all counseling students. Of the 74 institutions, 37 institutions (50%) offered one or more elective substance abuse courses, 34 institutions (45.9%) required a substance abuse course, 29 institutions (39.2%) infused substance abuse training into the content of one or more core courses, two institutions (2.7%) indicated no training was provided, and no institutions (0%) required two or more substance abuse courses.

Some institutions require the completion of an addiction course only for students enrolled in a specific program option. For the purposes of this study, the authors included the CMHC, Community Counseling, and Mental Health Counseling programs in this section of the survey. As stated earlier, the 2009 CACREP standards (a) offer accreditation for the CMHC program and (b) no longer offer or renew accreditation for the Community Counseling or Mental Health Counseling programs. Faculty currently offering CACREP-accredited Community or Mental Health Counseling programs may decide to make changes in curricula to align with the CMHC standards and seek accreditation. At the time of the study, institutions may not have an accredited CMHC program yet, but offer the Community or Mental Health Counseling programs. Therefore, the authors identified these programs in this part of the survey.

In the present study, 27 of the 74 institutions (36.5%) required a course only for students in certain specializations. Liaisons were then asked to indicate for which students the course(s) was required. Nine of the 74 institutions (12.2%) required a course for students in the CMHC program option; 8 institutions (10.8%) required a course for Mental Health Counseling students; 7 institutions (9.4%) required a course for Community Counseling students; 4 institutions (5.4%) required a course for Marriage, Couple, and Family Counseling students; 4 institutions (5.4%) required a course for School Counseling students; and 2 institutions (2.7%) required a course if students were enrolled in an addictions specialization or certificate program. None of the 74 institutions (0.0%) required a course for Career Counseling students or Student Affairs and College Counseling students.

Faculty expertise. The liaisons indicated the number of full-time counselor education faculty members that "have expertise in substance abuse counseling (e.g., experience in the field, completed research, hold credentials)." Of the 443.5 full-time faculty members reported by the liaisons, there are 142 members (32%) with such expertise. The mean per institution was 1.9 faculty members and the range was 0 to 6 faculty members. Eight liaisons (11%) reported having no faculty members with addiction-related expertise.

Addiction course instructor status. The liaisons provided information about the instructor of the addiction course that was required or offered at their counselor education program. The participants indicated if the instructor was an adjunct or a full-time faculty member and whether the instructor had addiction-related expertise. The majority, or 64.6% of the 48 liaisons, reported a full-time faculty member with addiction expertise teaches the course, 27.1% ($n = 13$) reported an adjunct faculty instructor with expertise teaches the course, 6.2% ($n = 3$) reported a full-time faculty member without expertise in addictions taught the course, and 2.1% ($n = 1$) indicated an adjunct faculty instructor without expertise in addictions taught the course.

Future Plans in Addiction Training

Of the 74 participants, 45 liaisons (60.8%) reported there were no plans to add faculty with addiction expertise at their institutions in the next two years. Twenty-two (29.7%) indicated "I don't know" and 7 liaisons (9.5%)

indicated their institutions had plans to add faculty with addiction expertise. The researchers noted that 4 of the 7 institutions planning to add faculty (57.1%) are also planning on offering the Addictions Counseling program.

The CACREP liaisons also reported if their institutions had plans to require one or more addiction-related courses in the next two years. Of the institutions that did not currently require a course, 8 of these 32 institutions (25%) reportedly had plans to require a course in the next two years. In regards to the total sample of 74 institutions, 10.8% intended on requiring an addiction course in the near future. Eighteen of the 74 liaisons (24.3%) indicated their institutions did not currently offer an elective course in addictions. Of those 18 institutions, 7 liaisons (38.8%) reported there were plans to offer such a course in the next two years. In other words, 9.4% of the 74 institutions intended on offering an addiction course in the near future.

The last inquiry related to future planning asked participants whether their institutions offer, or have plans to offer, the new Addiction Counseling program option. Twelve liaisons (16.2%) reported their institutions did plan to offer the Addiction Counseling program in the future.

Liaisons' Opinions Related to Addiction Training

The liaisons were asked how important substance abuse training is in counselor preparation programs. Thirty-six of the 74 respondents (48.6%) indicated this type of training was "Crucial;" 31 (41.9%) indicated it was "Very Important;" 6 (8.1%) indicated it was "Important;" 1 (1.4%) indicated it was "Somewhat Important;" and none of the liaisons (0.0%) indicated it was "Not Important."

Training to all students. The 2009 CACREP standards require all students, regardless of program option, to know the "theories and etiology of addictions and addictive behaviors, including strategies for prevention, intervention, and treatment" (Section II, Standard G.3.g., CACREP, 2009, p. 12). Ninety-two percent of the liaisons ($n = 68$) indicated this competency is "sufficient," 5.4% ($n = 4$) indicated "excessive," and 2.7% ($n = 2$) indicated "insufficient." To follow up, participants were asked which implementation method should be used to address this Human Growth and Development core competency.

The three main choices were infusion, a stand-alone course, or a combination of both. Thirty of the 74 liaisons (40.5%) reported counselor education programs should require a stand-alone addiction course and 17 participants (22.9%) reported programs should require a course and infuse the training into at least one core course. In essence, 63% of the respondents believed a course should be required.

Importance of addiction-related content. A matrix was created listing the 11 components on the left and over the top was a listing of the five program options (i.e., CMHC; Career; Marriage, Couple and Family; School; and Student Affairs and College Counseling). There was also the availability for the liaisons to check "None of these program options." The participants were asked to "indicate which master's-level counselor education program options *should* include each of the following substance abuse components into the training of their students." Screening, prevention, and assessment tools were rated the top three necessary areas of instruction for all students, regardless of specialty area. Diagnosis, co-occurring disorders, and pharmacology were rated the least necessary areas (see Table 2).

Training by program option. In the 2009 CACREP standards, there is a significant difference noted in the number of addiction-related competencies listed by program option. For example, Career Counseling has no addiction-related competencies, while CMHC has seven. The participants' responses indicated support for these disparities in the standards. For instance, the liaisons perceived all of the 11 curriculum components to be most important in the instruction of CMHC students. The following is the order in which the liaisons considered addiction training to be most important:

1. CMHC (97.5%)
2. School Counseling (66.2%)
3. Marriage, Couple, and Family Counseling (65.5%)
4. Student Affairs and College Counseling (53.9%)
5. Career Counseling (24.8%)

In other words, on average, 97.5% of the liaisons perceived all of the 11 curriculum components as necessary in the training of CMHC students. In regards to Career Counseling students, the 11 components were perceived as necessary instruction by 24.8% of the sample, on average. Table 2 shows the percentage of the sample that endorsed the necessity of each of the components, by program option. The authors wish to point out the previously accredited Community and Mental Health Counseling programs were not included in this part of the survey.

Discussion and Implications

Addiction training may not be as deficient today as researchers have previously suggested (e.g., Dawes-Diaz, 2007; Harwood et al., 2004; Salyers et al., 2005). According to the results of this study, many CACREP-accredited programs are providing instruction on the various addiction-related curriculum components which are considered important in counselor preparation. Content areas such as screening, diagnosis, counseling strategies, prevention, and intervention are being taught by over 70% of institutions with CACREP-accredited programs. These findings are noteworthy because they demonstrate most counselor education programs in this study are already educating their students on some of the content areas listed in the 2009 Human Growth and Development core competency. In other words, based on the data found in this investigation, less than one-third of the programs may have to incorporate new addiction-related content into curricula due to the core competency requirement.

Perceived Importance of Current Training Requirements

The core competency related to addiction training for all counselors is perceived as sufficient by the majority of the participants. While 92% of survey respondents found this competency to be appropriate as stated, the researchers found some discrepancies in perceived importance of the content identified in the competency. Interestingly, some of the curricular components specified in the core competency are *considered less important* than other components not specified in the competency. Additionally, some of the required content is not currently being taught by 30% or more of the CACREP-accredited programs in the survey. Therefore, the core competency may require training on various content areas, but the content may not be perceived as necessary, nor is it currently taught by a large percentage of programs. For instance, etiological theory content is now required training for all students, yet it was ranked fifth in perceived importance among the 11 curricular components listed, and it is not currently taught by 33% of institutions. Moreover, process addictions content (also required for all counselor education students) was ranked seventh out of the 11 curricular components, and half of institutions in this study did not provide education related to process addictions at the time of the survey. Another point of interest was the data found on the perceived importance of intervention training, which is also a required content area in the core competency. Of the 11 listed components, intervention ranked sixth in importance.

The researchers found screening was ranked the highest in perceived importance and it was also the most frequently taught component by institutions in the sample (78%); however, screening is not required training for all counselor education students. Additionally, content on assessment tools was ranked third, and assessment is not included in the core competency either. In essence, all students in CACREP-accredited programs are to be trained on addiction-related content which the liaisons deemed as important; although, other curricular components (e.g., screening and assessment) may be perceived as more crucial training.

Another significant finding was 8% of the faculty in the sample indicated their students do not receive instruction on any of the 11 curricular components. Potentially, many counselor education programs in existence today will have to incorporate instruction on etiological theories, addictive behaviors, prevention, intervention, and treatment into their curricula for all students in order to be in compliance with the 2009 CACREP Human Growth and Development core competency. Examination of the individual curricular components listed in this core competency (e.g., prevention, intervention, etiological theories, and addictive behaviors) revealed these various aspects are not perceived as crucially important in the education of any students other than CMHC students. For instance, 73% of the CACREP liaisons believed instruction on process addictions is not necessary for Career Counseling students, and one-third of the liaisons believed this content is also not essential for the training of students in the Marriage, Couple, and Family Counseling option. Also, 50% of participants indicated content related to etiological theories does not need to be part of the curricula for Student Affairs and College Counseling. Similarly, 47% of the liaisons think instruction on intervention is also not necessary for Student Affairs and College Counseling trainees. In other words, due to the 2009 Human Growth and Development core competency requirements, all students in CACREP-accredited programs are to be educated on addiction-related content during their training; however, this content (e.g., addictive behaviors, prevention, intervention, etiological theories) may be considered excessive by some faculty.

Faculty Implications

Close to 90% of the liaisons in this study reported their institutions have at least one full-time counselor educator with addictions expertise, and some have up to six members. Moreover, 9% of these institutions were planning to add faculty with addiction expertise within the next two years, and all reportedly had members with expertise. This investigation also found the majority of addiction courses were taught by full-time faculty members with expertise.

The implications of having faculty with knowledge, clinical experience, and research interests pertaining to addictions are significant, particularly with the release of the 2009 CACREP standards. If 16% of the institutions in this study were planning on implementing the new Addiction Counseling option, expertise would assist in the process of obtaining accreditation. Moreover, many counselor education programs are changing the Community Counseling and Mental Health Counseling program curricula to align with the new CMHC program option standards. More than likely, this transition will include incorporating more addiction-related content into courses than in the past and possibly even creating new addiction courses. This investigation found almost 11% of the institutions were planning to add a required addictions course in the counselor education department in the next two years, and 75% of institutions adding a course were doing so to fulfill the 2009 CACREP addiction-related standard requirements. In addition, 39% of the institutions in the sample not offering an elective addictions course have plans to do so in the next two years. These various curricular changes would be more efficient transitions if institutions had faculty with addiction expertise, and this study determined almost all institutions in the sample had someone with such expertise.

On the other hand, over 10% of the institutions had no full-time faculty with expertise, and therefore one in ten of these institutions may have to seek out guidance from faculty in other university departments, adjunct faculty, or other counselor educators in CACREP-accredited programs. Communication among faculty is vital during this time of transition. Journal publications, conference presentations, CACREP training sessions, the ACA-ACES syllabus clearinghouse, and discussions on list-serves (e.g., CES-net) provide opportunities for consultation and the exchange of ideas within the counselor education profession.

When institutions lack the faculty expertise and choose to infuse addiction training into existing courses (in lieu of adding a course), there are methods to aid counselor educators in aligning coursework with the CACREP standards. One possibility is the use of a guest lecturer who is an expert in addictions (e.g., another faculty member or a community service provider). Another option is to develop creative ways to infuse the standards and demonstrate student competency outcomes. One of the CMHC competencies, for example, requires that a student "provides appropriate counseling strategies when working with clients with addiction and co-occurring disorders" (CACREP, 2009, p. 31). In lieu of having he or she demonstrate the necessary addiction-related competencies in the classroom, one solution is to have the internship supervisor indicate whether the student has gained the appropriate addiction-related skills.

Recommendations

Regardless of the method counselor education programs choose to implement the new 2009 standards, CACREP has acknowledged the need for all counselor trainees to gain more addiction-related knowledge and skill. This next section provides recommendations specific to: (a) implementation methods, (b) curricular components, and (c) future research.

Implementation Methods

This study found 62% of the CACREP liaisons in the sample recommended a stand-alone course. This suggested course may cover the following addiction-related content: etiologies and theories, various substances and behaviors to which one can be addicted, routes of administration, screening and assessment, treatment approaches, continuum of care, and co-occurring disorders. The content listed above will cover the necessary instructional content cited within the several CMHC addiction-related competencies and the Human Growth and Development core competency.

Some counselor education programs may choose to meet the new accreditation standards by infusing the instruction into one or more core courses. Faculty may be able to modify the instruction and coursework of two or three existing courses to align curricula with the addiction-related competency requirements. Practicum and internship may be the appropriate stages in training where the skill-based addiction competencies can be demonstrated; however, the knowledge-based training requirements should occur before the clinical parts of counseling programs. For instance, a CMHC student can demonstrate he or she has learned "the disease concept and etiology of addiction and co-occurring disorders" (CACREP, 2009, Standard C.4., p. 30) in a Foundations of Clinical Mental Health Counseling course and then can demonstrate he or she "provides appropriate counseling strategies when working with clients with addiction and co-occurring disorders" (CACREP, 2009, Standard D.8, p. 31) during practicum or internship.

Curricular Components

While the Human Growth and Development core competency may be sufficient, some content may be more appropriate for the training of CMHC students than for students in program options such as Career Counseling. Graduates from Student Affairs and College Counseling programs should also be trained in more addiction-related content (e.g., screening, assessment) due to the prevalence of alcohol and drug use on college campuses (Maggs, Williams, & Lee, 2011; Seigers & Carey, 2010). In addition, the inclusion of addiction-related content pertaining to screening may be very appropriate for the training of all counselors (Madson et al., 2008) and should be added to the core competency in future revisions. Education on various addiction assessment tools was found to be important for the training of all counselors, except Career Counselors. Currently, the

2009 CACREP standards require assessment instruction for students in the CMHC program, but this type of education may be included in the other specializations in the future (e.g., Marriage, Couple, and Family and School Counseling programs). Finally, the CACREP liaisons believe that the ability to diagnose for substance abuse is important for CMHC students, but it does not need to be included in the core area for all students. Therefore, addiction diagnosis is not recommended training for any other counseling program options.

Limitations

The information received from the participants was self-report, based on memory, and subjective. Also, the depth of addiction-related education is a difficult variable to measure. The amount of time an instructor devotes to this training can vary drastically. Training may be found to be happening, but to what extent or depth is unknown. Moreover, the findings could reflect a self-selection bias. Counselor educators who felt confident in this area or had a personal interest in addictions-related education may have been more likely to participate in the survey. On the other hand, if potential participants had a negative view or bias toward this area of training or if their programs are not making significant changes in curricula related to addictions, those liaisons may have opted not to participate.

Future Research

Since the revised edition of the CACREP standards was released in 2009 and this current investigation was completed in 2010, future studies can determine how training is being implemented and how the results differ from this study. The researchers assume many programs were in transition during the time of this study with regard to curricular changes, particularly in addictions training content. Therefore, researchers can survey institutions a couple years from now to find out how many institutions adopted the Addiction Counseling program option and if the number of programs requiring or offering an addictions course has changed.

One aspect of training not researched in this study is where in the curriculum it takes place. Over five years ago, Salyers et al. (2005) found that practicum and internship are commonly the courses where the instruction is occurring. Future researchers can determine since the release of the 2009 CACREP standards, if the content is now infused into other courses more frequently.

As noted above, this investigation did not address how much time is involved or the extent of training. Is the duration of training devoted to a course (e.g., 45 hours), one class period (e.g., 3 hours), or one hour of a class period? Are the competencies taught primarily knowledge or skill-based, or are there objectives focused on addressing attitudes, beliefs, and biases? Future research can update the data found in the Chasek, Jorgensen, and Maxson (2011), Morgan et al. (1997), and Whittinghill et al. (2004) studies. Researchers could examine the syllabi of addiction courses and therefore, course design can be investigated. By doing so, researchers can determine if instructors are using didactic lecture, research-based projects, application assignments, reflective assignments, or experiential activities, and what type of competencies are being taught.

This investigation examined faculty members' perceptions and opinions related to addiction training. A few years ago, Dawes-Diaz (2007) asked graduates about their satisfaction with the addiction instruction they received and determined what addiction content was taught at that time. The sample included graduates from non-accredited CACREP programs. Future research could replicate the Dawes-Diaz study and focus on graduates from CACREP-accredited programs. Due to the new requirements pertaining to addictions, it is assumed the data obtained from graduates of CACREP programs would differ from graduates of programs which may not adhere to the CACREP standards.

Of the 218 institutions offering CACREP-accredited programs at the time of this study, liaisons from 74 institutions completed the survey. Thus, the response rate was approximately 34%. The implications and recommendations made by this researcher are based on data collected from approximately one-third of the institutions which have accredited counseling programs. Therefore, the authors suggest CACREP facilitate further data gathering and assessment in an effort to gain a larger sample size and reinvestigate the research questions posed in this study.

In conclusion, the 2009 CACREP standards symbolize a recognition that addiction instruction was lacking in the past and now there are educational requirements in this subject matter for all counselors-in-training. A stand-alone addictions course is the preferred method of implementation. For students wishing to specialize in this area, there is an Addiction Counseling program option now offered and a dozen programs reportedly will seek accreditation in the future. CACREP program faculty also indicated plans to add addiction courses and more faculty members with addiction expertise in the next two years. These proposed changes in counselor education appear to reflect the need to align with the 2009 CACREP standards, as well as the acknowledgement for the need to provide this type of training to future practitioners.

References

Burrow-Sanchez, J., Lopez, A., & Slagle, C. (2008). Perceived competence in addressing student substance abuse: A national survey of middle school counselors. *Journal of School Health, 78*, 280–286.

Chasek, C. L., Jorgensen, M., & Maxson, T. (2011). Assessing counseling students' attitudes regarding substance abuse and treatment. *Journal of Addictions and Offender Counseling, 33*, 107–114.

Council for Accreditation of Counseling and Related Educational Programs (CACREP). (2009). *CACREP accreditation standards and procedures manual*. Alexandria, VA: Author.

Crespi, T., & Rueckert, Q. (2006). Family therapy and children of alcoholics: Implications for continuing education and certification in substance abuse practice. *Journal of Child & Adolescent Substance Abuse, 15*, 33–44.

Dawes-Diaz, M. L. (2007). *Education and training in substance abuse: Counselor perceptions and recommendations* (Doctoral dissertation). Available from ProQuest Dissertations and Theses database. (UMI No. 3293150)

Harwood, H., Kowalski, J., & Ameen, A. (2004). The need for substance abuse training among mental health professionals. *Administration and Policy in Mental Health, 32*, 189–205.

Hosie, T. W., West, J. D., & Mackey, J. A. (1990). Perceptions of counselor performance in substance abuse centers. *Journal of Mental Health Counseling, 12*, 199–207.

Lee, T. K. (2011). *Implementation of the 2009 CACREP Standards addiction competencies*. (Doctoral Dissertation). Retrieved from ProQuest Database. (UMI 3455075.)

Madson, M. B., Bethea, A. R., Daniel, S., & Necaise, H. (2008). The state of substance abuse treatment training in counseling and counseling psychology programs: What is and is not happening. *Journal of Teaching in the Addictions, 7*(2), 164–178.

Maggs, J. L., Williams, L. R., & Lee, C. M. (2011). Ups and downs of alcohol use among first-year college students: Number of drinks, heavy drinking, and stumble and pass out drinking days. *Addictive Behaviors, 36*, 197–202. doi: 10.1016/j.addbeh.2010.10.005

Morgan, O., Toloczko, A. M., & Comly, E. (1997). Graduate training of counselors in the addictions: A study of CACREP-approved programs. *Journal of Addictions and Offender Counseling, 17*, 66–76.

Ong, L. Z., Lee, D. Y., Cha, G., & Arokiasamy, C. (2008). Training needs for substance abuse treatment and assessment among rehabilitation counselors: California state project. Journal of Teaching in the Addictions, 7, 109–122.

Salyers, K., Ritchie, M., Luellen, W., & Roseman, C. (2005). Inclusion of substance abuse training in CACREP-accredited programs. *Counselor Education and Supervision, 45*, 30–42.

Seigers, D. K., & Carey, K. B. (2010). Alcohol use, psychopathology, and treatment utilization in a university mental health clinic. *Journal of College Student Psychotherapy, 24*, 328–337. doi: 10.1080/87568225.2010.509250

Toloczko, A. M., Morgan, O. J., Hall, D., Bruch, L. A., Mullane, J. & Walck, C. (1998). Graduate training of rehabilitation counselors in the addictions: A study of CORE-approved programs. *Rehabilitation Education, 12*(2), 115–127. doi:10.2190/R7Q1-7521-7865-6222

Von Steen, P. G., Vacc, N. A., & Strickland, I. M. (2002). The treatment of substance abusing clients in multiservice mental health agencies: A practice analysis. *Journal of Addictions and Offender Counseling, 22,* 61–71.

Whittinghill, D. (2006). A preliminary investigation of the components of a curriculum for the preparation of master's level addiction counselors. *Journal of Drug Education, 36,* 357–371. doi:10.2190/R7Q1-7521-7865-6222

Whittinghill, D., Carroll, J., & Morgan, O. (2004). Curriculum changes for the education of professional substance abuse counselors. *Journal of Teaching in the Addictions, 3,* 63–76.

Table 1

Total Number and Percent of Sample Teaching Specific Addiction Curriculum Components

Curriculum Component	Count	Percent of Sample
Screening	58	78.4%
Diagnosis	57	77.0%
Counseling Strategies	54	73.0%
Prevention	53	71.6%
Intervention	52	70.3%
Assessment Tools	51	68.9%
Etiological Theories	50	67.6%
Co-occurring Disorders	49	66.2%
Treatment Options	47	63.5%
Pharmacology	39	52.7%
Process Addictions	37	50.0%
None of the Above	6	8.1%

Table 2

Percent of Participants Indicating Necessity of Curriculum Component by Program Option

Curriculum Component	CMHC	Career	Marriage, Couple, and Family	School	Student Affairs and College	No Programs
Screening	98.6%	50.0%	77.0%	91.9%	73.0%	1.3%
Prevention	97.3%	29.7%	66.2%	86.5%	64.9%	1.3%
Assessment Tools	97.3%	29.7%	70.3%	73.0%	64.9%	1.3%
Treatment Options	97.3%	27.0%	66.2%	68.9%	55.4%	0.0%
Etiological Theories	100.0%	25.7%	64.9%	68.9%	50.0%	0.0%
Intervention	97.3%	21.6%	66.2%	64.9%	52.7%	1.3%
Counseling Strategies	98.6%	13.5%	68.9%	66.2%	51.3%	0.0%
Process Addictions	95.9%	25.7%	67.6%	62.2%	48.6%	1.3%
Diagnosis	100.0%	24.3%	59.5%	54.0%	50.0%	0.0%
Co-occurring Disorders	98.6%	16.2%	62.2%	54.0%	43.2%	0.0%
Pharmacology	91.9%	9.5%	51.3%	37.8%	39.2%	5.4%

5

Training Students in Counselor Education Programs in Process Addictions
A Pilot Study

Judith A. Nelson, Angie D. Wilson, and Leigh F. Holman[1]

The addictions field continues to grow and is expanding beyond the area of substance use disorders. *Process addictions* are now an integral aspect of addictions treatment, diagnosis, and assessment. An initial study was conducted to initiate an understanding of levels of knowledge students in counselor education programs have in diagnosing, assessing and treating clients with process addictions, indicators of where and how they learned about process addictions, and of how students believe they will integrate their level of the treatment of process addictions into clinical practice. This article provides a brief overview of process addictions, a summary of original research, implications of this study, discussion, and recommendations for future research.

---

1. Judith A. Nelson, Department of Educational Leadership and Counseling, Sam Houston State University; Angie D. Wilson, Department of Psychology, Counseling, & Special Education, Texas A&M University—Commerce; Leigh F. Holman, Department of Counselor Education, Argosy University—Dallas Campus. Correspondence concerning this article should be addressed to Judith A. Nelson, Department of Educational Leadership and Counseling, Sam Houston State University, PO Box 2119, Huntsville, TX 77341-2119. E-mail: elc_jan@shsu.edu.edu

The American Counseling Association (ACA), as well as the ACA divisions the American Mental Health Counseling Association (AMHCA) and the Association for Assessment and Research in Counseling (AARC) provide ethical guidelines that indicate counselors should not practice outside of their level of competency. According to Freimuth (2005), addictive behaviors or process addictions (PA) (also called behavioral addictions) are common in clinical populations and often are not explicitly identified as the client's presenting problem. According to Grant, Potenza, Weinstein, and Gorelick (2010):

> Several behaviors, besides psychoactive substance ingestion, produce short-term reward that may engender persistent behavior despite knowledge of adverse consequences, i.e., diminished control over the behavior. Diminished control is a core defining concept of psychoactive substance dependence or addiction. This similarity has given rise to the concept of non-substance or "behavioral" addictions, i.e., syndromes analogous to substance addiction, but with a behavioral focus other than ingestion of a psychoactive substance. The concept of behavioral addictions has some scientific and clinical heuristic value, but remains controversial. (p. 233)

Examples of these addictive behaviors include pathological gambling, compulsive buying, sexual addiction, and Internet addiction. Clients with addictions have high rates of co-occurring diagnosis (Centre for Addiction and Mental Health [CAMH], 2010). Therefore, all counselors are likely to have clients with addictive behaviors at some point.

Malat, Collins, Dhayanandhan, Carullo, and Turner (2010) utilized the Addictive Behaviors Questionnaire (ABQ) on a sample of persons being treated for mental illness and a comorbid addiction. Their study resulted in 61% of their sample population endorsing at least one process addiction, and 31% of their sample endorsing two or more process addictions as problem behaviors. The authors noted that the most common process addictions reported by the participants in their study included: overeating, unhealthy relationships, excessive TV watching, and shopping in excess. According to researchers at the CAMH (2010), "the best predictor for a client having a given process addiction is evidence for their already having another process addiction" (p. 7). Process addictions often overlap and can be interchanged in order to meet the need of the client; therefore, treating one but not all process addictions often negatively impacts the client's success in treatment, and clinicians should be prepared to screen for several process addictions with one client (CAMH, 2010).

Although counseling clients with substance use disorders is taught in most counselor education programs, process addictions are new to counselor education standards, and ambiguity continues to be an issue among counselor educators regarding what constitutes a process addiction or if they even exist. There continues to be confusion among names for PAs which contributes to them being overlooked in counselor education programs, for example, in the DSM-V (American Psychiatric Association [APA], 2013), process addictions are referred to as behavioral addictions or non-substance addictions. Although PAs are recognized in the DSM-V as behavioral or non-substance addictions a specific section or category is "not included because at this time there is insufficient peer-reviewed evidence to establish the diagnostic criteria and course descriptions needed to identify these behaviors as mental disorders" (APA, 2013, p. 481). As such, counselors, counselor educators, and students in counselor education programs may need additional training in the assessment, diagnosis, and treatment of process addictions. Additionally, according to Freimuth's (2005) research, education alone is not sufficient to increase accuracy of identifying addictive behaviors. Counselors' beliefs, attitudes, and biases need to be identified and examined in order to improve their ability to correctly identify individuals who need further assessment.

What Are Process Addictions?

Although the term *addiction* has often been restricted to substances, this is primarily because of politics, professional turf wars, and public relations campaigns, according to Alexander and Schweighofer (1988) in their history of the term *addiction*. They asserted that similar to substance addictions "compulsive involvements with [behaviors] can consume a person's entire existence and can have tragic consequences," (p. 154) thus indicating that behavioral addictions exist. Donovan and Marlatt (1988) argued that addictions are not defined by the focus of the addiction (e. g. drugs) but by the process that addictions have in common including eating disorders, gambling, drug addiction, etc. Although some people are addicted to substances and others to behaviors, they all involve an *addictive process*. Thus, process addictions (PA) (Smith & Seymour, 2004), also called compulsive behaviors (Inaba & Cohen, 2011) and behavioral addictions (Grant, Potenza, Weinstein, & Gorelick, 2010), involve a compulsion "around doing behaviors" (Shallcross, 2011, p. 32).

More recently, medical and neuropsychological evidence provides support for our understanding of addiction as characterized by neurological and hormonal changes that occur as a result of the continued ritualized use of the substance or behavior (Zhang, Tian, von Deneen, Liu, & Gold, 2012). Zhang et al. (2012) stated in *Neuropsychiatry* that…

> acquired continued and compulsive overeating is one process addiction similar to other activities or behaviors, such as excessive video gaming, pathological gambling, hypersexuality or excessive internet use where the addict shows loss of control, an inability to stop or modify the activity, and a range of signs and symptoms that can be as debilitating as those associated with substance abuse or addiction. (p. 156)

Additionally, the authors offered research indicating similar neurological and endocrine changes among food, gambling, and Internet addictions to substance addictions. What begins as a functional, pleasurable experience becomes maladaptive when the patterns of behavior begin to interfere with the person's activities of daily living. Researchers have demonstrated evidence for the existence of a variety of PAs including gambling (Ashley & Boehlke, 2012; Jamieson, Mazmanian, Penney, Black, & Nguyen, 2011); Internet addiction (Jiang & Leung, 2012); exercise addiction (Parastatidou, Doganis, Theodorakis, & Vlachopoulos, 2012); food addictions (APA, 2012a; Wonderlich, Gordon, Mitchell, Crosby, & Engel, 2009); and sex addiction (APA, 2012b).

Why Are Process Addictions Important to Study?

Process addictions are a growing concern in counseling (Holden, 2001; Martin & Petry, 2005; Grant et al., 2010), as evidenced by several process addictions being referenced in the APA (2000) Diagnostic and Statistical Manual of Mental Disorders (4th ed., text rev.) and in the development references for the DSM-V (APA, 2013). Additionally, the Council for Accreditation of Counseling and Related Educational Programs (CACREP; 2009) standards revision included for the first time an expectation that clinical mental health counseling programs train students to screen for and assess process addictions. However, the standards specific to addictions counseling programs only refer to *addictions* without a clear definition regarding whether process addictions or only substances are included.

The need for training in process addictions assessment, diagnosis, and treatment is supported by Sussman, Lisha, and Griffiths (2011) in their review of 83 studies and estimated prevalence rates for PA. They found rates for gambling addiction at 2%, Internet addiction at 2%, sex addiction 3%, exercise addiction 2%, and eating addiction 2% among the general American population. Additionally, they also estimated substance abuse co-morbidity rates at 20–30% for gambling addiction and 10% for Internet addiction. However, in an informal review of textbooks by the International Association of Addiction and Offender Counselor's (IAAOC) Process Addictions Committee, none of the addictions texts treated PA as equal to substance addictions. Many texts had no information about PA, whereas others had cursory information on a handful of PA. Additionally, little was found in the professional literature relevant to teaching PA to counseling students. As such, the purpose of this study was to survey students currently enrolled in counselor education programs regarding their level of exposure to and perceived self-efficacy in screening, assessing, diagnosing, and treating a variety of PA. Students' perceptions of the importance of being trained in these skills were also explored.

Methodology

A mixed methods design was employed using the formulation stages found in Leech and Onwuegbuzie (2010) including identifying the goal, objective, rationale, purpose, and research questions. Our goals were to conduct research that would have an institutional and/or organizational impact on how students in counselor education programs are trained in process addictions and to inform constituencies about the status of this training. We chose exploration and description as our research objectives, and our rationale for using mixed research was significance enhancement (Collins, Onwuegbuzie, & Sutton, 2006). We believed that a mixed design would ultimately provide richer data than using only a quantitative or qualitative design. Using a mixed-methods design (Creswell, 2009; Leech

& Onwuegbuzie, 2010), an online survey was employed in which both open-ended and closed-ended questions were utilized to answer the following research questions in a pilot study relevant to process addictions: (a) What is the extent of pre- and post- service education and training in process addictions for students in counselor education programs? (b) What is the extent of assessment, diagnosis, and treatment of process addictions by counseling students with or without specific training? (c) To what extent do students in counselor education programs feel they are prepared to work with clients presenting with PA? The mixed research was conducted concurrently (Creswell, 2009). As such, no particular sequence was implemented because the quantitative and qualitative data held equal priority in the study, and the data were integrated at the time of data collection.

Using both qualitative and quantitative methods for evaluating the data allowed us to explore rich information provided by participants and compare their responses. Onwuegbuzie and Johnson (2006) coined the term *legitimation* regarding the process of evaluating criteria before, during, and upon the completion of a study to ensure that rigorous methods are employed throughout the research process. Our research team utilized the following recommendations for legitimation (validity) in mixed-methods research. For example, members of the PA Committee in the IAAOC who are counselor educators, researchers, and practitioners reviewed the survey multiple times and made comments to improve the clarity of the items. Additionally, members of the research team provided feedback regarding interpretation of the data to achieve *inside-outside legitimation*. Also, the quantitative and the qualitative questions were introduced to the participants simultaneously within the survey; therefore, neither method took precedence over the other. As such, potential sequencing problems were minimized. Lastly, the political outcomes of our study were taken carefully into consideration. Although the participants were students in counselor education programs, clearly the stakeholders without a voice in this study were the potential clients of these students and clients of practicing counselors. Keeping the needs of counseling clients uppermost in our minds as we conducted our research provided a political lens that has the potential to impact clients positively in therapeutic counseling settings.

The study was a survey design which provided a numeric description of trends, attitudes, and opinions of a population by studying a sample of that population (Creswell, 2009). In addition, open-ended questions in the survey provided richer data than if only the quantitative data had been collected. This design was used to provide rapid turnaround in data collection and to be able to reach students in two large geographic areas. We surveyed a sample of students currently enrolled in counselor education programs in order to determine if a national study of PA would be appropriate and essential to inform the counseling profession relevant to counselor training. Descriptive data were reported from the survey results, and qualitative data were also analyzed and reported.

Participants

The study was conducted in two states, North Carolina and Texas. Upon receiving approval from the Institutional Review Boards of the three investigators' universities, email invitations and a link to the survey were sent to individuals who were students in counselor education programs at various universities in both states. The participants were enlisted by the three investigators through professional listservs, websites of professional organizations, personal communication with counseling professionals, and word of mouth. The invitation asked participants to click on the URL address of the survey to read the informed consent and to begin the survey. Not knowing how many counseling students actually received the invitation, calculating the response rate was not possible. The total sample for our pilot study included 56 students in counselor education programs. The student participants included 68% ($n = 38$) pursuing a Master of Arts degree in Clinical, Mental Health Counseling; 2% ($n = 1$) pursuing a master's degree in a counseling related field with an addiction certification; 11% ($n = 6$) pursuing an education specialist degree in a counseling related field; and 20% ($n = 11$) pursuing a doctorate in a counseling related field. No student reported pursuing a master's degree in addictions. With regards to accreditation of the respondents' counselor education programs, 88% ($n = 48$) reported being enrolled in a CACREP accredited program. In addition, 11% ($n = 6$) of students reported that they were unaware of their program's accreditation status, 2% ($n = 1$) of respondents reported that their program was regionally accredited, while one participant did not respond to the question regarding CACREP accreditation. The majority of respondents (68%) reported their progression in their graduate program being between the fourth semester and practicum or internship.

Instrument

A survey instrument (see Appendix A) was developed by counselor educators and practicing counselors for the purpose of conducting the study of students in counselor education programs on their opinions and experiences with PA. The survey questions were based on a thorough review of the literature and were relevant to the participants' knowledge of process addictions and their experiences in training programs and in the courses being taught at training facilities. The survey questions developed were grounded in current survey methods research guidelines (Dillman, Smyth, & Christian, 2009), were sent to all members of the IAAOC Process Addictions Committee to assess for content validity, and finally were revised based on the members' feedback. The survey included both closed-ended and open-ended questions and was designed to be completed in 10 to 15 minutes. Committee members who are researchers and practitioners in professional counseling completed the survey at least two times to generate feedback on problems of clarity with the language of the survey questions, technical problems with the survey, and any other problems that might result in low participation rates. Comments and concerns were forwarded to the research team working on the project, and changes to the survey were made as needed.

In addition to the descriptive survey questions, open-ended text boxes were provided for participants to elaborate on their responses. Also, one grand tour question (Spradley, 1979) was asked of the participants who agreed to be interviewed. According to Spradley, using grand tour questions constitutes an emergent quality of the interview process to result in subsequent questions. The question was: What are your thoughts or feelings about working with clients who present with PA?

Data Collection

Zip SurveyTM was used to post the surveys and collect responses as well as to analyze the demographic and quantitative data. To access participants, we identified professional and university listservs and posted the link to the survey on the listservs. The postings indicated that we were interested in surveying students in counselor education programs. Upon opening the link, the participant read the informed consent and agreed that they understood the nature of the study by continuing with the survey questions. The participants were assured in the informed consent that their responses were anonymous and confidential. In addition, 10 participants provided their contact information and agreed to be interviewed by either telephone or SKYPE™. Five participants were able to be reached for the interviews. The interviews were conducted using an unstructured, open-ended interview protocol in order to capture the exact words of the students regarding PA.

Data Analysis

Quantitative data analysis. The survey, statement of anonymity and confidentiality, as well as the informed consent was posted in Zip SurveyTM, and participants were prompted to review this information before proceeding with the study. The quantitative data also was collected and analyzed within the Zip SurveyTM program. The quantitative results are descriptive data and are reported as such in the results section.

Qualitative data analysis. The qualitative responses from the open-ended text box responses on the survey and from the interviews were analyzed using a coding process in which the participants' responses were organized into chunks (Rossman & Rallis, 1998). This process involved reading the text and labeling the chunks with a term or category that often included actual language used by the participants. The researchers met on several occasions to reach consensus on their separate analyses of the qualitative data. Additionally, both quantitative and qualitative data were compared with one another to achieve triangulation (Creswell, 2009; Onwuegbuzie & Johnson, 2006).

Results

Quantitative Results

In addition to providing responses about their programs' accreditation and their progression in their respective programs, the 56 students also answered several survey questions regarding PA. Specifically, the participants responded to questions regarding their comfort levels working with PA, assessing, diagnosing, and treating nine different forms of PA. Seventy-eight percent ($n = 43$) of respondents reported that their counseling program offered a course on addictions counseling, however, only 4% ($n = 2$) of participants reported that their programs had a course specifically designated to teaching process addictions. No respondents reported a course in PA being a part of the core curriculum of their counselor education program. Although the majority of respondents reported that their programs do not have courses designated to teach PA, 23% ($n = 13$) of participants reported PA had been integrated in other courses. Seven percent ($n = 4$) of students reported that they had taken a course on how to recognize, screen, diagnose, and treat process addictions while 93% ($n = 51$) reported they had not.

With regards to comfort level in assessing, diagnosing, and treating process addictions; 7% ($n = 4$) of respondents reported feeling very comfortable; 15% ($n = 8$) reported feeling comfortable; 29% ($n = 16$) reported feeling ambivalent; 38% ($n = 21$) reported not feeling comfortable; and 11% ($n = 6$) selected not applicable. Students reported being trained to assess, diagnose, and treat eating disorders more than the other process addictions listed on the survey. Eating disorders, addiction to unhealthy relationships, and sexual addiction were the three PA with which students reported the most learning experience. Twenty-seven percent ($n = 21$) of respondents had been trained to assess and diagnose eating disorders, and 24% ($n = 17$) had been trained to treat eating disorders. Training for assessment, diagnosis, and treatment of all PA categories listed on the survey was consistent. Despite their limited preparation and knowledge of PA 69% ($n = 38$) of respondents categorized the training of counselors to assess, diagnose, and treat process addictions as very important, and 29% ($n = 16$) of respondents categorized it as important.

Qualitative Results

Participants were given the opportunity to provide qualitative responses to some questions. The following themes emerged: (a) students had no familiarity with process addictions; (b) students had heard of process addictions and knew it had to do with behavior rather than substances, but had no specific knowledge of them; (c) students have had little or no training on process addictions; (d) students have had training on information in the diagnostic criteria, but no training specifically on process addictions. When asked for additional comments one student stated "I think this is a very important but overlooked area in our counseling program. I wish that I had more training on how to assess and treat process addictions." Another student wrote "I appreciate this interview because I think it will make me more aware of process addictions in my remaining coursework and also in my practicum and internship experience." When asked about textbooks and classroom resources utilized to explain PA, one student responded "I was encouraged to do independent reading in areas that [were] of interest to me, and many times the reading focused on these types of addictions (PA)."

The follow-up phone interviews revealed similar themes as were found in the survey data. All of the participants indicated that they had not had specific training in the area of PA, but had been trained to identify sexual addictions or eating disorders. However, one participant stated that she was learning how to treat PA in her internship where the clients sometimes presented with sexual addiction or eating disorders. Another interviewee felt that he was learning a great deal in his internship about Internet addiction and gaming, but did not have specific training in coursework other than identifying sexual addiction in the sexual concerns class. Working with adolescents, he found that many of them use electronic devices to the point of distraction resulting in an inability to relate well to their families. In fact, as the interview progressed, he speculated that this may become an area of expertise for him. He indicated that he was not aware of counselors who specialize in this area but that there is a great need for expertise in working with process addictions, particularly gaming, among adolescent populations.

Discussion

The results of this survey identified several areas of concern regarding PA and the training of professional counselors. Many of the students were not familiar with the term PA and had no specific training in PA. Most ($n = 51$) reported that they had not been trained to recognize, screen, diagnose, and treat PA. Although new to some students, PA represented neither new phenomena nor new disorders. In fact, PAs have been a growing concern in the addictions field (Grant et al., 2010; Holden, 2001; Martin & Petry, 2005). Several PA are well researched and are referenced in the DSM-IV-TR and the DSM-V Development (APA, 2012b) including gambling disorder, Internet addiction, hypersexual disorder, exercise addiction, and binge eating disorder. While it is not possible to generalize to all students in counselor education programs, the results of this study may indicate a need for a national study to determine the status of training in PA in programs across the United States.

One of the challenges in training students in counselor education programs is that many counselor educators reported not being current in their own training on PA (Crozier & Agius, 2012). These researchers conducted a similar study of counselor educators and PA and found that only 43% ($n = 9$) of the counselor educators surveyed felt *comfortable* or *very comfortable* teaching students about PA, therefore, many counselor educators may not be providing training on PA to their students due to their own perceived lack of self-efficacy in teaching students about this topic. Additionally, in our current study, students reported very few programs that offered courses in PA ($n = 2$). Some students even indicated some confusion about terminology and were not familiar with the term PA, indicating that PA may not have been introduced at all in their programs.

Limitations

There were several limitations to this study of students in counselor education programs. The convenience sample included students in counselor education programs in North Carolina and Texas whose programs were listed on the Internet, who were members of professional listservs, and whose programs were CACREP or CORE certified; this may have limited the pool of potential respondents. The survey was also sent through professional listservs, making the response rate in-calculable. Also, the survey instrument may not have captured all the essential information about PA from students in counselor education programs. For example, the term *process addictions* used in the survey may have confused some respondents since approximately 40% reported preferring the term behavioral addictions. Another limitation is that approximately 60% of respondents reported they did not know if PA was integrated into other courses in their counselor education programs. Nevertheless, given the lack of research about training counseling students about PA and the increasing necessity for training, the study provides useful information for counselor educators and supervisors.

Recommendations

Training in counselor education programs. We support the training of counselor educators in PA through workshops, conferences, and special training opportunities. Also, as suggested by Freimuth's (2005) research, pre-service counselors' education should include an honest assessment of their attitudes, beliefs, and biases related to addiction and addicted populations. An informed counselor educator population would support the initial findings of this study that students want more training on PA and believe it is important to be trained in PA. In addition to didactic training, students would benefit from learning how to assess and diagnose PA in their practicum courses and ultimately know how to either treat or refer clients presenting with PA.

Process addictions should be included in ethics courses since competency and practicing outside one's scope of training is an issue of concern when students and practicing counselors indicate a lack of self-efficacy in screening, assessing, diagnosing, or treating PA. Due to the unique nature of PA and the prevalence rates of PA in the general population, classes on assessment and appraisal should include screening procedures as well as more in-depth assessment of specific PA.

We would support the inclusion of PA specific assessment measures among the resources provided on the website of the Association for Assessment and Research in Counseling. Also, any addiction-specific class should fully integrate PA within the class along with substance addictions. Co-morbidity of these addictions should be addressed as should symptom substitution, using one addiction to supplement use as an emotion regulation tool when the client is abstinent from the primary addiction. Screening and assessment of each type of addiction could be taught in one unit. Specialized training and treatment protocols for different types of addictions could be covered in separate units while also discussing the similarities in treatment approaches and addiction-specific treatment issues shared by substance use disorders and PA.

Additional training in process addictions. Although special certifications exist for professional qualification to treat specific types of process addictions, such as the Certified Sexual Addiction Therapist training, counselor educators really only need to be aware of these programs of continuing education and make use of those in which they are interested clinically. IAAOC sponsors a webinar series providing continuing education on PA in general and on specific process addictions such as sexual addictions. The IAAOC PA committee also continues to develop resources for counselor educators on specific PA including reading lists and power point presentations available on its website, which counselor educators can access and even use as teaching resources. Due to the deficits in training identified by this pilot study and in light of professional ethical competency and scope of practice standards, counselor educators should actively seek to attend process addictions conference workshops at conventions of the Association for Counselor Education and Supervision (ACES), IAAOC, the American Mental Health Counselors Association, and the American Counseling Association, as well as state and regional counseling conventions. Also, IAAOC should consider partnering with other divisions of ACA such as ACES and AARC to produce online training and resources for counselor educators to become more knowledgeable about process addictions and as teaching tools for educating students about process addictions.

Call for a national study. Based on the results of this mixed research conducted to explore training students in counselor education programs on PA, we believe the following recommendation should be considered. We recommend a national study using a similar research design to explore the status of PA training in a larger number and improved diversity of counselor education programs. Such a study would require funding and access to counselor listservs in order to reach a broad representation of students in counselor education programs.

References

Alexander, B. K., & Schweighofer, A. F. (1988). Defining "addiction." *Canadian Psychology/Psychologie Canadienne, 29*(2), 151–162. doi: 10.1037/h0084530

American Psychiatric Association. (2000). *Diagnostic and statistical manual of mental disorders* (4th ed., text rev.). Washington, DC: Author.

American Psychiatric Association. (2012a). *DSM-5 Development: K 05 binge eating disorder?* Retrieved from http://www.dsm5.org/proposedrevision/pages/proposedrevision.aspx?rid=372#

American Psychiatric Association. (2012b). *DSM-5 Development.* Retrieved from http://www.dsm5.org/Pages/Default.aspx

American Psychiatric Association. (2013). *Diagnostic and statistical manual of mental disorders* (5th ed.). Arlington VA: Author.

Ashley, L. L., & Boehlke, K. K. (2012). Pathological gambling: A general overview. *Journal of Psychoactive Drugs, 44*(1), 27–37. doi:10.1080/02791072.2012.662078

Centre for Addiction and Mental Health (2010). *An introduction to process addictions.* Retrieved from http://www.problemgambling.ca/EN/Documents/AnIntroductiontoProcessAddictions.pdf

Collins, K., Onwuegbuzie, A. J., & Sutton, I. L. (2006). A model incorporating the rationale and purpose for conducting mixed methods research in special education and beyond. *Learning Disabilities: A Contemporary Journal, 4,* 67–100.

Council for Accreditation of Counseling and Related Educational Programs. (2009). *Council for Accreditation of Counseling and Related Educational Programs 2009 Standards.* Retrieved from http://www.cacrep.org/doc/2009%20Standards%20with%20cover.pdf

Creswell, J. (2009). *Research design: Qualitative, quantitative, and mixed methods approaches* (3rd Ed.). Los Angeles, LA: Sage.

Crozier, M. & Agius, M. (2012). Counselor educators and process addictions: How we know what we know. *North Carolina Perspectives, 7*(1), 32–40.

Dillman, D., Smyth, J., & Christian, L. (2009). *Internet, mail, and mixed-mode surveys: The tailored design method* (3rd Ed.). Hoboken, NJ: John Wiley & Sons.

Donovan, D. M., & Marlatt A. G. (Eds.) (1988). *Assessment of addictive behaviors.* New York, NY: The Guilford Press.

Freimuth, M. (2005). *Hidden addictions.* Lanaham, MD: Roman and Littlefield Publishers.

Grant, J. E., Potenza, M. N., Weinstein, A., & Gorelick, D. A. (2010). Introduction to behavioral addictions. *The American Journal of Drug and Alcohol Abuse, 36*(5), 233–241. doi:10.3109/00952990.2010.491884

Holden C. (2001) 'Behavioral' addictions: Do they exist? *Science, 294* (5544), 980–982.

Inaba, D. & Cohen, W. (2011). *Uppers, downers, all arounders: Physical and mental effects of psychoactive drugs* (7th Ed.). Medford, OR: CNS Productions.

Jamieson, J., Mazmanian, D., Penney, A., Black, N., & Nguyen, A. (2011). When problem gambling is the primary reason for seeking addiction treatment. *International Journal of Mental Health and Addiction, 9*(2), 180–192. doi:10.1007/s11469-009-9268-3

Jiang, Q., & Leung, L. (2012). Effects of individual differences, awareness-knowledge, and acceptance of Internet addiction as a health risk on willingness to change internet habits. *Social Science Computer Review, 30*(2), 170–183. doi:10.1177/0894439311398440

Leech, N. L., & Onwuegbuzie, A. J. (2010). Guidelines for conducting and reporting mixed research in the field of counseling and beyond. *Journal of Counseling & Development, 88*, 61–69. doi: 10.1002/j.1556-6678.2010.tb00151.x

Malat, J., Collins, J., Dhayanandhan, B., Carullo, F. & Turner, N. (2010). Addictive behaviors in comorbid addiction and mental illness: Preliminary results from a self-report questionnaire. *Journal of Addiction Medicine,* 4(1), 38–46.

Martin, P. R., & Petry, N. M. (2005). Are non-substance-related addictions really addictions? *The American Journal on Addictions,* 14(1), 1–7. doi: 10.1080/10550490590899808

Onwuegbuzie, A. J., & Johnson, B. (2006). The validity issues in mixed research. *Research in Schools,* 13(1), 48–63.

Parastatidou, I. S., Doganis, G., Theodorakis, Y., & Vlachopoulos, S. P. (2012). Addicted to exercise: Psychometric properties of the Exercise Dependence Scale-Revised in a sample of Greek exercise participants. *European Journal of Psychological Assessment,* 28(1), 3–10. doi:10.1027/1015-5759/a000084

Rossman, G. B., & Rallis, S. F. (1998*). Learning in the field: An introduction to qualitative research.* Thousand Oaks, CA: Sage.

Shallcross, L. (June, 2011). Don't turn away. *Counseling Today,* 53(12), 30–38.

Smith, D., & Seymour, R. (2004). The nature of addiction. In R. Coombs (Ed.), *Handbook of addictive disorders: A practical guide to diagnosis and treatment* (pp. 3–30). Hoboken, NJ: Wiley and Sons.

Spradley, J. P. (1979). *The Ethnographic Interview.* Belmont, CA: Wadsworth, Cengage Learning.

Sussman, S. Lisha, N., & Griffiths, M. (2011). Prevalence of the addictions: A problem of the majority or the minority? *Evaluation & the Health Professions,* 34(1), 3–56. doi: 10.1177/0163278710380124

Wonderlich, S. A., Gordon, K. H., Mitchell, J. E., Crosby, R. D., & Engel, S. G. (2009). The validity and clinical utility of binge eating disorder. *International Journal of Eating Disorders,* 42(8), 687–705. doi:10.1002/eat.20719

Zhang, Y., Tian, J., von Deneen, K., Liu, Y., & Gold, M. S. (2012). Process addictions in 2012: Food, internet and gambling. *Neuropsychiatry,* 2(2), 155–161.

Appendix A: Survey Instrument Sample Items

Does your program offer a course on addictions counseling (or some variation)?

Does your program have a coursed dedicated to teaching process addictions?

Have you taken a course on how to recognize, screen, diagnose, and treat process addictions?

Is the topic of process addiction integrated into another course?

If the topic of process addictions is integrated into another course, please indicate which course:

Rate your comfort level in assessing, diagnosing, and treating process addictions:

Which of the following process addictions were you trained to assess/screen for? Check all that apply.

Which of the following process addictions were you trained to diagnose?

Which of the following process addictions were you trained to treat?

Describe your training with respect to process addictions:

Rate the importance of training counselors to assess/screen, diagnose, & treat process addictions:

Please write any additional comments, questions, or recommendations related to process addictions in the space below.

6

Competency Based Alcohol and Drug Clinical Supervision Model

CHRISTINE CHASEK[1]

A competency based supervision model is proposed combining the framework developed by the Center for Substance Abuse Treatment, the Blended Model of Supervision, and the Integrated Developmental Model based on supervisee needs. The application and structure of the newly defined Competency Based Alcohol and Drug Clinical Supervision Model is presented.

Substance use, abuse, and dependency in the United States have long been national problems. The U.S. Department of Health and Human Services, Substance Abuse and Mental Health Services Administration (SAMHSA), and the Office of Applied Studies (2007) report that an estimated 51.1%, or 126.8 million, American's age 12 and over use alcohol and 9%, or 22.3 million, can be classified with substance use disorder based on the criteria in the *Diagnostic and Statistical Manual of Mental Disorders*, 5th Edition (American Psychological Association [APA], 2013). In addition, the rate of illicit drug use of American's age 12 and

---

[1]. Christine L. Chasek, Department of Counseling and School Psychology, University of Nebraska Kearney. Correspondence concerning this article should be addressed to Christine L. Chasek, Department of Counseling and School Psychology, University of Nebraska Kearney, 905 West 25th Street, College of Education, Kearney, NE 68849. E-mail: chasekc1@unk.edu

older is 8% of the population or 19.9 million users. The number of people in need of substance abuse services and mental health counseling are reflected in these statistics. To respond to the growing number of client in need of treatment services, addiction counselors are needed. The Occupational Outlook Handbook for 2012–13 predicts that the growth in the addiction counseling field is expected to be 27%. This is classified as growing much faster than the average for all other occupations (United States Department of Labor, 2013). In proportion to the growing number of addiction counselors, the demand for alcohol and drug clinical supervision will also grow.

Substance abuse counseling is unique in the counseling field due to issues pertaining to the training and education of addictions counselors. It is not uncommon in the field of alcohol and drug counseling for treatment providers to have a variety of levels of education, training, and experience in addictions counseling as well as personal experience with addiction (Anderson 2000; Laschober, de Tormes Eby, & Sauer, 2012; Powell & Brodsky, 2004; West & Hamm, 2012). The field has addressed this concern with a gate-keeping function related to education, training, and certification of addiction counselors. The education and training qualifications related to licensing and regulation addictions counseling are tightly controlled and set forth by each individual state. In order to be certified as an addictions counselor, a provider must have completed an educational component related to addictions counseling and must receive clinical supervision by an approved supervisor when entering the field (Anderson 2000; Center for Substance Abuse Treatment [CSAT], 2006; Powell & Brodsky, 2004; West & Hamm, 2012). This requirement places a great deal of responsibility on clinical supervisors to provide supervision that is competent and relevant. While there is a great deal of responsibility on placed on clinical supervisors, a review of the literature found very little research on the development of substance abuse clinical supervisors or the factors that promote supervisor development (Culbreth & Cooper, 2008; Schmidt, 2012). This is concerning given the great deal of responsibility placed on substance abuse supervisors.

The Center for Substance Abuse Treatment (CSAT, 2007) has addressed this demand for competent clinical supervision by developing a competency based model for clinical supervisors that provides a framework for understanding, learning, and implementing the multiple functions and tasks of addictions clinical supervisors. Culbreth and Cooper

(2008) examined factors that predict high level of clinical supervisor development. They found that overall supervisor self-efficacy was positively correlated with more experience as a counselor and more experience as a supervisor. Knowledge and technique in clinical supervision was also found to be a significant predictor of overall supervisor development suggesting that the field focus on the development of clinical supervisors by training them in supervision models. In a review of the clinical supervision literature, Schmidt (2012) similarly found that experience and education were positively correlated with competency in alcohol and drug clinical supervision. Clinical supervisors who had more education in supervision models were better able to evaluate and support supervisee development. Becoming a fully competent alcohol and drug clinical supervisor then is a developmental process that requires a firm grounding in a supervision model. The newly defined Competency Based Alcohol and Drug Clinical Supervision Model outlined in this paper is consistent with the current practice in the addictions field, addresses the developmental process of addiction counselors, and is based in the competency framework set out by CSAT.

Competency Based Alcohol and Drug Clinical Supervision

The definition of clinical supervision as adopted by CSAT in the competency based framework of alcohol and drug clinical supervision is defined as:

> . . .a social influence process that occurs over time, in which the supervisor participates with supervisees to ensure quality clinical care. Effective supervisors observe, mentor, coach, evaluate, inspire, and create an atmosphere that promotes self-motivation, learning, and professional development. They build teams, create cohesion, resolve conflict, and shape agency culture, while attending to ethical and diversity issues in all aspects of the process. Such supervision is key to both quality improvement and the successful implementation of consensus- and evidence-based practices. (CSAT, 2007, p. 3)

CSAT encourages supervisors to understand the developmental process of supervisees and demands that an atmosphere of learning and personal development is incorporated into the supervision process. Powell and Brodsky (2004) have developed a model of clinical supervision in alcohol and drug counseling that addresses the development of the addiction counselor and is based in the competency model. The Blended Model of Clinical Supervision was developed to address the unique needs of the addictions field in training and supervising addictions counselors. The Model is considered to be the standard supervision model in the addictions counseling field.

The Blended Model of Clinical Supervision rests on several assumptions regarding how people change particularly as the change applies to addiction. The philosophy of change that informs the Blended Model of Clinical Supervision is comprised of seven beliefs:

1. People have the ability to bring about change in their lives with the assistance of a guide.
2. People do not always know what is best for them, for they may be blinded by their resistance to and denial of the issues.
3. The key to growth is to blend insight and behavioral change in the right amounts at the appropriate time.
4. Change is constant and inevitable.
5. In supervision as in therapy, the guide concentrates on what is changeable.
6. It is not necessary to know a great deal about the cause or function of a manifest problem to resolve it.
7. There are many correct ways to view the world (Powell & Brodsky, 2004, pp. 151–155).

In supervision, the goal of the Blended Model is to promote behavioral change (defined as skills acquisition) and affective growth (defined as insight) based on the stage of the development of the supervisee.

In addition to the competency based framework of supervision outlined by CSAT (2007) and the Blended Model of clinical supervision described by Powell and Brodsky (2004), a developmental framework is needed to understand the developmental level of supervisees. The understanding of the developmental process of alcohol and drug supervisees can be informed by the three overriding structures of the Integrated Development Model of clinical supervision: (a) self and other awareness, (b) motivation, and (c) autonomy (Anderson, 2000; Bernard & Goodyear,

2009). The self and other awareness structure refers to the supervisee's ability to be aware of and effectively use his or her own feelings and a simultaneous awareness of the client's world. The motivation structure refers to the supervisee's interest, investment, and effort in expanding their clinical training and experience. The autonomy structure refers to the degree of independence the supervisee is demonstrating. In each structure the supervisee is assessed according to their developmental level. The levels in the Integrated Model are classified as Level 1, the beginning counselor or counselor-in-training, Level 2, the counselor with some post graduate clinical experience, and Level 3, the seasoned licensed counselor. This concept is applied in the Blended Model of Clinical Supervision through categorizing the supervisee based on developmental level in several dimensions related to the practice of addictions counseling.

The Blended Model of Clinical Supervision is comprised of nine dimensions: influential, symbolic, structural, replicative, counselor in treatment, information gathering, jurisdictional, relationship, and strategy. The conceptual descriptions of the dimensions and a visual representation of the dimensions are summarized below.

1. Influential: Supervisees are influenced both affectively and behaviorally, depending on the individual's stage of development, needs, and cognitive abilities as well as contextual variables. A Level 1 counselor will need more focus on developing the core functions of alcohol counseling and basic helping skills. As the counselor progresses and develops more focus will be on theoretical issues and affective concerns in counseling.

	Influential	
Level 3	Level 2	Level 1
Affective		Cognitive

2. Symbolic: Emphasis is placed on the manifest content, not the unconscious material, to bring about desired change. In the supervision process, the supervisor is concerned with skill acquisition, behavioral change, and cognitive issues rather than issues rooted in the counselor's past. To avoid role confusion and dual relationships, supervisors make referrals for counseling services if it becomes apparent that the supervisee is in need of counseling services.

Symbolic

X

Latent   Manifest

3. **Structural:** Early in the supervision process, the supervisor is very structured, teaching the core functions and directing the supervision process. The structure of supervision is proactive in the beginning with significant direction and structure and then moves to reactive with more consultation and collegial supervision as the counselor develops. The locus of control shifts over time to more self-directed instruction as the supervisee develops.

Structural

Level 3	Level 2	Level 1

Reactive   Proactive

4. **Replicative:** The Blended Model acknowledges the parallel process; counselors behave in supervision in a manner that is parallel to clients in therapy. However, the supervisor in the Blended Model rarely addresses the actions and unconscious influences that impact the counselor except if those issues interfere with clinical functioning. The focus of supervision is to help the counselor be a more effective clinician rather than a functional individual. If counseling is needed, a referral to counseling is made outside of the supervision process.

Replicative

X

Parallel   Discrete

5. **Counselor in Treatment:** The Blended Model holds that counseling in supervision by the supervisor is appropriate. The role of the supervisor in the supervision process is to monitor the supervisee's functioning. Should the supervisee need counseling, the supervisor is directed to refer the supervisee to counseling or to a recovery program/self-help group.

Counselor in Treatment

X

Related   Unrelated

6. Information Gathering: Direct methods of supervision are preferred over indirect methods of supervision when supervisee's are in the early stages of development. This helps to determine the training needs of the counselor. As the counselor grows in the three developmental structures of motivation, self-and other-awareness, and autonomy, the more indirect methods of observation are appropriate to address more insight-oriented issues and to foster theoretical developmental.

	Information Gathering	
Level 3	Level 2	Level 1
Indirect		Direct

7. Jurisdictional: Jurisdiction refers to the ethical and legal issues in supervision. Ultimate responsibility for ethical and legal issues rests with the supervisor. Legal and ethical issues must be reviewed and monitored in every supervision session.

	Jurisdictional	
Level 3	Level 2	Level 1
Therapist		Supervisor

8. Relationship: The counselor-supervisor relationship is determined by the level of development of the counselor and the practice setting. The relationship with Level 1 counselors and counselors in structured settings, such as inpatient treatment facilities, is more hierarchical. As counselors progress in their development and as the setting becomes less directive the relationship becomes more consultative and less hierarchical.

	Relationship	
Level 3	Level 2	Level 1
Facilitative		Hierarchical

9. Strategy: The teaching of technique or theory in the Blended Model is dependent on the level of development of the supervisee. Teaching techniques and the core functions of drug and alcohol counseling are necessary when the supervisee is in the early stages of development. As the supervisee develops and grows, theory

should be the focus of supervision in order to help the supervisee integrate technique to theory.

	Strategy	
Level 3	Level 2	Level 1
Theory		Technique

The nine dimensions of the Blended Model provide a structure that guides the supervisor in providing drug and alcohol clinical supervision that addresses the developmental level of the supervisee. Incorporating a competency based framework as outlined by CSAT (2007) and the developmental level assessment of supervisees as determined by the Integrated Development Model (Bernard & Goodyear, 2009) provides clinical supervisors with the knowledge base and the techniques in clinical supervision that have been found to be significant predictors of overall supervisor effectiveness. Clinical supervisors who apply the principles of the newly defined Competency Based Alcohol and Drug Clinical Supervision Model are operating out of a competency based framework which has been determined to be critical for ensuring quality clinical care and quality supervision.

Application

In the Competency Based Alcohol and Drug Clinical Supervision Model the developmental level of the supervisee drives the implementation of the model. The first step in applying the Competency Based Alcohol and Drug Clinical Supervision Model is the classification of the supervisee by developmental level. To determine the developmental level of each supervisee an interview can be conducted prior to the initiation of the supervisory relationship. Each supervisee is then classified into the appropriate developmental level and interventions can be developed according thorough the supervision process. The classification of the supervisee's developmental level is based on their training and clinical experience in the drug and alcohol field and knowledge of alcohol and drug counseling.

Applying the Competency Based Alcohol and Drug Clinical Supervision Model in clinical supervision guides the interventions and supervision activities with supervisees. In order to create an atmosphere that promotes self-motivation, learning, and professional development, supervisees must be given the opportunity to share their experiences and goals for professional development. This experience can be accomplished by having each supervisee develop their goals and professional development needs at the first supervision session. As an activity, each supervisee can be instructed to write out their philosophy of addiction and addiction treatment in order to individualize the learning process and to determine each supervisee's theory of change related to alcohol and drug counseling. This is in line with a competency based framework as an attempt to determine the opinions, beliefs, and knowledge that each supervisee brings to the supervision process. The philosophy statements can be reviewed frequently throughout the supervision process and updated and changed as new learning occurred and as each supervisee develops in their practice. Supervisees can also be challenged to incorporate the core functions of drug and alcohol counseling and any new learning or insight from clients, colleagues or from supervision. In the Competency Based Alcohol and Drug Clinical Supervision Model, a constructivist approach is used to engage supervisees in the learning process and to increase their self-awareness and professional identity as an addiction counselor.

The structure of the supervision process in the Competency Based Alcohol and Drug Clinical Supervision Model can be provided in a variety of formats; however an important component of the model is live supervision especially for counselors at lower levels of development. Research has found that live supervision is effective at increasing the self-efficacy of counselors and promoting professional growth (Schmidt, 2012). The format of the Competency Based Alcohol and Drug Supervision Model that incorporates live supervision with group and self-report supervision is essential for supervisee development.

A group supervision format is often necessary for supervisors in clinical practice who have multiple responsibilities and a minimum of time available. The suggested group supervision format is a ninety minute weekly group meetings with all supervisees and sixty minutes of individual supervision per week for one supervisee. The individual time for supervisees is rotated each week so a different supervisee had the individual time each week (See Table 1). The individual time can be utilized in a variety of ways depending on the supervisee developmental level. For Level 1 supervisees the individual time should be spent in direct observation of clinical skills and role playing or modeling of counseling sessions to evaluate clinical skills and techniques. For Level 2 and 3 supervisees the individual time was spent in theory development, advanced counseling techniques in drug and alcohol counseling, and consultation.

In the group supervision format, challenges can arise as a result of having supervisees' at all developmental levels. To address some of these challenging issues, attempts need to be made to vary the content of the supervision session from technique to theory and from development of counseling skills to consultation. Level 3 counselors can also be utilized in a manner of teaching and role modeling to the other supervisees. Level 3 counselors can present cases according to the core function areas in alcohol and drug counseling, show videos of counseling sessions where specific techniques are demonstrated, and provide feedback to the other counselors as a learning tool for self and others.

Two critical functions must be carried out in supervision in the Competency Based Alcohol and Drug Clinical Supervision Model. Ethical issues and licensing information must frequently be reviewed with all supervisees to ensure that clinical services are ethically sound and that move the counselor closer to meeting the regulations for licensing. The other critical function relates to the formal evaluation of supervisees during and after the supervision experience. This formal evaluation is a gate keeping function to ensure that clinical services are ethically sound and the client receives benefit from the services and is not harmed. The ultimate goal of the newly defined Competency Based Alcohol and Drug Clinical Supervision Model is to ensure that quality clinical care is occurring while meeting the supervisee's developmental and clinical training needs.

References

American Psychiatric Association. (2013). *Diagnostic and statistical manual of mental disorders*, (5th ed.). Arlington, VA: Author.

Anderson, C. (2000). Supervision of substance abuse counselors using the integrated developmental model. *The Clinical Supervisor, 19*(2), 185–195.

Bernard, J. M., & Goodyear, R. K. (2009). *Fundamentals of clinical supervision* (4th ed.). New Jersey: Pearson.

Center for Substance Abuse Treatment. (2006). *Addiction Counseling Competencies: The Knowledge, Skills, and Attitudes of Professional Practice*. Technical Assistance Publication (TAP) Series 21. DHHS Publication No. (SMA) 06-4171. Rockville, MD: Substance Abuse and Mental Health Services Administration.

Center for Substance Abuse Treatment. (2007). *Competencies for Substance Abuse Treatment Clinical Supervisors*. Technical Assistance Publication (TAP) Series, Number 21-A. DHHS Pub. No. (SMA) 07-4243. Rockville, MD: Substance Abuse and Mental Health services Administration.

Culbreth, J. R., & Cooper, J. B. (2008). Factors impacting the development of substance abuse counseling supervisors. *Journal of Addictions & Offender Counseling, 29*, 22–35.

Laschober, T. C., de Tormes Eby, L. T., Sauer, J. B. (2012). Clinical supervisor and counselor perceptions of clinical supervision in addiction treatment. *Journal of Addictive Diseases, 31*, 382–388.

Powell, D., & Brodsky, A. (2004). *Clinical Supervision in Alcohol and Drug Abuse Counseling: Principles, Models, Methods*. (Rev. ed.). San Francisco, CA.: Jossey-Bass.

Schmidt, E. A. (2012). Clinical supervision in the substance abuse profession: A review of the literature. *Alcoholism Treatment Quarterly, 30*(4), 487–504.

U. S. Department of Health and Human Services, SAMHSA, & Office of Applied Studies. (2007). *SAMHSA's latest national survey on drug use and health*. Retrieved from http://www.oas.samhsa.gov/NSDUHlatest.htm

United States Department of Labor. (2013). *Occupational Outlook Handbook, 2012-2013*. Retrieved from http://www.bls.gov/ooh/ community-and-social-service/print/substance-abuse-and-behavioral-disorder-counselors.htm

West, P. L., & Hamm, T. (2012). A study of clinical supervision techniques and training in substance abuse treatment. *Journal of Addictions & Offender Counseling, 33*, 66–81.

Table 1

Competency Based Alcohol and Drug Clinical Supervision Model Supervision Structure for Individual and Group Supervision by Supervisee

Counselor	Week 1	Week 2	Week 3	Week 4	Week 5	Week 6	Week 7
Counselor A	Group	Video/Live Individual Group	Group	Group	Group	Group	Group
Counselor B	Group	Group	Video/Live Individual Group	Group	Group	Group	Group
Counselor C	Group	Group	Group	Video/Live Individual Group	Group	Group	Group
Counselor D	Group	Group	Group	Group	Video/Live Individual Group	Group	Group
Counselor E	Group	Group	Group	Group	Group	Video/Live Individual Group	Group
Counselor F	Group	Group	Group	Group	Group	Group	Video/Live Individual Group

Note: The counselor who is doing video/live supervision will have 60 minutes of individual supervision time. During the group time, the counselor who is scheduled for live or video supervision will be the focal point of the group supervision.

7

Multiple Relationships with Clients

Applying the Concept of Potentially Beneficial Interactions to the Practice of Addiction Counseling

Kevin Doyle[1]

Counselors who work with clients with substance use disorders face numerous possibilities for interactions with current and former clients. The current ACA Code of Ethics continues to permit potentially beneficial interactions, a concept introduced in the previous Code. An overview of these interactions is presented, along with proposed guidelines for counselors and supervisors to ensure ethical behavior.

The issue of multiple relationships, also referred to as dual relationships, has appeared frequently in the counseling and mental health literature for decades, reflecting the challenges practitioners face in trying to navigate non-professional relationships with their clients. Occurring on a time continuum, these relationships can be in place before the beginning of the counseling relationship, develop during counseling, or, perhaps most frequently, develop after the termination of counseling. In 2005, the American Counseling Association (ACA) Code of Ethics added an

---

1. Kevin Doyle, Counselor Education Department, Longwood University. Correspondence concerning this article should be addressed to Kevin Doyle, Longwood University, College of Education and Human Services, 201 High Street, Farmville, VA 23909, doyleks@longwood.edu

important element to the discussion of dual relationships, the concept of "potentially beneficial interactions." The revised Code eliminates this phrase but preserves the concept in general (ACA, 2014). These "potentially beneficial" interactions are those that might have previously been considered either marginally or clearly unethical, but due to the potential for benefit to a client or former client are now considered in a different light. Little has been written, however, about this issue as it relates to counselors who work with clients with substance use disorders (SUDs). For counselors who are personally in recovery, where the dynamics of dual relationships play out regularly in settings such as self-help groups like Alcoholics Anonymous (AA) and Narcotics Anonymous (NA), such interactions may be particularly problematic. For counselors working in substance use disorder settings, further exploration of the issue of potentially beneficial interactions is both warranted and needed.

Review of the Literature

Doyle (1997) described some of the possible relationships that counselors in recovery from substance use disorders might have with their clients, with a concentration on social, employment, and self-help group interactions, such as sponsorship. He noted that not all dual relationships are problematic, identifying the concept of *avoidability* as a central one in the discussion of the ethical nature of the relationships. The article also identified issues related to confidentiality and anonymity, self-help group meetings, sponsorship relationships, social relationships, and employment as important considerations in professionals' consideration of appropriate and inappropriate interactions with clients. Given the prevalence of counselors in recovery at the time of the article (nearly 60% of members of the National Association of Alcoholism and Drug Abuse Counselors [NAADAC] self-identified as being personally in recovery at that time), these issues were frequent and not particularly avoidable. However, codes of ethics at that time had not evolved to the point where potentially beneficial relationships were acknowledged, as they are currently.

Kaplan (2005), writing from a social work perspective, echoed several themes from the Doyle (1997) article and added a number of additional considerations. She noted that some practitioners faced the possibility of additional confusion due to their membership in more than one professional association, such as the National Association of Social Workers, ACA or NAADAC, each of which might treat the issue of dual relationships somewhat differently. The author encouraged professionals to utilize the tried and true techniques of consultation and supervision, as well as consulting their codes of ethics, while acknowledging that there might not be uniformity among them. She also pointed out that the self-help groups themselves offer some guidance to their members about issues such as self-disclosure, explaining that professionals who are in AA are encouraged to consider their motives for sharing their personal stories with clients. She also correctly identified the potentially problematic issues that may occur when professionals in recovery share information that is intended to be private at self-help meetings at which clients or former clients are in attendance.

Some research has also focused on the beliefs that counselors in recovery have about multiple relationships (Hollander, Bauer, Herlihy, & McCollum, 2006). The authors reported findings indicating that substance abuse counselors in person recovery were less likely to find ethical issues with dual relationships, supporting the notion that ongoing discussion and research are needed to ensure that full consideration of any ethical ramifications of these relationships is conducted by practitioners, particularly those in recovery, as well as those supervising them.

Kaplan (2006), writing from his position as ACA's Chief Professional Officer shortly after the publication of the 2005 ACA Code of Ethics, noted that the long-used term *dual relationships* was not used at all in the 2005 code, which also introduced the concept of potentially beneficial interactions with clients in Standards A.5.c, and A. 5. d., within Section A: The Counseling Relationship (ACA, 2005). Utilizing an interview with Ethics Committee members Rocco Cottone and Michael Kocet, Kaplan reported that the 2005 code "allows professional counselors to interact with clients outside of a counseling session under certain conditions (personal communication, March 27, 2006, as cited in Kaplan, 2006)." He further identified three types of relationships covered by the code: romantic/sexual relationships (which continued to be prohibited by Standards A.5.a. and A.5. b.), ongoing contact/relationships with clients, and professional role changes, and indicated that only the second type was envisioned as appropriate for the "potentially beneficial" provision. Kaplan's interview includes a discussion of commonly discussed client interactions such as weddings and graduations, the issue of bartering, and interactions among a group of people centering around a common interest (muscular dystrophy, in this case). While potentially helpful, the discussion does not touch upon some of the very real issues faced by counselors working in the substance use disorder arena.

Hecksher (2007) identified several relevant issues relating to the interactions between counselors in recovery and their clients. Noting that some of the professionals in recovery might be better categorized as paraprofessionals due to their qualifications being based more on their personal experience than their training, Hecksher pointed out some of the dynamics that might occur in a self-help group meeting attended by both clients and professionals. Difficulties sharing openly in the meeting, for example, might occur due to the fear of being judged by the other party due to the nature or content of the disclosure. Hecksher also raised the issue of the possible loss of objectivity if a professional were to become friends or acquaintances with a client due to the shared experience of self-help group membership. Objectivity is a vital component of ethical practice, and the possibility of its being compromised in this manner is worthy of additional exploration and consideration.

Dual/Multiple Relationship Issues in Substance Abuse Counseling

There are numerous potential dual/multiple relationships that may occur in the context of working with individual with substance use disorders, and that are worthy of further discussion in the context of what is potentially beneficial to a client or former client. Several that are particularly common are: counselors in recovery, staff/collegial relationships, social issues, and issues for supervisors.

Counselors in Recovery

Counselors in recovery from a substance use disorder have long faced particular challenges in navigating possible ongoing relationships with current and former clients, most notably in self-help group activities. Among these are issues such as determining when and if to speak at meetings when current or former clients are in attendance, considering whether to serve as a sponsor for current or former clients, and deciding whether to acknowledge being acquainted with a current or former client (Doyle, 1997). Clearly, there are potentially beneficial interactions per the ACA Code of Ethics, Sections A.6. (2014). Clients may see counselors in recovery as role models and be given hope that not only is recovery possible, but so also is the possibility of high-functioning professional performance. Given the difficulties faced by individuals in early recovery, this phenomenon may be very significant to a client. Likewise, what a counselor in recovery has to offer in an AA, NA, or other self-help group meetings may be just what that client might need to hear at that time. Requiring the counselor to be silent in such a situation might actually be detrimental to the client (or former client). In a similar vein, it is not far-fetched to consider that a counselor serving as a sponsor to a newcomer might be very beneficial, particularly if the counselor has long-term recovery, is the same gender as the person being sponsored (or *sponsee*), and if there are not many other options in a given community. Finally, the simple acknowledgement of a newcomer's presence could be very beneficial for a client who is new to a meeting or fellowship. If a counselor chooses to ignore someone he or she recognizes from a treatment setting, this could be counterproductive to a client feeling welcome. This is not insignificant as the initial response to meeting attendance can be very important in determining whether a client is willing to commit to ongoing engagement.

Staff/Collegial Relationships

One potentially beneficial relationship for a client occurs in the scenario when he or she establishes stable recovery and, as is not unusual, decides to pursue a career in the addiction counseling arena. Numerous studies have documented the high prevalence of recovering individuals in the addiction counseling profession (although this number has fallen in recent years) (NAADAC, 2007). Obviously, it is beneficial for an individual in recovery to become gainfully employed, assuming that he or she has the qualifications and is adequately prepared for the position being undertaken. Clearly the days of recovery status being the primary qualification for employment is long gone, and rightfully so. When an individual builds upon his or her recovery experience, however, with academic preparation, which might also include counselor certification or licensure, an effective employee can result. The new employee might even apply for a job at the treatment program from which he or she received services. If some of the same staff still work there, the potential for dual/multiple relationships exists, but this need not be problematic Individuals in such a situation may benefit from some guidelines to assist both parties in successful navigation.

Social Issues

Another area in which potentially problematic relationships may occur is in the social arena. Particularly in smaller communities where the issue of avoidability is a very real one (ACA, 2014; NAADAC, 2011), counselors may encounter their current and former clients in a variety of social settings. Determining which of these are problematic and which are potentially beneficial for those working in addiction counseling, as well as counselors in general, has not been a simple task. An important additional variable in social settings for counselors working with clients with substance use disorders is that of alcohol (and possibly other substances as well). For example, if a counselor encounters a former client in a social setting in which alcohol is present, should the counselor change his or her use of alcohol to reflect the knowledge of the client's recovery status? And should the counselor treat the former client any differently; for example, not offer the person any alcohol based on his/her knowledge of the person's treatment?

Issues for Supervisors

Finally, all of the above are relevant issues for supervisors who might find themselves supervising counselors who are personally in recovery. As the SAMHSA Technical Assistance Publication 21-A *Competencies for Substance Abuse Treatment Clinical Supervisors* (2007) states, supervisors should "learn about their supervisees' cultures, lifestyles, beliefs and other key factors that may influence their job performance," (p. 29), and one can think of little that is more important to a supervisee's identity than his or her recovery status. Therefore, supervisors, whether they are personally in recovery or not, who supervise counselors who are, have an obligation to consider how a supervisee's recovery status impacts his or her work performance. Most notably for this discussion, they should also consider how to help their supervisees in recovery to navigate some of the potentially problematic ethical issues that may result from the scenarios already noted.

Proposed Guidelines for Addiction Counselors Regarding Potentially Beneficial Interactions

Given the lack of discussion in the literature regarding the concept of potentially beneficial interactions with current and former clients, some initial thoughts on this issue appear to be needed to "jump start" the professional dialogue. The proposed guidelines that follow are intended for this purpose, rather than as any definitive word on this issue. It is hoped that these proposals will stimulate professional discussion, debate, and perhaps even controversy, with the intent of assisting those engaged in practice treating individuals with substance use disorders, particularly those who are also personally in recovery, as they consider the ethical ramifications of their client interactions.

Counselors in Recovery

As noted above, counselors who work with individuals with substance use disorders and who are also in recovery personally would be well-advised to consider ahead of time how their interactions with current and former clients might be problematic as well as potentially beneficial. The following are proposed guidelines for counselors in recovery for the three specific situations noted above: speaking/sharing at self-help group meetings where clients are in attendance, sponsoring current or former clients, and acknowledging current/former clients at self-help meetings.

Rather than suggesting that counselors in recovery not speak at meetings when current or former clients are in attendance, a more reasonable suggestion might be that counselors use good judgment in determining what topics about which to share. Speaking about problems at their workplace (i.e. the local treatment center) or with their supervisor (the local center director), for example, might be ill-advised when clients of the center are in attendance. Keeping one's comments general or about broad topics might thus be a wiser and safer strategy. If a counselor in recovery needs to share about issues similar to those noted above, however, he or she might consider speaking privately with a sponsor, sharing at a smaller, closed meeting, or consulting with a trusted friend or colleague who is also in recovery.

As for the issue of sponsoring current or former clients, the prevailing wisdom seems to be clear that counselors should not sponsor current clients and should be cautious about sponsoring former ones. Clearly the potential for role confusion is very high if a counselor was to consider sponsoring a current client, and in many ways this practice would be counterproductive. Part of what should happen during the treatment process is for clients to begin to use community resources, such as self-help fellowships, and to transition their recovery program from the formal treatment program and staff to these types of community groups (whether they be 12-Step programs or not). When it comes to sponsoring former clients, some of the above admonitions still may apply, but the longer the separation from the counseling relationship, the more likely the relationship *might* meet the "potentially beneficial" clause in the ACA 2005 Code and the current language of the 2014 Code. To date, there is no consensus on this, nor is there a specified timeframe after which it would be acceptable to sponsor a former client. Factors such as avoidability, size of the community, other potential sponsors, how close the counseling relationship was, and others should be considered, and a counselor would be wise to seek supervision and/or consultation around this issue before deciding to proceed. Counselors, of course, should always be aware of employer policies covering these issues and follow them while under the purview of the employer—or advocate for changing them.

Finally, the question of whether to acknowledge a client or former client at a self-help meeting may be problematic for some counselors in recovery. Should a counselor simply turn away and avoid a current or former client, fearing a confidentiality violation or an inappropriate interaction? It is conceivable that such avoidance could in reality be detrimental to a client, as noted earlier, so the common admonition to "do no harm" may be applicable here. A more ethical approach might be to acknowledge the client politely without any specific notation of a prior connection to him or her, thereby not providing any clue to another connection for any bystander to notice, but validating the importance of the client being welcomed and encouraged. The counselor would need to consider whether or not to use the client's name and should be prepared to answer vaguely if questioned by another member about how he or she might know the client.

Staff/Collegial Relationships

The issue of staff/collegial relationships is one that fits the proverbial notion of "a good problem to have." In other words, when clients remain in recovery and eventually become colleagues of addiction counselors who were involved in their treatment, it means both that treatment was successful and that the counselors have remain employed for a period of time beyond treatment completion—both positive outcomes. Treatment programs have a variety of policies about the eligibility of recovering individuals to be hired (minimum of one year in recovery, minimum of two years in recovery, etc.), but regardless of policy it is clearly possible that a former client of a program may find his or her way back as a prospective employee/applicant and may successfully obtain an employment position. Indeed, one may argue persuasively that this is a desirable eventuality. In that instance, then, the former client would become the colleague of his or her former counselors. This is both ethical and not particularly troublesome, as long as the hiring was conducted in accordance with agency hiring policies and the candidate was not given any preferential consideration. Counselors who were involved in the individual's treatment might wish to consider having a private discussion with him or her assuring the new employee that their current relationship is collegial and no longer related to the previous counseling relationship. It is conceivable that a counselor might even end up supervising a former client, or being supervised by one (although this is probably less likely). In either case, having what might be similar to an "informed consent discussion" with the individual might be advisable. Consideration might also be given to exploring other available supervision options, particularly if the counselor has an inclination that he or she might have difficulty being objective regarding the former client (i.e. due to pride over his/her accomplishment).

Social Issues

The ACA Code (2014) is clear that any social relationships of a romantic or sexual nature with current clients are inappropriate and unethical. The Code imposes a five-year minimum restriction on such relationships with former clients, with the stipulation that to be ethical there must be documentation that such relationships are not exploitative, while the NAADAC Code includes a permanent restriction on such relationships. Social relationships in general, however, may run the gamut from highly unethical to non-problematic. The 2005 ACA Code added the concept of a relationship being "potentially beneficial," while the 2014 Code implies the same concept without using the exact words. When counselors work with clients with substance use disorders, social relationships in their community may be complicated by the presence of legal (such as alcohol) or illegal substances. It is more difficult to envision highly ethical examples of the latter (illegal substances) due to the illegality, but the former could be inclusive of such socially acceptable events as wedding receptions, dinner parties, or other social occasions where alcohol is served. Should a counselor who is not personally in recovery avoiding using or serving alcohol at such events where a former client now in recovery is in attendance? Should a counselor in such a situation avoid serving a former client he or she knows to have been in treatment for an alcohol use disorder? Certainly there is an issue of autonomy here in that it may no longer be the place of the counselor to impose his or her values (such as abstinence) on a former client. One suggestion is for the counselor to use a high amount of discretion in avoiding such situations and excuse himself/herself if at all possible from being forced to manage such a delicate interaction. A counselor would be well-served to either abstain from drinking personally or to engage in only minimal, legal use as well in his or her personal use when around current or former clients, out of respect for his or her clients.

Issues for Supervisors

The final point of discussion relates to the obligation that supervisors have to be sensitive to issues regarding potentially beneficial interactions that their supervisees in recovery might have. It would be easy for supervisors who are not personally in recovery to defer to others in recovery when their supervisees raise issues about ethical behavior and the question of potentially beneficial interactions. The most ethical of supervisors, however, will take the time necessary to consider these issues, consult with colleagues, peruse the relevant literature, and offer appropriate guidance to their supervisees. Nothing is more frustrating to a counselor than when his or her supervisor is unable or unwilling to be of assistance when the counselor overcomes the normal reluctance to raise difficult issues in supervision. Supervisors who are unfamiliar with the dynamics of recovery, self-help groups, sponsorship, and similar issues should take the time to familiarize themselves in order to provide the appropriate supervision they are ethically bound to provide—and that their supervisees deserve.

Conclusion and Directions for Future Research

Counselors working with clients with substance use disorders should carefully consider the implications of the provision of the ACA Code of Ethics that permits potentially beneficial interactions with clients. Given the high potential for problematic interactions, particularly for counselors in recovery who may interact with current and former clients at venues such as AA or other self-help group meetings, counselors would be well-served to consult with other professionals when such interactions occur or may occur. Likewise, supervisors should spend the time needed to familiarize themselves with these issues so that that might be most effective with their supervisees. The proposed guidelines presented above are an attempt to begin a more thorough discussion among practitioners about ethical behavior, within the context of the ACA Code,

References

American Counseling Association. (2005). *ACA Code of Ethics*. Alexandria, VA: Author. Retrieved from www.counseling.org/ethics.

American Counseling Association. (2014). *ACA Code of Ethics* . Alexandria, VA: Author. Retrieved from www.counseling.org/ethics.

Doyle, K. (1997). Substance abuse counselors in recovery: Implications for the ethical issue of dual relationships. *Journal of Counseling and Development. 75*(6), 428–432.

Hecksher, D. (2007). Former substance users working as counselors: A dual relationship. *Substance Use & Misuse. 42*(8), 1253–1268.

Hollander, J., Bauer, S., Herlihy, B., & McCollum, V. (2006). Beliefs of board certified substance abuse counselors regarding multiple relationships. *Journal of Mental Health Counseling, 28*(1), 84–94.

Kaplan, D. (2006). Allowing dual relationships. *Counseling Today*. Retrieved from ct.counseling.org/2006/03/ct-online-ethics-update-9/

Kaplan, L. E. (2005). Dual Relationships: The challenge for social workers in recovery. *Journal of Social Work Practice in the Addictions, 5*(3), 73–90.

NAADAC: The Association for Addiction Professionals. (2007). *Member Survey*. Retrieved from www.naadac.org.

NAADAC: The Association for Addiction Professionals. (2011). *Code of Ethics*. Retrieved from www.naadac.org.

Substance Abuse and Mental Health Services Administration (SAMHSA). (2007). *Technical Assistance Publication 21-A: Competencies for Substance Abuse Treatment Clinical Supervisors*. Rockville, MD: Author.

8

Brief Alcohol Counseling Interventions in a Trauma Setting with Latina/o Clients

NATHANIEL N. IVERS, LAURA J. VEACH, REGINA R. MORO, JENNIFER L. ROGERS, AND MARY CLAIRE O'BRIEN[1]

Alcohol screenings and brief counseling interventions (ASBCIs) administered at trauma centers can help reduce risky drinking behaviors. However, few guidelines exist for culturally modifying ASBCIs for Latinas/os. Utilizing the cultural concepts of locus of control, individualism-collectivism, and communication styles, we present guidelines to consider when providing ASBCI to Latina/o clients.

Few guidelines exist for modifying and applying evidence-based counseling interventions across cultures (Griner & Smith, 2006). This

1. Nathaniel N. Ivers, Department of Counseling, Wake Forest University; Laura J. Veach Department of Counseling, The University of North Carolina at Charlotte, and Department of Surgery, Wake Forest School of Medicine; Regina R. Moro, Counseling Department, Barry University; Jennifer L. Rogers, Department of Counseling, Wake Forest University; Mary Claire O'Brien, Department of Emergency Medicine, Wake Forest School of Medicine. This research was supported by the Substance Abuse Policy Research Program of the Robert Wood Johnson Foundation (Grant # 65032; PI: O'Brien; *Policy Implementation Regarding Brief Interventions in the Trauma Unit*, "The Teachable Moment"). Correspondence concerning this article should be addressed to Nathaniel N. Ivers, Wake Forest University, PO Box 7406; Winston-Salem, NC 27109. E-mail: iversnn@wfu.edu

holds particularly true for alcohol treatment (Lee et al., 2011). Although many researchers have expressed the importance of culturally-adapted alcohol interventions, few have provided specific guidelines on how to adapt brief alcohol counseling to culturally diverse populations. The objective of this article is to present guidelines for counselors to utilize when providing a one-time alcohol screening and brief counseling intervention (ASBCI) at the hospital bedside of Latina/o clients who are hospitalized for physical, traumatic injuries. To accomplish this objective, we provide (a) a brief overview of alcohol consumption patterns and alcohol-related injury rates; (b) a description and rationale for ASBCIs; (c) a review of pertinent research examining the effectiveness of ASBCIs with Latina/o clients; and (d) specific guidelines to consider when providing ASBCIs to Latina/o clients.

Risky Alcohol Consumption Patterns and Trauma

An estimated 65% of adults in the United States drink alcohol, with approximately 9% drinking in abusive or addictive patterns (National Institute of Alcohol Abuse and Alcoholism [NIAAA], 2010). An additional 19% of individuals drink alcohol in non-diagnosed, risky ways, such as binge drinking (NIAAA, 2010). Risky drinking, according to the NIAAA (2013), is a pattern of alcohol consumption in which an individual's blood alcohol content (BAC) increases to 0.08% or greater within a two hour time period. In general, this corresponds to five or more standard drinks per occasion for males and four or more standard drinks per occasion for females.

Individuals who drink in risky patterns are more susceptible to alcohol-related injuries, such as falls or car accidents (Moore, 2005; NIAAA, 2013). Alcohol is considered the "single greatest contributor to injury in the United States" (Desy, Howard, Perhats, & Li, 2010, p. 538), and the "third largest factor of premature mortality, disability, and loss of health" worldwide (World Health Organization [WHO], n.d.). Up to 30% of patients treated in emergency departments and 40–50% of severely injured trauma patients test positive for alcohol use (D'Onofrio & Degutis, 2002).

Alcohol Screening and Brief Counseling Intervention

Mounting evidence suggests that brief alcohol interventions in hospital trauma centers can reduce drinking behaviors and injury associated with risky alcohol consumption (Gentillelo et al., 1999; Soderstrom et al., 2007). Alcohol screening entails administering a brief screening questionnaire to explore drinking patterns. The gold standard screening questionnaire is the 10-item Alcohol Use Disorder Information Test (AUDIT) developed and tested worldwide by the WHO (Babor, Higgins-Biddle, Saunders, & Monteiro, 2001). Once identified as a risky drinker by a screening tool such as the AUDIT, clients are offered a brief counseling intervention. In brief counseling interventions, counselors do not diagnose but do provide clients with their alcohol screening results, elicit client perspectives regarding their drinking patterns, assist clients in goal-setting for changing their alcohol behaviors, when desired, and highlight the client's choices in considering changes, if any. ASBCIs involve one 30 minute session in the patient's hospital room, after the patient is medically stable (O'Brien, Reboussin, Veach, & Miller, 2012). Individuals with more serious alcohol issues, such as alcohol dependence, are also provided a referral to more intensive addiction treatment as part of the ASBCI.

Outcome studies support the use of ASBCIs in trauma centers and emergency departments. Gentilello et al. (1999) analyzed the effect of an alcohol screening and brief intervention on trauma patients' alcohol use and recidivism rates. The researchers compared the re-injury rates and alcohol consumption behaviors of patients who received the alcohol screening and brief intervention and those who did not. Results indicated that those who received an intervention experienced a 48% reduction in subsequent hospitalizations for re-injury, as well as a significant decrease in alcohol intake (i.e., reduction of 21.8 standard drinks), as compared with the control group. Brief alcohol interventions also have shown potential for decreasing the following: arrests for driving under the influence (DUI; Schermer, Moyers, Miller, & Bloomfield, 2006), criminal justice arrests, symptoms of depression and anxiety, suicide attempts, and the use of mood altering drugs (Substance Abuse and Mental Health Services Administration [SAMHSA], 2012). After additional promising research in alcohol screening and brief interventions with trauma patients (Crawford et al., 2004; Gentilello, Ebel, Wickizer, Salkever, & Rivara, 2005), in 2006, the American College of Surgeons added a prevention requirement to their trauma center accreditation standards, requiring all Level I Trauma Centers to conduct alcohol screening, brief interventions, and referrals to treatment when clinically indicated.

Culture and Brief Alcohol Interventions

Although extant empirical literature on ASBCI is encouraging, studies examining the effectiveness of alcohol screenings and brief interventions with culturally diverse populations are limited (e.g., Field & Caetano, 2010; Field, Caetano, Harris, Frankowski, & Roudsari, 2010; Madras et al., 2009). The few studies that exist (Field & Caetano, 2010; Field et al., 2010; Madras et al., 2009) suggest that brief alcohol interventions can be effective at reducing alcohol consumption for ethnic minority clients. Madras and colleagues (2009) showed that brief alcohol interventions may be effective without cultural adaptations; whereas, other findings (i.e., Field & Caetano, 2010; Field et al., 2010), indicate that cultural adaptations of brief alcohol interventions are vital and can positively influence treatment outcomes for culturally diverse clients.

Field et al. (2010) reported that a brief alcohol intervention was effective in reducing alcohol consumption in African American, Latina/o, and European American participants at six- and twelve-month follow-ups. Cultural factors in the administration of the intervention, in particular the fact that the majority of the study clinicians were Latina/o and spoke Spanish, may have influenced treatment outcomes for Latina/o participants. Field et al. (2010) stated that ethnic agreement between counselor and participant may explain the positive response of Latinas/os following the intervention. In particular, they suggested that "cultural scripts," which consist of values and beliefs exhibited by cultural groups in social interactions, may have positively influenced the effectiveness of the brief alcohol intervention with Latinas/os.

As a follow-up to the previous study, Field and Caetano (2010) examined the influence of ethnic matching between clinician and client on the effectiveness of brief alcohol interventions with Latinas/os. Among other things, results indicated that Latina/o clients whose clinicians were also Latina/o exhibited significant reductions in their drinking behaviors. In particular, the results revealed that ethnic match was most efficacious with foreign-born and less acculturated Latina/o clients. Field and

Caetano (2010) explained these results in terms of cultural competence, stating that ethnic matching was beneficial because of several mechanisms, including "cultural scripts, ethnic specific perceptions pertaining to substance abuse, and ethnic specific preferred channels of communication" (p. 8). Inattention to these cultural factors by non-Latino clinicians may generate misunderstandings, miscommunication, and missed opportunities to express empathy (Field & Caetano, 2010).

Not all clients have access to culturally concordant counselors. This underscores the importance of multicultural counseling training. A key aspect of multicultural counseling competence pertains to counselors' ability to adapt treatments to the unique needs and circumstances of their culturally diverse clients (Veach & Moro, 2012). This is important because multiculturally competent counselors, regardless of ethnicity, may be equipped to provide comparable, positive treatment outcomes to those produced with ethnic agreement between counselor and client (Field & Caetano, 2010).

Cultural Considerations with Latina/o Clients

Culture is an abstract, dynamic, ubiquitous, and multilayered construct that is difficult to conceptualize (Hall, 1989) and for which it is challenging to provide guidelines. Nevertheless, due to the importance of modifying culturally sensitive and effective alcohol screenings and brief interventions for Latina/o clients, we provide key cultural guidelines for clinical consideration. This is by no means an exhaustive list, but a starting point. To enhance the feasibility of this task, we conceptualize and organize guidelines using three integral cultural concepts which are prevalent in the multicultural literature (e.g., Hall, 1989; Sue & Sue, 2008): locus of control, individualism-collectivism, and communication styles. Guidelines to consider when providing ASBCI to Latina/o clients are drawn from these cultural concepts. After a brief overview of these concepts, each will be discussed in relation to the provision of ASBCI to Latina/o clients.

For counseling to be effective, it is imperative that counselors recognize and adapt their interventions to the cultural worldviews of their Latina/o clients (Torres-Rivera, Wilbur, Phan, Maddux, & Roberts-Wilbur, 2004). The term Latina/o is used in this article to represent

Spanish-speaking individuals residing in the U.S. who have immigrated or whose ancestors immigrated from Cuba, the Dominican Republic, Central America, Mexico, Puerto Rico, or South America. As we discuss common cultural beliefs and values associated with Latinas/os, it is important to note that wide cultural variations exist between subgroups (e.g., Guatemalans and Peruvians) and within subgroups (Gloria & Peregoy, 1996). Consequently, although we provide guidelines to consider for culturally adapting ASBCI to Latinas/os, it is essential that counselors take care in applying these guidelines while also assessing for individual and sub-group differences, as well as acculturation levels. That being said, a cluster of cultural commonalities exist among Latinas/os (Gloria & Peregoy, 1996), including beliefs about locus of control, collectivism, and communication styles. These cultural factors can potentially influence counseling and, thus, should be considered when providing ASBCI to Latina/o clients.

Locus of Control

Locus of control refers to the perceived degree of personal autonomy one exercises in shaping the circumstances of one's life. Locus of control is not a bimodal distribution, but rather it approximates a normal curve, with extremes of internal and external locus of control situated at the tails of the distribution (Rotter, 1975). External locus of control, at times referred to as fatalism, is the belief that external forces, such as fortune, fate, or the will of otherworldly beings such as a deity or spirits, have a significant influence on a person's life circumstances. Internal locus of control, on the other hand, refers to the belief that one is mostly the master of one's own life circumstances and destiny. Although within-group differences are prevalent, culture plays a prominent role in shaping individual perceptions of what one can control in one's life.

With respect to Latino culture, some Latinas/os, based on their religious beliefs and *espiritualidad* (spirituality), may possess a fatalistic view of life, wherein they believe that life circumstances are determined by external forces (Gloria & Peregoy, 1996). Similar to other cultural concepts, evidence of *fatalismo* (fatalism) is embedded in colloquial language (Gloria & Peregoy, 1996; Ivers, 2012). A familiar example is the use of the phrase, *si Dios quiere* (if it is God's will; Gloria & Paragoy, 1996; Ivers,

2012), in reference to future commitments. Fatalism is also evident in familiar passive voice phrases used in Spanish, such as *se me olvidó* (it forgot itself to me) or *se me rompió* (it broke itself on me). These phrases omit the agent in control of or responsible for these actions (Ivers, 2012).

Spiritual or healing practices common in Latino cultures, such as Santeria, Curanderismo, and Espiritismo, may influence Latina/o clients' perceptions of their alcohol use, as well as their beliefs about their ability to change their drinking behaviors (Gloria & Paragoy, 1996). In particular, Latina/o clients who believe in or practice one of these spiritual or healing practices may consider their alcohol consumption levels to be influenced by or the result of other worldly, spiritual powers (Gloria & Paragoy, 1996). Consequently, Latina/o clients with fatalistic views may believe that their ability to change their alcohol drinking patterns is limited or unfeasible.

It is important that counselors who conduct ASBCI consider the locus of control of their Latina/o clients. ASBCI with clients who possess an external locus of control may necessitate modifications in counseling interventions. A central feature of ASBCI is goal-setting to explore reduction of risky alcohol consumption. An emphasis on goal-setting may be less effective with Latina/o clients who hold fatalistic views about their life circumstances in general and their alcohol consumption behaviors specifically. In these situations, it is important that counselors avoid communicating that goal-setting is mandatory or required. Openness to exploring clients' locus of control can minimize confusion, enhance rapport, and misperceptions of counselor insensitivity toward Latina/o clients' religious or spiritual values. Instead, counselors might consider the following guidelines.

Withhold assumptions about client avoidance, resistance, and lack of motivation. Due to the stigmatizing nature of alcohol issues, counselors providing ASBCIs commonly encounter defense mechanisms such as ambivalence, avoidance, resistance, and motivational challenges. With respect to some Latina/o clients, behaviors that appear like resistance and lack of motivation may, in fact, be manifestations of a fatalistic worldview (Gloria & Peregoy, 1996). For example, clients who avoid answering or struggle to answer questions about their goal for reducing their drinking may be resistant and may lack motivation; or, they may not believe they have the autonomy to make changes in their alcohol consumption.

Examine clients' spiritual and cultural beliefs. Broaching the subject of clients' cultural and spiritual beliefs may be beneficial when providing ASBCIs to Latina/o clients who possess a fatalistic worldview. Ideally, if permitted and feasible, consultation and collaboration with clients' religious or spiritual healer could be included in treatment (Gloria & Peregoy, 1996; Sue & Sue, 2008). Procuring the help of religious leaders or spiritual healers could facilitate counselors' understanding of clients' alcohol drinking in the context of their religious, spiritual, and cultural paradigms, as well as inform treatment adaptations (Gloria & Peregoy, 1996).

In many situations, due to the logistics of providing brief alcohol treatment, it may prove difficult to consult with religious leaders and spiritual healers. In these circumstances, it may be beneficial for counselors to discuss directly the topic of spiritual and cultural beliefs with their client (Torres-Rivera et al., 2004). The following prompts might be helpful: (a) I noticed that when I mentioned goal-setting you appeared a little uncomfortable. Please talk more about that. (b) You expressed earlier your belief that God has helped you through this accident; tell me more about your faith. (c) How do your religious or spiritual beliefs influence your drinking behaviors? (d) You mentioned that God is in control of your life. In light of this injury/accident, what do you believe God's will is for you in regard to drinking? (e) With respect to drinking alcohol, talk more about ways you might align yourself more closely with your spiritual practice or God's will.

Individualism versus Collectivism

The cultural construct of individualism-collectivism, according to Triandis (2001) is the "most significant cultural difference among cultures" (p. 907). Similar to locus of control, individualism-collectivism exists on a continuum. Individualism, as the name suggests, is a cultural concept in which emphasis is placed on individuals rather than groups. Autonomy, independence, individual development, personal fulfillment, and self-interest, for example, are stressed above group cohesion and group welfare, and individuals give priority to personal goals over group goals. In contrast, collectivism is characterized by an emphasis on group cohesion. Individuals identify themselves in terms of their group affiliation, and group welfare and group goals are valued over individual goals or achievement.

Latinas/os, as a group, are generally considered more collectivistic in nature than are European Americans. Nonetheless, individual differences and acculturation to U.S. norms may influence Latina/o clients' values regarding collectivism. Counselors should assess Latina/o clients' individualistic-collectivistic identity before making assumptions.

Familismo (familism) is a core Latina/o cultural value associated with collectivism (Field & Caetano, 2010; Gloria & Peregoy, 1996). Familismo is characterized by a strong, close-knit connection and commitment to the family and its welfare. Familismo often extends beyond the nuclear family to include aunts, uncles, cousins, Godparents, and close family friends. Latina/o families that value familismo are often directly and intimately involved in family members' lives, including each other's physical and mental healthcare. It is not uncommon, for example, for family members to attend each other's medical appointments and support each other in treatment plan adherence (Young, 2009). Below are some guidelines to consider when working with Latinas/os who possess collectivistic values, particularly familismo.

Develop Confianza (Trust) and Rapport through Self Disclosure.
Familismo may play an important role in alcohol treatment for Latina/o clients (Field & Caetano, 2010). Latinas/os are often reticent to discuss their alcohol-related problems with people outside of their family, including mental health professionals, due to its potential to influence negatively the reputation and welfare of the family. Instead, Latinas/os may be less embarrassed and more willing to talk to a family member or close friend about their concerns or problems with alcohol (Field & Caetano, 2010). Discussing a topic such as risky alcohol drinking may feel particularly threatening to undocumented Latina/o immigrants, due to their vulnerable legal status in the U.S. To reduce potential client mistrust, reticence, and guardedness, it is essential that alcohol counselors emphasize trust and rapport-building before engaging fully in an ASBCI with Latina/o clients.

Cultivating *personalismo* may greatly facilitate the process of building rapport and establishing trust with Latina/o clients which, in turn, may increase Latina/o clients' willingness to share information about their alcohol drinking behaviors. Personalismo is an important, complimentary value to familismo, characterized by warmth, friendliness, and a mutual respect for individuals' uniqueness, worth, and dignity (Galanti, 2003; Gloria & Peregoy, 1996). Counselors can cultivate personalismo through active listening, empathic responses, genuine expressions of concern, and mutual sharing (Galanti, 2003; Gloria & Peregoy, 1996). Concerning mutual sharing, to develop personalismo, counselors may consider self-disclosing more frequently than they are accustomed to, as well as spending more time getting to know their Latina/o clients before delving into alcohol screening questions. Latina/o clients may feel more comfortable discussing potentially risky alcohol behaviors after an interpersonal connection with their counselor has been established. In addition, personalismo may improve treatment outcomes. Although not specific to alcohol, Galanti (2003) discussed a situation in which a Latina/o patient became more compliant with diet and fluid restrictions associated with diabetes and renal failure only after the patient and her nurse had developed a close, personal relationship. This relationship was developed in part by the nurse encouraging her patient to discuss personal matters unrelated to the medical care provided.

Focus on Group or Family Welfare. Latina/o clients who possess collectivistic values may respond differently to an ASBCI than would their individualistic counterparts. As mentioned earlier, a core component of brief alcohol sessions is the development of therapeutic goals. However, these goals are generally focused primarily on the individual client. This emphasis on the individual may not resonate with collectivistic, Latina/o clients and, therefore, may be less effective. Instead, counselors might consider focusing less on individual goals and more on helping collectivistic clients discover ways to improve family cohesion and welfare by engaging in safer alcohol drinking behaviors. One of the central concerns of Latina/o clients revolves around how their alcohol drinking behaviors affect their family negatively (Field & Caetano, 2010). Counselors may be able to use this central concern to explore the motivation, as it pertains to the family, to make healthy changes regarding their alcohol use. The following are a few phrases that counselors might employ to help collectivistic Latina/o clients make positive changes regarding their alcohol consumption: (a) how is your alcohol use affecting your family? (b) It sounds like your family is really important to you. Talk more about ways that reducing your drinking could benefit you and your family. (c) In whom can you confide when you are feeling down/low/anxious/stressed/lonely (whatever the trigger is)? (d) Share more about those in your life who can support you in your goal of drinking less.

Assess Social Supports. Latina/o immigrants who possess a strong sense of familial connectedness and who leave important social networks to immigrate to the U.S., may feel a sense of loneliness and isolation in the U.S. (Lee et al., 2006). Latinas/os may respond to these feelings by increasing their alcohol consumption (Lee et al). In a qualitative analysis, Lee et al. (2006) reported that Latina/o immigrants who self-identified as frequent heavy drinkers tended to drink more heavily in the U.S. than they did in their countries-of-origin. Participants reported drinking alcohol to remember happy memories of the past, as well as to escape feelings of isolation. They also reported drinking alone more frequently in the U.S. than they did in their countries-of-origin.

When clinically indicated, it may be beneficial for counselors to help Latina/o clients recognize how losing their social support or not having consistent interactions with their family can trigger risky drinking. It also may be beneficial to discuss ways in which clients can cope with feelings of loneliness, nostalgia, and isolation. Moreover, where appropriate, counselors may consider referring Latina/o clients to alcohol support groups, such as Alcoholics Anonymous. Triandis (2001) indicated that collectivistic individuals living in individualistic societies often benefit from participation in and associations with groups, such as clubs, and church organizations.

Communication Styles

A wide variety of communication styles exist between cultures, from nonverbal gestures and encouragers to verbal intonations, nuances, and emotional expressivity. It is important that counselors recognize and interpret appropriately the distinct communication styles of their culturally diverse clients. Hall (1989) conceptualized cultural variations in communication styles in terms of low- and high-context communication. In low-context communication, individuals rely more heavily on words to communicate. In high-context communication individuals rely less on words and more on other factors, such as gestures, implicit messages, and silence, to interpret the meaning of interactions.

Hall (1989) contended that some cultures are higher- or lower-context in their communication styles than others. Hall (1989) also pointed out that all cultures, regardless of their preferred communication style, have latent rules about when and how individuals should engage in low- or high-context communication. For example, in the U.S., communication in court proceedings are exceptionally low-context; whereas, interactions with good friends and family members are often higher-context. In interactions with friends, individuals often rely less on words to interpret meaning from conversations and more on other factors such as paralanguage, nonverbals, and context. This greater reliance on context to communicate with friends is true of higher- and lower-context cultures. However, more is demanded of friends in higher-context cultures, such as Japanese culture—particularly around the expectation for friends to adeptly understand and interpret each other's implicit thoughts and feelings (Hall, 1989).

Cultural variations regarding communication styles may influence the effectiveness of ASBCIs with Latina/o clients. Many Latinas/os, especially less acculturated immigrants, possess a higher context communication style than is customary in the U.S. This, coupled with Latina/o values of *simpatía*—a desire for harmony in relationships—and *respeto*—a respect for the elderly and authority figures—may influence an ASBCI. The combination of these values may manifest themselves in the following ways: (a) Latina/o clients, in order to cultivate a harmonious relationship as well as to respect a counselor's perceived authority, may say what they believe the counselor would like to hear at times rather than expressing their true feelings; (b) Latina/o clients may believe it would be rude to disagree with a counselor or decline services directly, but will do so indirectly using paralanguage and nonverbals. This is high-context communication. Disagreements and refusals are expressed contextually using nonverbals, nuances, and intonations. Members of the same culture would likely understand immediately the true meaning being communicated without it being spoken. However, in cross-cultural exchanges, these unspoken, underlying meanings may be missed altogether. This is especially possible for ethnic majority counselors who are more accustomed to lower-context communication which relies more heavily on the spoken word. Thus, another important guideline to consider when providing ASBCIs to Latina/o clients is to recognize the potential for high-context communication. This means that counselors should become fluent not only in Latina/o clients' verbal language, but also in nonverbal communications, nuances, and paralanguage.

Conclusion

Our nation's medical trauma centers serve diverse populations, yet a dearth of literature exists that examines the process of providing culturally competent alcohol screening and brief counseling interventions to clients from underrepresented cultural backgrounds. The objective of this article was to attend to this gap, particularly by highlighting cultural variables that may impact the clinical process when engaging with Latina/o clients. Utilizing the concepts of locus of control, individualism-collectivism, and communication styles, we provided some basic guidelines for clinical consideration with Latina/o clients. Perceived client resistance or lack of motivation may be influenced by a deeply spiritual fatalism. Incorporating an awareness of this may increase therapeutic alliance and allow for spiritually-informed goal-setting. Cultivating a personal and respectful relationship with Latina/o clients may increase client willingness to share information about drinking problems. Tying changes in drinking patterns to family or group welfare may increase motivation for Latina/o clients, and awareness of social supports (or lack thereof) in this often-immigrant population is critical. Finally, we advise that counselors stay particularly attuned to the high-context, nonverbal communication taking place during a session, as an understanding of and empathic response to that which is spoken and un-spoken are integral to rapport-building and positive outcomes. These considerations are intended to be a starting point from which researchers and clinicians can begin a much-needed conversation regarding multiculturally competent practice in the rapidly-growing world of ASBCI in medical settings. There is much to learn regarding the complex and nuanced process of tailoring practices to the idiosyncratic needs of clients. Our hope is to begin the process of laying a foundation for a conceptual and research literature focused on providing the highest-quality and most-effective ASBCI for all clients, including those from underserved populations.

References

Babor, T. F., Higgins-Biddle, J. C., Saunders, J. B., & Monteiro, M. G. (2001). *The Alcohol Use Disorders Identification Test: Guidelines for use in primary care* (2nd ed.). Geneva, Switzerland: World Health Organization.

Crawford, M. J., Patton, R., Touquet, R., Drummond, C., Byford, S., Barrett, B., ... & Henry, J. A. (2004). Screening and referral for brief intervention of alcohol-misusing patients in an emergency department: A pragmatic randomised controlled trial. *The Lancet, 364*(9442), 1334–1339. doi:10.1016/S0140-6736(04)17190-0

Desy, P. M., Howard, P. K., Perhats, C., & Li, S. (2010). Alcohol screening, brief intervention, and referral to treatment conducted by emergency nurses: An impact evaluation. *Journal of Emergency Nursing, 36*(6), 538–545. doi:10.1016/j.jen.2009.09.011

D'Onofrio, G., & Degutis, L. C. (2002). Preventive care in the emergency department: Screening and brief intervention for alcohol problems in the emergency department: A systematic review. *Academic Emergency Medicine, 9*(6), 627–638.

Field, C. A., & Caetano, R. (2010). The role of ethnic matching between patient and provider on the effectiveness of brief alcohol interventions with Hispanics. *Alcoholism: Clinical and Experimental Research, 34*(2), 262–271. doi:10.1111/j.1530-0277.2009.01089.x

Field, C. A., Caetano, R., Harris, T. R., Frankowski, R., & Roudsari, B. (2010). *Addiction, 105*(1), 62–73. doi:10.1111/j.1360-0443.2009.02737.x

Galanti, G. (2003). The Hispanic family and male-female relationships: An overview. *Journal of Transcultural Nursing, 14*, 180–185. doi:10.1177/1043659603014003004

Gentilello, L. M., Ebel, B. E., Wickizer, T. M., Salkever, D. S., & Rivara, F. P. (2005). Alcohol interventions for trauma patients treated in emergency departments and hospitals: A cost benefit analysis. *Annals of Surgery, 241*(4), 541–550. doi:10.1097/01.sla.0000157133.80396.1c

Gentilello, L. M., Rivara, F. P., Donovan, D. M., Jurkovich, G. J., Daranciang, E., Dunn, C. W., ... Ries, R. R. (1999). Alcohol interventions in a trauma center as a means of reducing the risk of injury recurrence. *Annals of Surgery, 230*(4), 473–483. doi:10.1097/00000658-199910000-00003

Gloria, A. M., & Peregoy, J. J. (1996). Counseling Latino alcohol and other substance users/abusers. *Journal of Substance Abuse Treatment, 13*(2), 119–126.

Griner, D., & Smith, T. B. (2006). Culturally adapted mental health intervention: A meta-analytic review. *Psychotherapy: Theory, Research, Practice, 43*(4), 531–548.

Hall, E. T. (1989). *Beyond culture*. New York: Doubleday.

Ivers, N. N. (2012). The effect of ethnicity on multicultural competence. *Journal of Professional Counseling, Practice, Theory, & Research, 39*(2), 40–52.

Lee, C. S., López, S. R., Colby, S. M., Tejada, M., García-Coll, C., & Smith, M. (2006). Social processes underlying acculturation: A study of drinking behavior among immigrant Latinos in the Northeast United States. *Contemporary Drug Problems, 33*(4).

Lee, C. S., López, S. R., Hernández, L., Colby, S. M., Caetano, R., Borrelli, B., & Rohsenow, D. (2011). A cultural adaptation of motivational interviewing to address heavy drinking among Hispanics. *Cultural Diversity and Ethnic Minority Psychology, 17*(3), 317–324. doi:10.1037/a0024035

Madras, B. K., Compton, W. M., Avula, D., Stegbauer, T., Stein, J. B., & Clark, H. W. (2009). Screening, brief interventions, referral to treatment (SBIRT) for illicit drug and alcohol use at multiple healthcare sites: Comparison at intake and six months. *Drug and Alcohol Dependence, 99*(1–3): 280–295. doi:10.1016/j.drugalcdep.2008.08.003.

Moore, E. E. (2005). Alcohol and trauma: The perfect storm. *The Journal of Trauma: Injury, Infection, and Critical Care, 59*, 53–75.

National Institute of Alcohol Abuse and Alcoholism. (2013, February). *Alcohol overdose: The dangers of drinking too much.* Retrieved from: http://pubs.niaaa.nih.gov/publications/AlcoholOverdoseFactsheet/overdoseFact.pdf

National Institute of Alcohol Abuse and Alcoholism. (2010). *Rethinking Drinking* (NIH Publication No. 10–3770). Rockville, MD: Author.

O'Brien, M. C., Reboussin, B., Veach, L. J., & Miller, P. R. (2012). *Robert Wood Johnson Grant # 65032: The Teachable Moment Study* [Unpublished research report].

Rotter, J. B. (1975). Some problems and misconceptions related to the construct of internal versus external control of reinforcement. *Journal of Consulting and Clinical Psychology, 43*(1), 56–67.

Schermer, C. R., Moyers, T. B., Miller, W. R., & Bloomfield, L. A. (2006). Trauma center brief interventions for alcohol disorders decrease subsequent driving under the influence arrests. *Journal of Trauma: Injury, Infection, and Critical Care, 60*, 29–34.

Soderstrom, C. A., DiClemente, C. C., Dischinger, P. C., Hebel, J. R., McDuff, D. R., Auman, K. M., . . .Kufera, J. A. (2007). A controlled trial of brief intervention versus brief advice for at-risk drinking trauma center patients. *Journal of Trauma: Injury, Infection, and Critical Care, 62*(5), 1102–1112. doi:10.1097/TA.0b013e31804bdb26

Substance Abuse and Mental Health Services Administration. (2012). *State of SBIRT 2003–2012: Review and discussion of SAMHSA funded SBIRT initiatives* [PDF file].

Sue, D. W., & Sue, D. (2008). *Counseling the culturally diverse: Theory and practice* (5th ed.). Hoboken, NJ: John Wiley & Sons.

Torres-Rivera, E.,Wilbur, M. P., Phan, L. T., Maddux, C. D., & Roberts-Wilbur, J. (2004). Counseling Latinos with substance abuse problems. *Journal of Addictions & Offender Counseling, 25*(1), 26–42. doi:10.1002/j.2161-1874.2004.tb00191.x

Triandis, H. C. (2001). Individualism-collectivism and personality. *Journal of Personality, 69*(6). 907–924. doi:10.1111/1467-6494.696169

Veach, L. J., & Moro, R. R. (2012). Cultural considerations: Alcohol screening and brief intervention in a southern US level-1 trauma center. *Addiction Science & Clinical Practice, 7*(Suppl 1), A41.

World Health Organization. (n.d.). Retrieved from http://www.who.int/substance_abuse/facts/alcohol/en/index.html#

Young, J. (2009). Clinical pediatrics in the Mexican immigrant community: Insights into the impact of culture on the health of Mexican American children, Part 1. *Contemporary Pediatrics, 26*(2), 30–33.

Appendix

Fatalistic, Religious Beliefs Vignette

I (first author) once worked with a Mexican-American client who expressed discomfort when I suggested we work on constructing therapeutic goals. He indicated his belief that setting goals was inappropriate because it was "playing God." Not having encountered clients with a fatalistic paradigm before, I was uncertain about how to respond, so I asked my client to tell me more. He discussed in detail his religious beliefs, which were rooted in an evangelical Christian tradition. I then asked the client to further elaborate on his religious beliefs with the following prompt: "What do you believe God's will for you is with regard to your presenting problem?" The client thought about it for a minute and then explained that he believed that God would want him to feel relief from his problem. I then asked how, working together, we might be able to help him work towards fulfilling God's will. This line of questioning, from my perspective, appeared to resonate more fully with the client's religious and cultural values, while at the same time providing an opportunity for us to address his presenting problem.

High-Context Communication Vignette

As part of the Teachable Moment research team, I (first author) had the opportunity to invite Spanish-speaking Latina/o trauma center patients who met specific criteria to participate in our study. On one occasion, I met with an individual who initially consented verbally to participate. However, after being given the consent form, he indicated that he had had second thoughts about participating in the study, particularly because he was not comfortable signing the consent form because of the type of paper on which it was printed. I, of course, respected his wishes and did not enroll him in the study. Later, I wondered about his reason(s) for not wanting to sign his name to that standard type of paper. Was this a religious or spiritual belief of which I was unaware? Was this an idiosyncratic preference of this individual? I'm still not certain. However, my guess is that the individual valued respeto and simpatía. Thus, rather than openly refuse my invitation which, to him, may have been seen as rude and disrespectful and potentially harmful to our relationship, he allowed me to save face by indirectly expressing his desires not to participate.

9

Incorporating Family Systems Models into Substance Abuse Interventions with Latino Adults

Aaron S. Hymes[1]

Substance abuse with Latino adults remains a problem in the United States of America. Family systems theory (Bowen, 1991) focuses on interdependence in the family leading to balance and decreased dysfunction. Family systems theory incorporated into substance abuse interventions with Latino adolescents shows positive outcomes yet has not been applied to interventions with Latino adults. This article seeks to describe the need to incorporate family systems theory into substance abuse interventions used with Latino adults.

Drinking and drug-related problems are recognized to exist on a large scale and to represent the greatest challenges for the prevention and ill-health in both developed and developing countries (Orford et al., 1998). The World Health Organization (WHO; 2012) reported demographic trends suggesting the total number of drug users in developing

1. Aaron S. Hymes, Doctoral Student, Department of Counseling, University of North Carolina at Charlotte.Correspondence concerning this article should be addressed to Aaron S. Hymes Department of Counseling, College of Education, University of North Carolina at Charlotte, Charlotte, NC 28223. E-mail: ahymes@uncc.edu

countries would increase significantly. In 2012 the WHO (2012) reported there were 27 million problem drug users, representing approximately 0.6% of the world adult population. The WHO (2012) goes on to estimate there were between 99,000 and 253,000 deaths globally in 2010 as a result of illicit drug use, with drug-related deaths accounting for between 0.5% and 1.3% of all-cause mortality among those aged 15–64. As recently as 2009, some 4.5 million people worldwide were receiving treatment for problems related to illicit drug use, though the need for treatment is much higher (WHO, 2012). These statistics suggest the prevalence of substance abuse is a global concern and current models of substance abuse treatment are less than effective in decreasing this global epidemic. According to the National Survey on Drug Use and Health (NSDUH) from 2012 there were no significant differences in drug use for any minority group between the years 2002 through 2011 except Latinos (Substance Abuse and Mental Health Services Administration [SAMHSA], 2012). SAMHSA reported in the NSDUH between the years 2002 and 2011 the current drug use rate among Latinos increased from 7.2% to 8.4%

The prevalence of consistently high treatment dropout rates and lack of engagement of Latino clients suggests the need to reshape our westernized view of substance abuse interventions. As noted historically by Sue and Sue (1977) and more recently by Kim (2011), the termination rate among racial and ethnic minority clients has been observed at approximately 50%, or one out of every two culturally different clients fails to return to counseling services. Alvarez, Jason, Olsen, Ferrari and Davis (2007) supported this further reporting a number of studies have found Latino ethnicity as a predictor of premature termination from substance abuse treatment services. As the counseling field continues to move toward culturally responsive treatment modalities it has become paramount to recognize the role of culture for increased substance abuse intervention effectiveness. Rowe and Liddle (2003) noted living in a family where one member has a drinking or drug problem is a very common predicament worldwide supporting the rise of chronic family stress. This points toward the need for the development of culturally relevant substance abuse treatment designs aimed toward the incorporation of family systems approaches. Family systems substance abuse interventions lend to deconstruction of substance abuse through the identification of dysfunctional family patterns and the development of family driven strategies to block the unhealthy patterns contributing to the substance abuse behaviors. Thus, this article seeks to describe the need to incorporate family systems theory into substance abuse interventions for use with Latino adults.

Need to Address Latinos' Substance Abuse Needs

There appears to be a gap in substance abuse intervention literature focusing on cultural responsiveness. Scholars in the field have called attention to the gap that exists in family systems therapy focusing on the incorporation of cultural variables involved in family systems and substance abuse (Orford, 1990; Rowe & Liddle, 2009). The scarcity of substance abuse literature stressing the need to appreciate the historical and cultural roots of family life and drinking has been long acknowledged (Orford, 1990). More recently, Rowe and Liddle (2009) reported the development of family-based treatments for adult substance abusers was extremely limited and significantly lags behind the field of family-based adult alcoholic treatment. In fact, most substance abuse interventions for adults are based on an individualistic, Anglo perspective that fails to lend a voice to cultural minorities being affected. This is concerning as the United States (U.S.) is rapidly moving toward a major shift in demographics as outlined previously.

The rates of substance abuse among Latino youth indicate an increase that may be surpassing that of Caucasians (Prado et al., 2007). This was expanded upon by Goldbach, Thompson, Holleran & Stelker (2011) who noted first generation Latinos born in the U.S. are 6.4% more likely to need treatment when compared to those not born in the U.S. They further stated findings from the Monitoring the Future Study, which indicates that by 8th grade, Latino youth report greater use of all substances except amphetamines, and by 12th grade have the highest rates of crack use when compared to other racial/ethnic groups (Goldbach, et al., 2011). Although Latinos are being referred to substance abuse services at a higher rate, those who do seek substance abuse services are likely to terminate at higher rates, receive culturally inappropriate services (Waldron, Turner, Brody, & Hops, 2008), and experience a sense of neglect or being unimportant when compared with the majority (Baca & Koss-Chioino, 1997).

Sue and Sue (1977) proposed counselors must remain aware of possible misinterpretations and aspects of counseling perceived as antagonistic to the worldview held by the client. The multicultural competencies proposed by Sue, Arredondo, and McDavis (1992) are poignant of the need for counselors to increase cultural awareness and how culture shapes treatment effectiveness. The competencies outline the need to better understand the role of cultural factors and for treatment modality development and approaches aimed at increased cultural responsiveness as a profession. These competencies may also increase perceived creditability of counselors by clients, which may serve to positively affect sustained engagement in treatment by clients and families.

Even in light of the multicultural counseling movement the area of culturally sensitive substance abuse interventions has little empirical evidence (Gil, Wagner, & Tubman, 2004) illuminating the need for culturally relevant interventions to encourage the engagement of minorities and marginalized groups (Gragg & Wilson, 2011). The need for increased empirical evidence of culturally relevant substance abuse treatment interventions is evident. A significant increase in minority substance use, specifically in Latino's, and low retention rate is disheartening and of serious note as the United States continues to become a melting pot of ethnicity.

Proponents of cultural competencies suggest our conceptualizations of mental illness needs adjustment, Suggested areas of adjustment include changes to treatment planning and the targeted goals of treatment plans (Cunningham, Foster & Warner, 2010). Cunningham, Foster, and Warner (2010) go on to suggest counselors need to make adaptions in how they interact with ethnically dissimilar clients in a cross-cultural context. Becoming stagnant in our cross-cultural conceptualizations will lend itself to the continued use of treatment interventions not suited to the Latino population receiving it. It is our role as professionals to provide the appropriate treatment interventions aimed at producing positive outcomes in our client's lives. A failure to account for cultural factors and adapt our interventions in accordance is blurring the lines of ethics as laid out in the multicultural competencies. Thus, this article presents a model of substance abuse treatment intervention with Latino adults that incorporate a family systems model.

Latinos' Cultural Values

Substance abuse treatment models have largely focused on Westernized treatment modalities and have failed in conjoining with variables unique to differing cultures (see Gil, et al., 2004; Gragg & Wilson, 2011; Triandis, 2001; Orford, et al., 1998). In failing to incorporate cultural variables into treatment models, we are choosing to remain blind to the impact of culture on those seeking substance abuse interventions. Castro & Alacón (2002) suggested "cultural variables" (p. 784) defined as specific beliefs, values, norms and behaviors that capture the core life experiences of racial/ethnic minority peoples. Three cultural variables of the Latino culture that are important to a family systems approach are Familismo, allocentrism, collectivism and cultural mistrust.

The concept of Familismo has been identified as a significant element of Latino culture. *Familismo* is characterized by strong identification, social and family support and respect for nuclear and extended family (Antshel, 2002; Dillon, De La Rosa, Sastre & Ibanez, 2012). The concept of Familismo specifically suggests family as a significant factor in decision making for Latino clients. Antshel (2002) noted family is likely to play a role in the decision-making and planning processes of treatment and both nuclear and extended family may service as a support for the client receiving care. Furthermore, Familismo serves as a protective measure against threats to the health, status and honor of the family (Altarriba & Bauer, 1998; Dillon et al, 2012; Loya, Reedy, & Hinshaw 2010). Dillon et al. (2012) also noted Familismo as a significant cultural factor effective in preventing substance abuse among Latinos living in the United States. The importance of the Familismo variable cannot be understated in working with Latinos and must be accounted for in substance treatment interventions due to its impact. Familismo ties into the cultural variable of allocentrism but is not to be confused as being one in the same.

Allocentrism is an important concept to view through the lens of treatment retention with Latino substance abuse clients. Altarriba and Bauer (1998) noted *allocentrism* as the need of Latinos to have relationships that are nurturing, loving and respectful. Of interesting note is the focus on trust among group members. Our westernized substance abuse models appear to be in conflict with allocentrism as they focus on healing in an individualized stance and can be quite confrontational in nature. Building trust and honoring allocentrism for Latino clients can become a difficult process utilizing only treatments designed to focus on a westernized set of cultural variables.

Collectivism has been defined by scholars as a group of people who are interdependent and embedded in their social contexts, leading to sacrificing of self-interest for the benefit of the group or collective (Vargas & Kemmelmeier, 2012). As noted by Gil, et al. (2004) some studies suggest greater levels of acculturation predicts heavier substance use, in others less acculturation predicts heavier substance use, while US-born Latino youth were highly acculturated, they reported high Latino ethnic orientation, low levels of perceived discrimination and high levels of cultural mistrust. The element of cultural mistrust is interesting when applied to substance abuse treatment as it further complicates the already difficult process of building a therapeutic alliance. Cultural differences adding to a historically high level of perceived mistrust with this population will convolute the treatment process and may be a component to higher treatment dropout rates by minorities as compared to the majority. As Gil, et al. (2004) suggest little is known about how cultural mistrust and perceived discrimination affect attempts to prevent or treat adjustment problems, including substance abuse, among Latinos. Cultural mistrust appears to be a difficult variable within Latino culture as it seems to directly intertwine with interdependence of collectivism.

Again, it is noteworthy to remain aware of the cultural elements of collectivism and cultural mistrust and their effects on the traditional substance abuse treatment models currently available. Santisteban and Mena (2009; as cited in Gragg & Wilson, 2011) highlighted the need for interventions that take into consideration the unique needs of Latino youth when treating substance abuse. Treatment becomes more complicated for Latino families where rules and expectations surrounding treatment-seeking behaviors (Cardona et al., 2009; as cited in Gragg & Wilson, 2011) and culturally specific stressors (Falicov, 2009) are known barriers to successful engagement. The ability to provide substance abuse interventions becomes increasingly difficult if those struggling with substance abuse related issues are not engaging in treatment interventions. Further understanding of these variables and how they may be applied to culturally relevant substance abuse treatment models, especially from a family systems perspective, may prove beneficial in increasing treatment engagement and positive outcomes for substance abusers of differing cultures.

Culturally Responsive Substance Abuse Treatments for Latinos

Austin, Macgowan, and Wagner (2005) elaborated on how Brief Strategic Family Therapy (BSFT) was developed to treat substance abuse among Latino youths through the incorporation of family therapy. BSFT was developed for use with Cuban families in Miami as they tended to value connectedness over individual autonomy more closely related to collectivist views (Szapocnik, et al., 2012). The BSFT intervention is an integrative model combining structural and strategic family therapy theory and intervention techniques to address family interactions that are associated with the formation of adolescent substance use and related behavior problems (Robbins et al., 2011). BSFT is a family systems approach where family members are interdependent and the experiences and behavior of each family member affect the experiences and behavior of other family members (Szapocnik, et al., 2012). BSFT has demonstrated success in retaining families in treatment with Latino boys (Rowe & Liddle, 2003) and has been shown to reduce adolescent behavior problems that serve as precursors to substance abuse (Castro & Alacón, 2002). Rowe and Liddle (2003) stated the evidence for family-based therapy to reduce teen drug use and sustain treatment gains a year removed from treatment is "unequivocal" (p. 101). This appears in contradiction to reports by Austin, et al. (2005) who noted, BSFT was not clinically significant in reducing substance use among Latino youth, showed a high dropout rate from treatment and included no follow-up assessment to measure long-term treatment effects. Furthermore, there are no published manuals in working with this population (Baca & Chioino, 1997) and ethnic minority youths referred to substance abuse treatment experience high rates of release from treatment (Waldron, Turner & Hops, 2008) as a result of ineffective models designed to meet cultural needs.

There are a number of other family treatment modalities suggesting a varying spectrum of outcome effectiveness when applied to substance use interventions with adolescents (Rowe & Liddle, 2003; Gil, et al., 2004; Austin et al., 2005). For instance, Family Behavior Therapy (FBT) findings suggest it is an effective intervention for decreasing substance use among Caucasian male adolescents (Austin, et al., 2005) while reporting no generalizability to the Latino population. Henggler, Pickrel, and Brondino reported Multisystemic Family Therapy (MST) has demonstrated increased retention rates with youth and families and has reported approximately 98% treatment completion rate for substance abusing teens (as cited in Rowe & Liddle, 2003, p. 100; as cited in Austin et al., 2005, p. 77). However, it should be noted 1% of the sample in the Hedggler et al. (1999) study identified as Hispanic-American. Also of note is Family Focused Therapy (FFT), which suggests no significant differences in use of marijuana, or family functioning (Austin, et al., 2005). Recently, Alcohol Treatment Targeting Adolescents In Need (ATTAIN) was designed to provide interventions accounting for culture-specific factors. ATTAIN was also constructed to address the causes and risk factors associated with developing substance use behaviors (Gil, et al., 2004).

The effectiveness of BSFT, MST, and ATTAIN have shown varied levels of effectiveness with Latino adolescents. A limitation to empirically supported evidence may be the small sample sizes specific to Latino adolescents reported in these studies. However, it is interesting the need to incorporate family based substance abuse interventions with Latino adolescents was identified and has not continued in application to Latino adults. When applied to substance abuse interventions with Latino adults Family Systems theory may bridge this gap.

Substance Abuse and Family Systems Theory

Substance abuse treatment within the adult Latino culture appears to be a multifaceted issue lacking a suitable theory to serve as an umbrella for treatment engagement, treatment retention and treatment effectiveness as supported by a lack of literature available. Family systems theory (Bowen, 1991) could be the umbrella needed, as it postulates the importance of emotional interdependence among family members. This emotional interdependence among family members can lead to increased levels of anxiety resulting in changes at the level of functioning for both individual and the family system as a whole. Family systems theory incorporates concepts around patterns of behavior and reactions to these behaviors taking place within the family. The patterns of behavior may create balance in the family system or generate dysfunction within the family unit. This fits with the effects of substance abuse at the individual and family level, but appears to be in conflict with traditionally westernized models of adult substance abuse intervention that remain focused on change at the individual level. Latinos appear to be interdependent as a culture. Family systems theory's focus on the roles each member of a family plays in the context of the family unit may uncover areas of dysfunction supporting the continued behaviors of the substance abuser. Family systems theory is aimed toward bringing to light the family functions in direct opposition to these continued behaviors as well as those supporting continued dysfunction.

Orford (1990) states we largely work with families with drinking problems receiving treatment through a Westernized stress-victim model. The stress victim model postulates the stress family members experience leads them to view themselves as being victimized by the problem drinkers excessive drinking and behaviors. Further, the family members are left to cope with the behavior the best way they know how too. Orford (1990) posits that strictly looking through a stress victim lens doesn't account for the interactions of the family and the functions of the family the problem drinking may serve. Working from a stress victim approach has primarily been utilized in the West and Eastern Europe (Orford, 1990) and does not seem appropriate as a substance abuse intervention in a cross-cultural context. Castro and Alarcón (2002) support this notion in stating substance abuse providers are being asked or required to select and use model programs that have not been tested with multiple ethnic or racial groups, such as those found within the provider's own community. The concept of Familismo serves as an important cultural variable in Latino culture, yet it continues to be disregarded in substance abuse interventions with Latino adults.

The vast majority of literature focused on family systems substance interventions with the Latino population has focused on Latino adolescents. One of family therapy's significant contributions to treating adolescent drug abuse is the development of strategies and specialized methods for engaging youth and their families into treatment (Rowe & Liddle, 2001). Family therapy is often considered an especially culturally sensitive treatment modality that has been shown to be efficacious with Latino populations as well as with adolescent substance abusers. Parental support, nurturing and involvement have been shown to increase Latino adolescents' capacity to reject negative behaviors such as substance abuse (Goldbach et al., 2011). Effectively engaging an adolescent's system in treatment requires that therapists consider the influence of a family's culture on the process. Morgan and Crane (2010) noted intensive family-based treatments were more effective in retention with adolescents as compared to standard treatment procedures. Such a systemic approach has been found to be particularly valuable when working with minority families (Gragg & Wilson, 2011). If family systems focused substance abuse interventions are appropriate for Latino adolescents because of adherence to cultural variables why do the same cultural variables become non-factors when Latino's reach adulthood?

Steinglass (2009) states, " when substance abuse behavior is ongoing within a family, all members of the family are powerfully affected by this behavior, and it is therefore the whole family, rather than the abuser alone, that is the appropriate target for treatment" (p. 170). Building on the notion from Steinglass we can postulate the needs of the entire family unit when faced with a substance abusing family member. Interdependence of the family unit may serve as a barrier to treatment engagement as interventions focus on independence and boundary setting with substance abuse clients, which may prove a difficult task for the application of current westernized interventions. Awareness of the importance of Familismo, allocentrism, collectivism and cultural mistrust make it necessary to build substance abuse interventions from a family systems perspective.

Conclusions and Future Directions

When treating substance abuse with Latino adults, we appear to move back into our westernized model of treatment and disregard the importance of Familismo, although it has been identified as an important cultural variable across a large part of the literature. It makes one wonder how we can expect increased positive outcomes in providing substance abuse interventions to the Latino population if we continue in our failure to incorporate cultural variables shown to be significant. Incorporating a family systems model into substance abuse treatment with Latino adolescents has been found to produce significant results in reducing substance abuse. Simply, so much has been placed on prevention and treatment of Latino adolescents but has allowed Latino adults to fall through the proverbial cracks.

A key development to monitor will be the ongoing shift of substance abuse away from developed to developing countries, which would mean a heavier burden for countries relatively less equipped to tackle it (WHO,

2012). We remain in the early stages of understanding how to best match patients and families to different treatment approaches most of the evidence regarding the efficacy of family-based interventions comes from the United States of America and the United Kingdom. The applicability of these interventions to other parts of the world remains to be established. Although the outcome results for family therapy approaches to the treatment of substance misuse have been impressive, positive treatment responses are clearly not universal (Corless, Mirza & Steinglass, 2009).

Much of the work has been theoretical rather than focused on intervention outcome research and has specifically been lacking in assessing effectiveness with the Latino population (Jani, et al., 2009). Substance abuse has been identified as a problem affecting the family as much as the individual, despite treatment models continuing in their westernized stance. With the demographic shift of the United States of America moving closer to a minority-majority nation (United States Census Bureau, 2010), it is a necessity for outcome studies focused on substance abuse interventions accounting for cultural variables. If we fail at the level of intervention development, we have directly engaged in disservice to those we trained to serve. The formation of family focused mutual aid support groups like Al-Anon and Nar-Anon show recognition of the families need to engage in the healing process along with the substance-abusing individual. The continued growth of these groups speaks to the need for continued research into the effectiveness of family systems theory applied to substance abuse treatment.

A clear need has been established for effective substance abuse interventions in working with Latinos. Research has long identified the importance of family or Familismo as a significant variable for Latino's yet little has been done to infuse family systems theory into current substance abuse intervention models used in treatment. Application of cultural variables of significance to the Latino culture needs to be addressed in manualized substance abuse interventions and traditional counseling models.

An area needing further consideration in particular is acculturation. Goldbach et al. (2011) stated, "acculturation is a powerful determinant of attitudes and behaviors and needs to be considered in clinical work and research concerning substance abuse prevention and intervention" (p. 10). Research suggests the positive effect on concepts like worldview matching (Kim, 2011; Lynch, Vansteenkiste, Deci, & Ryan, 2011) increase client motivation in seeking treatment. According to Kim (2011) matching worldview supports stronger client-counselor working alliances and counselor empathy than mismatched worldview. An increase in cultural adaptations to current substance abuse interventions is needed as they will reduce the risk of acculturative stress and include the voices of the targeted population (Falicov, 2009) leading to increased positive outcomes. Greater emphasis needs to be placed on bi-lingual counselors serving the population of Latino substance abusers in all formats. In holding true to our focus on the significance of cultural variables we should, as a profession, make all necessary accommodations to promote the effectiveness of treatment on any population we serve. Effectively providing Latino adults with substance abuse interventions aimed at decreased substance use and sustained abstinence requires more than theoretical ponderings, it requires development and application.

Additionally, an area of focus needs to be change at the policy making level. Morgan and Crane (2010) noted a 5.9% annual rise in costs related to drug abuse since 1992 reaching an estimated total of $180.0 billion as recently as 1992. Policy makers must raise their awareness to the impact of culture and cultural variables and should assert for cultural considerations to be incorporated into all aspects of substance abuse research and interventions. Almost all forms of research require some source of funding and it appears we are not getting what we paying for as it relates to a current lack of outcome research focusing on culturally relevant substance abuse interventions. Castro and Alacón (2002) stated, "priority should be given to funding prevention and treatment research that focuses on generating new scientific knowledge about culture as it relates to the complex issues associated with substance abuse" (p. 801). Change begets change. Incorporation of cultural considerations at the level of policy making may increase funding of outcome research specifically focused on the development of substance abuse interventions tailored to Latino's. This is a call to action for counseling professionals to add to the multicultural counseling movement through the development of substance abuse models incorporating family systems theory for use with Latino adults.

References

Altarriba, J., & Bauer, L. (1998). Counseling the Hispanic client: Cuban Americans, Mexican Americans, and Puerto Ricans. *Journal of Counseling and Development, 76,* 389–396. doi: 10.1002/j.1556-6676.1998.tb02697.x

Alvarez, J., Jason, L.A., Olson, J. R., Ferrari, J. R. & Davis, M. I. (2007). Substance abuse prevalence and treatment among Latinos and Latinas. *Journal of Ethnicity in Substance Abuse, 6,* 115–141. doi: 10.1300/J233v06n02_08

Austin, A.M., Macgowan, M. J., & Wagner, E. F. (2005). Effective family-based interventions for adolescents with substance use problems: A systematic review. *Research on Social Work Practice, 15,* 67–83. doi: 10.1177/1048731504271606

Baca, L. M. & Koss-Chioino, J.D. (1997). Development of a culturally responsive group counseling model for Mexican American adolescents. *Journal of Multicultural Counseling and Development, 25,* 130–141. doi: 10.1002/j.2161-1912.1997.tb00323.x

Bowen, M. (1991). Alcoholism as viewed through family systems theory and family psychotherapy. *Family Dynamics of Addiction Quarterly, 1,* 94–102.

Castro, F. G. & Alarcón, E. H. (2002). Integrating cultural variables into drug abuse prevention and treatment with racial/ethnic minorities. *Journal of Drug Issues, 32,* 783–810. doi: 10.1177/002204260203200304

Corless, J., Mirza, K., & Steinglass, P. (2009). Family therapy for substance misuse: The maturation of the field. *Journal of Family Therapy, 31,* 109–114. doi: 10.1111/j.1467-6427.2009.00457.x

Cunningham, P. B., Foster, S. L., & Warner, S.E. (2010). Culturally relevant family-based treatment for adolescent delinquency and substance abuse: Understanding within-session processes. *Journal of Clinical Psychology: In Session, 66,* 830–846. doi: 10.1002/jclp.20709

Dillon, F., De La Rosa, M., Sastre, F., & Ibañez, G. (2012). Alcohol misuse among recent Latino immigrants: The protective role of preimmigration familismo. *Psychology of Addictive Behaviors.* doi: 10.1037/a0031091

Falicov, C. J. (2009). Commentary: On the wisdom and challenges of culturally attuned treatments for Latinos. *Family Process, 48,* 292–309. doi: 10.1111/j.1545-5300.2009.01282.x

Flicker, S. M., Turner, C. W., Waldron, H. B., Brody, J. L. & Ozechowski, T.J. (2008). Ethnic background, therapeutic alliance, and treatment retention in functional family therapy with adolescents who abuse substances. *Journal of Family Psychology, 22,* 167–170. doi: 10.1037/0893-3200.22.1.167

Gil, A.G., Wagner, E. F., & Tubman, J. G. (2004). Culturally sensitive substance abuse intervention for Hispanic and African American adolescents: empirical examples from the Alcohol Treatment Targeting Adolescents in Need (ATTAIN) project. *Addiction, 99,* 140–150. doi: 10.1111/j.1360-0443.2004.00861.x

Gragg, J.B. & Wilson, C. M. (2011). Mexican American family's perceptions of the multirelational influences on their adolescent's engagement in substance use treatment. *The Family Journal, 19,* 299–306. doi: 10.1177/1066480711405822

Goldbach, J. T., Thompson, S. J., & Holleran Stelker, L. K. (2011). Special considerations for substance abuse intervention with Latino youth. *The Prevention Researcher, 18,* 8–11.

Henggeler, S. W., Pickrel, S.G., & Brondino, M.J. (1999). Multisystemic treatment of substance-abusing and-dependent delinquents: outcome, treatment, fidelity, and transportability. *Mental Health Services Research*, 1, 171–184. doi: 10.1023/A:1022373813261

Jani. J., Ortiz, L. & Aranda, M. (2009). Latino outcome studies in social work: A review of literature. *Research on Social Work Practice*, 19, 179–194. doi:10.1177/1049731508315974

Kim, B.S. (2011). Client motivation and multicultural counseling. *The Counseling Psychologist*, 39, 267–275. doi: 10.1177/001 1000010375310

Loya, F., Reedy, R. & Hinshaw, S. (2010). Mental illness stigma as a mediator of differences in Caucasian and South Asian college students' attitudes toward psychological counseling. *Journal of Counseling Psychology*, 57, 484–490. doi: 10.1037/a0021113.

Lynch, M. F., Vansteenkiste, E. L., Deci, E. L., & Ryan, R. M. (2011). Autonomy as process outcome: Revisiting cultural and practical issues in motivation for counseling. *The Counseling Psychologist*, 39, 286–302. doi: 10.1177/0011000010388424

Morgan, T. B. & Crane, D. R. (2010). Cost-effectiveness of family-based substance abuse treatment. *Journal of Marital & Family Therapy*, 36, 486–498. doi: 10.1111/j.1752 0606.2010.00195.x

Orford, J. (1990). Alcohol and the family: An international review of the literature with implications for research and practice. In *Research Advances in Alcohol and Drug Problems*, Vol. 10, (pp. 81–155). New York, NY: Plenum Press.

Orford, J., Rigby, K., Miller, T., Tod, A., Bennett, G., & Velleman, R. (1992). Ways of coping with excessive drug use in the family: A provisional typology based on the accounts of 50 close relatives. *Journal of Community & Applied Social Psychology*, 2, 163–193. doi: 10.1002/casp.2450020302

Orford, J., Copello, A., Natera, G., Nava, A., Mora, J., Davies, J., Rigby, K., Bradbury, C., & Velleman, R. (1998). Stresses and strains for family members living with drinking or drug problems in England and Mexico. *Salud Mental*, 21, 1–13.

Prado, G., Pantin, H., Briones, E., Schwartz, S., Feaster, D., Huang, S., Sullivan, S., Tapia, M., Sabillon, E., Lopez, B. & Szapocznik, J. (2007). A randomized controlled trial of patient-centered intervention in preventing substance use and HIV risk behaviors in Hispanic adolescents. *Journal of Consulting and Clinical Psychology*, 74, 914–926. doi: 10.1037/0022-006X.75.6.914

Robbins, M.S., Feaster, D. J., Horigian, V. E., Pucinelli, M. J., Henderson, C., Szapocznik, J. (2011). Therapist adherence in brief strategic family therapy for adolescent drug abusers. Journal of Consulting and Clinical Psychology, 79, 43–53. doi: 10.1037/a0022146

Rowe, C. L., & Liddle, H. A. (2003). Substance Abuse. *Journal of Marital and Family Therapy*, 29, 97–120. doi: 10.1111/j.1752-0606.2003.tb.00386.x

Szapocznik, J., Schwartz, S. J., Muir, J. A., & Brown, C. H. (2012). Brief strategic family therapy: An intervention to reduce adolescent risk behavior. *Couple and Family Psychology: Research and Practice*, 1, 134–145. doi: 10.1037/a0029002

Steinglass, P. (2009). Systemic-motivational therapy for substance abuse disorders: An integrative model. *Journal of Family Therapy*, 31, 155–174. doi: 10.1111/j.1467-6427.2009.00460.x

Substance Abuse and Mental Health Services Administration. (2012). *Results from the 2011 National Survey on Drug Use and Health: Summary of National Findings* (HHS Publication No. (SMA) 12–4713). Retrieved from http:// http://www.samhsa.gov/data/nsduh/2k11results/nsduhresults2011.pdf

Sue, D. & Sue, D. (1977). Barriers to effective cross-cultural counseling. *Journal of Counseling Psychology, 24,* 420–429. doi: 10.1037/0022–0167.24.5.420

Sue, D., Arredondo, P., & McDavis, R. (1992). Multicultural counseling competencies and standards: A call to the profession. *Journal of Counseling and Development, 70,* 477–486. doi: 10.1002/j.2161–1912.1992.tb00563.x

Triandis, H. C. (2001). Individualism-collectivism and personality. *Journal of Personality, 69,* 907–924. doi: 10.1111/1467–6494.696169

United States Census Bureau. (2012). *U.S. census bureau projections show a slower growing, older, more diverse nation a half century from now.* Retrieved from: http://www.census.gov/newsroom/releases/archives/population/cb12-243.html

Vargas, J & Kemmelmeier, M. (2012). Ethnicity and contemporary American culture: A meta-analytic investigation of horizontal-vertical individualism-collectivism. *Journal of Cross-Cultural Psychology, 44,* 195–222. doi: 10.1177/0022022112443733

Waldron, H. B., Turner, C. W., Brody, J. L., & Hops, H. (2008). Ethnic matching and treatment outcome with Hispanic and Anglo substance-abusing adolescents in family therapy. *Journal of Family Psychology, 22,* 439–447. doi: 10.1037/0893–3200.22.3.439

World Health Organization. (2012). *World Drug Report.* Retrieved from http://www.unodc.org/documents/data-and-analysis/WDR2012/

10

Providing Forensic Services in Community Mental Health Agencies
Ethical Considerations and Forensic Training Needs of Community Mental Health Counselors

Courtney C. C. Heard[1]

This article addressed the training needs of community mental health counselors providing forensic services. Disparities in forensic mental health counseling training are contextualized through a discussion of forensic programs in operation in community mental health agencies.

Forensic mental health services are generally associated with psychiatry and psychology disciplines. This frame of reference is likely due to the extensive historical advocacy of these disciplines in promoting training and certifications for serving forensic populations (Sadoff & Dattilio, 2012). Sadoff and Dattilio (2012) discussed the importance of psychiatrists

1. Courtney C. C. Heard, Mental Health and Substance Abuse Division, Adult Mental Health Unit, Texas Department of State Health Services. The views and opinions expressed in this article are those of the author and do not necessarily reflect the official policy or position of the Texas Department of State Health Services. Correspondence concerning this article should be addressed to Courtney C. C. Heard via email at cheard0604@gmail.com.

and psychologists being formally trained as forensic experts, as there are a number of these professionals who have engaged in these duties without certification (e.g. providing forensic expert testimony). Organizations such as the American Board of Professional Psychology (ABPP) oversees the credentialing of the American Board of Forensic Psychology, who are responsible for establishing criteria "related to the definition, and requirements for education, training, competencies, and the examination, which leads to Board Certification in Forensic Psychology" (ABPP, 2012). Providing forensic services without formal training or certification may be detrimental to the individuals being evaluated for treatment, and potentially violates the integrity of the helping professions and judiciary systems represented (Sadoff & Dattilio, 2012). States such as Texas have codes of criminal procedure whose statues require that the evaluator be certified by the American Board of Psychiatry, or ABPP (Incompetency to Stand Trial, 2011).

These certifications often do not exist for licensed counselors working in community mental health agencies for forensic programs; though, there are some graduate programs with specializations in forensic counseling and who offer certifications in the area (e.g. George Washington and Argosy Universities). The American College of Certified Forensic Counselors serves as the certification commission of the National Association of Forensic Counselors (NAFC; NAFC, 2009). The NAFC is the sole organization who provides national certification as a forensic counselor (NAFC, 2009). The NAFC offers clinical and non-clinical certifications under the umbrella of forensic specializations, some of which include: Clinically Certified Forensic Counselor, Clinically Certified Forensic Interviewer, Certified Criminal Justice Specialist, and Certified Forensic Interviewer.

Counseling Literature: Disparities in Addressing Work with Forensic Populations

In a review of counseling literature, excluding counseling psychology, few articles were found whose authors addressed working with forensic populations, and none discussed certification, or licensing opportunities (Barros-Bailey, Carlisle, & Blackwell, 2010; Krieshok, 1987; Smith, 2006). Evans (1983) and Krieshok (1987) published articles addressing the emerging role of counselors and helping professionals in collaborating with the criminal justice system to offer linkage to community mental health treatment for offenders with mental illness. Smith (2006) and Barros-Bailey, Carlisle, and Blackwell (2010) discussed ethical considerations for working with forensic populations, specifically, as a vocational rehabilitative counselor. Miller, Linville, Todahl, and Metcalfe (2009) described the benefit of utilizing mock trials to teach forensic competencies when training marriage and family therapists. However, some of these authors addressed only one component of forensic work, to include expert testimony, not service delivery (Krieshok, 1987; Miller et al., 2009).

The bulk of counseling literature addressing forensic populations is published in the *Journal of Addictions and Offender Counseling*, made available by the International Association of Addictions and Offender Counselors, a sub-division of the American Counseling Association (ACA). A review of the literature published in this journal from 1990 to present yielded no articles whose authors addressed ethical considerations for working with forensic populations; however, two articles were located whose author addressed reducing malpractice suits, and legal and ethical issues when providing services to clients with chemical dependency needs (Manhal-Baugus, 1996a; Manhal-Baugus, 1996b). Journal issues included a wealth of information regarding the treatment of persons with chemical dependency needs (Carroll, 1999; Culbreth, 1999; Whittinghill, Whittinghill, & Loesch, 2000). Mire, Forsyth, and Hanser (2007) reported that of the eleven million offenders in the United States (U.S.), eight hundred thousand are diagnosed with a mental illness, seventy-two percent of which have a co-occurring diagnosis. However, having a chemical dependency need and being involved in the criminal justice system are not mutually exclusive; thus, addressing the treatment needs of a population with chemical dependency issues, does not necessarily provide discourse on the treatment needs of the forensic population, or the training needs of counselors in addressing these issues.

Addictions Counseling: The Council for Accreditation of Counseling and Related Educational Programs (CACREP)

Based on reports of the percentages of offenders diagnosed with co-occurring disorders, one might assume that content related to counseling forensic populations could be infused in addictions programming. However, according to CACREP, "Addiction Counseling programs prepare graduates to work with persons and families affected by alcohol, drugs, gambling, sexual and other addictive disorders" (CACREP, 2013). By this description, addiction counseling programs accredited by CACREP have curriculum that encompass an array of addictions, there is not a sole focus on substance abuse. Addiction counseling programs accredited by CACREP are sixty semester credit hours, or, ninety quarter hours (CACREP, 2009). This is extensive training; thus, when considering the inclusion of forensic counseling coursework in a program, one must consider if a separate track in forensic community or clinical mental health counseling is needed, and if a distinct trajectory is not needed, would a separate course suffice, or could content be infused in existing coursework across specialty areas. Regardless, the number of incarcerated individuals identified with a mental illness, released to the community, and linked to community mental health services warrants an assessment of the training needs of counselors who will provide treatment to forensic populations.

Forensic Programming in Community Mental Health Agencies

It is estimated that each year 900,000 individuals are booked into U.S. jails and have a diagnosable mental illness or co-occurring diagnosis (Vogel, Noether, & Steadman, 2007). Upon release from these institutions, many of these individuals are on bond without legal supervision, probation, or parole, and referred to community mental health agencies for treatment (Dirks-Linhorst & Linhorst, 2012). Many do not appear for the initial appointment, often times, resulting in a re-arrest and/or no receipt of mental health services (Arboleda-Florez, 2003). Due to the increasing number of reoffending offenders not engaged in community treatment, criminal justice and mental health agencies have strengthened collaboration, established wrap-around services, and safeguarded for continuity of care post-institutional release (Hatcher, 2007; Theurer & Lovell, 2008). These services comprise an inter-disciplinary approach to treatment to include: probation or parole, mental health, substance abuse, housing, employment, and social security benefits coordinators. In the U.S. there are two primary forensic programs offered in community mental health agencies for offenders with mental illness: jail diversion programs and Forensic Assertive Community Treatment (FACT; Cuddeback, Pettus-Davis, & Scheyett, 2011; Cusack, Morrissey, Cuddeback, Prins, & Williams, 2010; Draine, Blank, Kottsieper, & Solomon, 2005; Steadman & Naples, 2005). Outpatient Competency Restoration (OCR) programs began to be implemented in 2005 and are available in certain states (e.g. Arizona, Arkansas, Connecticut, and District of Columbia).

Jail Diversion Program

Jail diversion programs were created in response to the increased number of offenders identified to have a mental diagnosis, particularly for those individuals identified as repeat offenders for misdemeanor offenses (e.g. criminal trespassing, criminal mischief, and petty theft). Jail diversion programs are believed to be beneficial in reducing recidivism before these minor offenses are enhanced to felony crimes, and provide individuals with linkage to long-term mental health treatment (Case, Steadman, Dupuis, & Morris, 2009).

The most frequently employed jail diversion strategies are pre-booking and post-booking (Mire et al., 2007). Pre-booking programs are designed to provide an intervention to individuals arrested for committing a crime prior to being booked in jail for the arrest. Pre-booking programs generally utilize police officers who have been trained in crisis intervention and recognizing symptoms of mental illness. When an individual is arrested, believed to have a mental illness, and in need of crisis stabilization services, officers take the individual to a community mental health agency to receive treatment, as an alternative to being placed in jail. Thus, pre-booking programs are a preventative strategy that may permit services to be provided to a broader range of individuals, other than people with mental illness in county jails (Draine et al., 2005). Post-booking programs involve the identification of individuals with a mental illness who are currently detained in jail. Successful completion of the jail diversion program may lead to charges being dropped, or reduced (Mire et al., 2007). The treatment process involves an agreement between the defense and state's attorney, judge, client, and treatment provider. Criteria for program admission are generally delegated to misdemeanor offenders; however, felony offenses may be considered.

Forensic Assertive Community Treatment Program

The inception of Assertive Community Treatment (ACT) teams began in the 1970s, to specifically target those individuals diagnosed with schizophrenia and a history of multiple psychiatric hospitalizations (Jennings, 2009). Traditional ACT services are based on the interdisciplinary model of treatment, encompassing a psychiatrist, nursing staff, social workers, and mental health professionals. These services are provided in outpatient mental health facilities to small caseloads of qualifying individuals (Cuddeback et al., 2011). The intensity of these services varies based on state mental health practices for agencies responsible for the delivery of services. For instance, in the state of Texas, ACT treatment is built into the general array of services offered at local mental health authorities. It is the most intensive level of care characterized by case-management caseloads of no more than 10, and each individual must be provided services equating to an average of 10 hours a month (Texas Department of State Health Services, 2013).

FACT teams provide the intensity of services associated with ACT; however, services are specifically provided to individuals with extensive arrest histories, chronic symptoms of mental illness, and/or a history of multiple psychiatric hospitalizations. These individuals are referred to programming from criminal justice agencies, and non-engagement in services may include legal sanctions (Cusack et al., 2010).

Outpatient Competency Restoration Program

An individual is deemed incompetent to stand trial if he or she lacks the rational and factual capacity to understand court proceedings, and sufficient present ability to consult with an attorney with rational understanding (Dusky v. U.S., 1960). Once an individual is found incompetent to stand trial (IST), all court proceedings must be discontinued until competency is restored. Prior to the development of OCR programs, once an individual was deemed IST, he or she was committed to a state hospital facility to undergo competency restoration training, for a period of time that varied based on state statutory requirements. States began to establish OCR programs roughly in 2005; however, a review of the literature suggests that the bulk of OCR programs currently in operation began pilots in 2008 (Behavioral Consultants, Inc., 2012; Hogg Foundation for Mental Health, 2011). As of 2009, 17 states have established OCR programs: Arizona, Arkansas, Connecticut, District of Columbia, Florida, Georgia, Hawaii, Idaho, Michigan, Nevada, Ohio, Tennessee, Texas, Virginia, Washington, and Wisconsin. OCR programs were established as an alternative to inpatient competency restoration treatment. These programs are geared towards serving individuals in the least restrictive setting, providing intensive case-management services, and engaging clients in long-term mental health care. The amount of time an individual is committed to these programs varies by state. For instance, the Texas Code of Criminal Procedure Chapter 46B: Incompetency to Stand Trial (2011) mandates that for a misdemeanor offense the individual is committed for 60 days and 120 days for a felony. In contrast, Wisconsin legislation does not delineate a difference in number of commitment days for misdemeanor and felony offenses. Individuals are committed for a period of 12 months, or "the maximum sentence specified for the most serious offense with which the defendant is charged, whichever is less" (Competency Proceedings, 2009).

Community Mental Health Forensic Counselors: Ethical Concerns

The above programs are examples of outpatient treatment opportunities for individuals identified to have a mental illness being reintegrated into the community. Generally, clinical services provided to these individuals in the form of daily assessments, initial diagnosis, and counseling are provided by masters-level practitioners (Castellano, 2011). These counselors may not have had any formal training in working with forensic populations, and may not have an awareness of how to address some of the issues that may arise when providing services (Scott, 2003). Furthermore, given the novelty of implementation of forensic programs in many community mental health agencies, there may be ambiguity regarding confidentiality of client information, awareness of mental health laws, inadequate collaboration in program design and implementation, and a lack of understanding concerning the functions of judicial and mental health organizations (Arboleda-Florez, 2003).

Client Identification

Identifying the client may be difficult when providing forensic services. Kalmbach and Lyons (2006) stated:

> The forensic practitioner may have as a client (a) the individual (via his or her attorney), (b) the custodian of the individual (e.g. The Texas Department of Criminal Justice), or (c) the Court (by way of the court order for evaluation). (pp. 263)

When court ordered treatment is mandated, the service provider acts as an agent of the court and must uphold the conditions of the order (Castellano, 2011). Thus, should the client fail to comply with the conditions of the program (e.g. curfew, attending counseling sessions, or engaging in substance abuse treatment), mental health professionals are contractually bound to report this information to the court, at the risk of the client being placed in jail (Castellano, 2011). This obligation possibly compromises the establishment of a therapeutic relationship between the client and the service provider.

Role Ambiguity

Distinguishing and explaining role changes to clients may be difficult when providing forensic services (Barros-Bailey et al., 2010). For instance, depending on the amount of funding delegated to service delivery, hiring individuals to perform each duty of the contract may not be possible (Knight, Broome, Simpson, & Flynn, 2008). There may be an individual who operates as the forensic evaluator, program administrator, case-manager, and counselor. The ACA Code of Ethics (2005) mandates "Counselors do not accept as counseling clients individuals they are evaluating, or individuals they have evaluated in the past for forensic purposes" (p. 13). Execution of these multiple roles potentially violates ACA standards of conduct for general and forensic practice, in the absence of suitable academic and occupational training, and availability of professional consultation in forensic counseling.

Confidentiality and Disclosure of Information

The ACA Code of Ethics addresses informed consent and confidentiality practices (ACA, 2005). When providing court-ordered services such as administration of assessments, or, mental status examinations, there is an absence of confidentiality regarding the disclosing of results to the court (Kalmbach & Lyons, 2006). Information is shared with the judge, assistant district attorney, and defense attorney. However, counselors remain obligated to inform the client of the absence of confidentiality, parties to which the results of the assessments will be shared, and potential consequences of the information included in the reports (Kalmbach & Lyons, 2006). There is opportunity for error in the inappropriate disclosure of information to parties unaffiliated with judiciary systems. Consent to disclose protected health information remains required for individuals outside of the purview of the judiciary system (HIPAA Administrative Simplification, 2013). Counselors must be aware of state and federal mandates for confidentiality and disclosure of protected health information, as well as ethical standards of conduct.

Supervisor Expertise

The relevance of supervision to the counseling profession has been highly documented and reinforced in the ACA Code of Ethics and CACREP standards (ACA, 2005; CACREP, 2009). However, it appears that the context in which supervision is discussed is pre-service, or prior to individuals securing employment as practitioners. Moreover, specifically as it pertains to supervision in forensic specialties, a review of counseling literature yielded four articles that addressed the importance of supervision and consultation. Each of these articles was written within the context of rehabilitation counseling, a disciplinary field that has sought to address the ethical practice of forensic rehabilitation counselors (Barros-Bailey et al., 2009; Barros-Bailey et al., 2010). Bourgeois, Decoteau, and King (2011) discussed the development of an ethical framework for supervision and consultation of forensic rehabilitation practitioners. These authors asserted that there are no existing specialized models of supervision, or consultation for rehabilitative counselors. Similarly, based on a review of the literature, these models do not appear to exist for community mental health counselors. Bourgeois et al. (2011) wrote "Without a supervisory or consultation structure in place, the forensic rehabilitation practitioner is at risk in terms of professional skill development, ethical practice, and erosion of professional objectivity" (p. 51). Also highlighted was the deficiency in various ethical codes of conduct in addressing the relevance of supervision and consultation in-service, or while operating as a practitioner (Bourgeois et al., 2011).

Addressing the Training, Supervision, and Ethical Guidance Needs of Community Mental Health Agency Forensic Practitioners

Ethical Codes of Conduct: Addressing Forensic Practice

The ACA Code of Ethics (2005) Section E addresses forensic work within the parameters of evaluation for legal proceedings. Though this is an important factor to consider when providing forensic services as a private practitioner, it does not encompass the broader scope of forensic counseling professional practice. It may be beneficial for the counseling profession to consider infusing ethical standards for forensic practice in other areas of the code of ethics (e.g. the counseling relationship and confidentiality, privileged communication, and privacy).

The American Mental Health Counselors Association (AMHCA), a sub-division of ACA representative of mental health counselors, addresses forensic practice in their code of ethics. However, forensic activity is only addressed in the area of assessment and diagnosis (AMHCA, 2010). These codes of ethics, primarily covering forensic activity as it pertains to expert testimony and evaluation/assessment, may be representative of the lack of awareness of the increased engagement of mental health counselors in forensic programming, particularly, in community mental health settings.

Supervision and Consultation in Forensic Practice

Bourgeois et al. (2011) discussed the lack of supervision in forensic practice as it pertains to rehabilitation counselors. Additionally, there are articles whose authors have highlighted the inadequate supervision of counselors' post-graduation (Borders & Usher, 1992; Navin, 1995).

Though it may not be required, it can be beneficial to have an administrative supervisor whose licensing credentials are similar, and who has experience working with forensic populations. Furthermore, where these conditions are unable to be met, it may be important for practitioners to engage in consultation in an attempt to ensure that ethical treatment is provided and program operations are legal (Bourgeois et al., 2011).

Incorporating Forensics in Academic Curriculum

CACREP accredits counseling programs who may have an accredited addiction counseling track (CACREP, 2009). Often times, when substance abuse addictions are discussed, there may be an assumption that the individual is involved in the criminal justice system; however, addictions and forensics are not mutually exclusive. The treatments provided to address substance abuse needs are not necessarily beneficial in addressing criminogenic thinking and behavior. Therefore, it may beneficial for counselor training programs to infuse forensic practices into training curriculum. There are several courses where it may be conducive to discuss forensic practices: addictions, mental health counseling, ethics, and assessment and diagnosis. Miller et al. (2009) provided an example of one method utilized to expose marriage and family therapists to forensic work as an expert witness. This method, along with additional experiential activities could be replicated across other counseling tracks.

Conclusion

It is estimated that between eight and 16% of all individuals booked into U.S. jails have a mental illness (Vogel et al., 2007). Declining bed availability at state mental health hospitals has triggered criminal justice institutions to become temporary or long-term housing and treatment facilities for persons with mental illness (Vogel et al., 2007). Those individuals booked into county jails for petty crimes (e.g. criminal trespassing, simple assaults, and criminal mischief), or serious offenses that do not warrant state jail or prison time will be released to the community (Hatcher, 2007; Mire et al., 2007; Steadman & Naples, 2005). Thus, there are several programs that have been established to treat offenders with mental illness, divert them from the criminal justice system, and provide long-term linkage to community mental health care. Jail diversion, FACT, and OCR were a few covered in this article. Many of these programs are established in community mental health agencies; thus, there are implications for training community mental health counselors who will provide forensic services as to avoid ethical and legal violations that can occur (Barros-Bailey et al., 2009; Bourgeois et al., 2011). Additionally, during pre-service and in-service there are several areas in which the forensic practice of community mental health counselors could be expanded and/or addressed: ethical codes of conduct for counselors, academic curriculum, and supervision and consultation. As the number of individuals identified to have a mental illness and involved in the criminal justice system steadily increases, it will be important to build counselor awareness of the diverse components to providing forensic services.

References

American Board of Professional Psychology. (2012). *Forensic Psychology*. Retrieved from http://www.abpp.org/i4a/pages/index.cfm?pageid=3313

American Counseling Association. (2005). *ACA Code of Ethics*. Retrieved from http://www.counseling.org/Resources/CodeOfEthics/TP/Home/CT2.aspx

American Mental Health Counselors Association. (2010). *AMHCA Code of Ethics*. Retrieved from http://www.amhca.org/assets/content/AMHCA_Code_of_Ethics_2010_update_1-20-13_COVER.pdf

Arboleda-Florez, J. (2003). Integration initiatives for forensic services. *World Psychiatry*, 2(3), 179–183.

Barros-Bailey, M., Carlisle, J., Graham, M., Neulicht, A. T., Taylor, R., & Wallace, A. (2009). Who is the client in forensics? *Journal of Forensic Vocational Analysis*, 12(1), 31–34.

Barros-Bailey, M., Carlisle, J., & Blackwell, T. L. (2010). Forensic ethics and indirect practice for the rehabilitation counselor. *Rehabilitation Counseling Bulletin*, 53(4), 237–242. doi: 10.1177/0034355210368728

Behavioral Health Consultants Inc. (2012, November). *The outpatient competency restoration program*. Presented at the Wisconsin Public Defenders' Annual Criminal Defense Conference, Milwaukee, WI.

Borders, L. D., & Usher, C. H. (1992). Post-degree supervision: Existing and preferred practices. *Journal of Counseling and Development*, 70, 594–599.

Bourgeois, P. J., Decoteau, J. P., & King, C. L. (2011). Filling in the gaps: Seeking an ethical framework for supervision and consultation of the forensic rehabilitation practitioner. *The Rehabilitation Professional*, 19(2), 49–56.

Carroll, J. (1999). Compatibility of Adlerian theory and practice with the philosophy and practices of alcoholics anonymous. *Journal of Addictions and Offender Counseling*, 19(2), 50–62.

Case, B., Steadman, H. J., Dupuis, S. A., & Morris, L. S. (2009). Who succeeds in jail diversion programs for persons with mental illness? A multi-site study. *Behavioral Sciences and the Law*, 27, 661–674. doi: 10.1002/bsl.883

Castellano, U. (2011). Courting compliance. Case managers as "double agents" in the mental health court. *Law and Social Inquiry*, 36(2), 484–514.

Competency Proceedings, 5 Wisconsin Legislative Documents §§ 971.14a.1 (2009).

Council for Accreditation of Counseling and Related Educational Programs (CACREP). (2013). *Choosing a graduate program*. Retrieved from http://67.199.126.156/template/page.cfm?id=5

Council for Accreditation of Counseling and Related Educational Programs (CACREP). (2009). *CACREP 2009 standards*. Retrieved from http://cacrep.org/doc/2009%20Standards%20with%20cover.pdf

Cuddeback, G. S., Pettus-Davis, C., & Scheyett, A. (2011). Consumers' perceptions of forensic assertive community treatment. *Psychiatric Rehabilitation Journal*, 35(2), 101–109. doi: 10.2975/35.2.2011.101.109

Culbreth, J. R. (1999). Clinical supervision of substance abuse counselors: Current and preferred practices. *Journal of Addictions and Offender Counseling*, 20(1), 15–26.

Cusack, K. J., Morrissey, J. P., Cuddeback, G. S., Prins, A., & Williams, D. M. (2010). Criminal justice involvement, behavioral health service use, and costs of forensic assertive community treatment: A randomized trial. *Community Mental Health Journal*, 46, 356–363. doi: 10.1007/s10597-010-9299-z

Dirks-Linhorst, P. A., & Linhorst, D. M. (2012). Monitoring offenders with mental illness in the community: Guidelines for practice. *Best Practices in Mental Health, 8*(2), 47-70.

Draine, J., Blank, A., Kottsieper, P., & Solomon, P. (2005). Contrasting jail diversion and in-jail services for mental illness and substance abuse: Do they serve the same clients?. *Behavioral Sciences and the Law, 23*, 171-181. doi: 10.1002/bsl.637

Dusky v. United States, 362 U.S. 402 (April 18, 1960).

Evans, J. (1983). The treatment specialist: An emerging role for counselors within the criminal court system. *The Personnel and Guidance Journal, 61*(6), 349-351. doi: 10.1111/j.2164-4918.1983.tb00040.x

Hatcher, S. S. (2007). Transitional care for offenders with mental illness in jail: Mapping indicators of successful community reentry. *Best Practices in Mental Health, 3*(2), 38-51.

Hogg Foundation for Mental Health. (2011). *Outpatient Competency Restoration (OCR)*. Retrieved from http://www.hogg.utexas.edu/uploads/documents/Outpatient_Competency_Restoration_011011.pdf

Incompetency to Stand Trial, Texas Code of Criminal Procedure §§ 46B.022-46B.073. (2011).

Jennings, J. L. (2009). Does assertive community treatment work with forensic populations? Review and recommendations. *The Open Psychiatry Journal, 3*, 13-19.

Kalmbach, K. C., & Lyons, P. M. (2006). Ethical issues in conducting forensic evaluations. *Applied Psychology in Criminal Justice, 2*(3), 262-289.

Knight, D. K., Broome, K. M., Simpson, D. D., Flynn, P. M. (2008). Program structure and counselor-client contact in outpatient substance abuse treatment. *Health Research and Educational Trust, 43*(2), 616-634. doi: 10.1111/j.1475-6773.2007.00778.x

Krieshok, T. S. (1987). Psychologists and counselors in the legal system: A dialogue with Theodore Blau. *Journal of Counseling and Development, 66*, 69-72.

Manhal-Baugus, M. (1996a). Confidentiality: The legal and ethical issues for chemical dependency counselors. *Journal of Addictions and Offender Counseling, 17*(1), 3-11.

Manhal-Baugus, M. (1996b). Reducing the risk of malpractice in chemical dependency counseling. *Journal of Addictions and Offender Counseling, 17*(1), 35-42.

Miller, J. K., Linville, D., Todahl, J., & Metcalfe, J. (2009). Using mock trials to teach students forensic core competencies in marriage and family therapy. *Journal of Marital and Family Therapy, 35*(4), 456-465. doi: 10.1111/j.1752-0606.2009.00148.x

Mire, S., Forsyth, C. J., Hanser, R. (2007). Jail diversion: Addressing the needs of offenders with mental illness and co-occurring disorders. *Mental Health Issues in the Criminal Justice System, 45*(1-2), 19-31. doi: 10.1300/j076v45n01_02

National Association of Forensic Counselors (2009). *NAFC Certifications Offered, Requirements, and Applications*. Retrieved from http://www.nationalafc.com/?NAFC_Certifications_Offered%2C_Requirements_and_Applications

Navin, S. (1995). Ethical practices of field-based mental health counselors and supervisors. *Journal of Mental Health Counseling, 17*(2), 243-253.

Sadoff, R. L., & Dattilio, F. M. (2012). Formal training in forensic mental health: Psychiatry and psychology. *International Journal of Law and Psychiatry, 35*, 343-347. doi: 10.1016/j.ijlp.2012.09.010

Scott, R. E. (2003). Forensic counseling: A new approach to school crime. *Education, 124*(2), 219-222.

Smith, S. (2006). Confronting the unethical vocational counselor in forensic practice. *Journal of Vocational Rehabilitation, 25*, 133–136.

Steadman, H. J., & Naples, M. (2005). Assessing the effectiveness of jail diversion programs for persons with mental illness and co-occurring substance use disorders. *Behavioral Sciences and the Law, 23*, 163–170. doi: 10.1002/bsl.640

Texas Department of State Health Services. (2013). *Texas Resilience and Recovery: Utilization Management Guidelines: Adult Mental Health Services.* Retrieved from http://www.dshs.state.tx.us/mhsa/trr/um/

Theurer, G., & Lovell, D. (2008). Recidivism of offenders with mental illness released from prison to an intensive community treatment program. *Journal of Offender Rehabilitation, 47*(4), 385–406.

U.S. Department of Health and Human Services Office for Civil Rights. *HIPAA administrative simplification regulation text.* Retrieved from http://www.hhs.gov/ocr/privacy/hipaa/administrative/privacyrule/adminsimpregtext.pdf

Vogel, W. M., Noether, C. D., & Steadman, H. J. (2007). Preparing communities for reentry with offenders with mental illness: The ACTION approach. *Mental Health Issues in the Criminal Justice System, 45*(1–2), 167–188. doi: 10.1300/J076v45n07_12

Whittinghill, D., Whittinghill, L. R., & Loesch, L. C. (2000). The benefits of a self-efficacy approach to substance abuse counseling in the era of managed care. *Journal of Addictions and Offender Counseling, 20*(2), 64–75.

11

The MO(o)D PIRATE Malingering Mnemonic Risk Assessment
General Implications and Guidelines for Correctional Counselors

PAUL A. CARROLA AND GERALD A. JUHNKE[1]

Corrections counselor frequently encounter inmates who report severe emotional and psychological symptoms and stressors. To date, no standardized, free, brief, face-to-face malingering risk assessment exists within the counseling literature and none has been published in the International Association of Addictions & Offenders Counselors flagship journal, the *Journal of Addictions & Offender Counseling*. To address this malingering risk assessment absence, the authors created the MO(o)D PIRATE Malingering Mnemonic Risk Assessment. The assessment is an evidenced informed instrument that considers 9 malingering risk factors identified within the literature or experienced by the author's combined span of 37 years counseling and consulting in corrections. The purpose of the assessment is to facilitate a thorough malingering risk assessment and generate general malingering intervention guidelines that can be used, in

---

1. Paul A. Carrola, Department of Educational Psychology and Special Services, University of Texas at El Paso. Gerald A. Juhnke, Department of Counseling, University of Texas at San Antonio. The authors declared no potential conflicts of interest with respect to the authorship and/or publication of this article. The authors received no financial support for the research and/or authorship of this article.

conjunction with clinical judgment, supervision, and a risk assessment committee, to aid corrections counselors.

The most recent data indicates nearly half the world's prison population is incarcerated in the United States (U.S.; Walmsley, 2011), and more than 1.5 million persons are incarcerated in U.S. state and federal prisons (Glaze, 2012). These data do not include inmates in U.S., county or city jails and detention centers. The total number of mentally ill incarcerated in U.S. prisons is estimated between 15 and 20% or between 225,000 and 300,000 inmates and is greater than the total number of mentally ill within all U.S. psychiatric and medical hospitals (Torrey, et al., 2010). This elevated percentage of mentally ill persons in U.S. prisons is in part attributed to the "deinstitutionalization" of inpatient mental health hospitals which began in the early 1950's (Torrey, et al., 2010) and is a major reason why corrections counselors need to be able to determine the differences between mentally ill inmates who truly warrant counseling in comparison to those who simply report severe emotional and psychological symptoms for secondary gains.

The prison subculture's unique nature defies conventional reasoning and creates an environment where destructive behaviors and emotional instability are often accepted and even rewarded. Counselors working within this subculture face unique challenges specific to addressing or resolving inmate behavioral conflicts and emotional crises. These challenges are influenced by individual inmate personalities and prison cultural dynamics created by other inmates, correctional staff, and prison administrators. At the forefront of these challenges is dealing with prisoners who knowingly and intentionally feign mental illness or self-report severe psychological symptoms to attain ulterior objectives and secondary gains (e.g., movement from the general prison population to a quieter or perceived safer observation cell). In clinical terms, this phenomenon is labeled malingering in the Diagnostic and Statistical Manual of Mental Disorders-5 (DSM-5; American Psychiatric Association, 2013). Recent literature has provided evidence of increased incidents of malingering in correctional settings compared to other forensic settings (i.e., pretrial evaluations; McDermott, Dualan & Scott, 2013). The consequences of the misidentification or misdiagnosis of malingering in the prison system range from the inappropriate use of mental health services to negative legal consequences for inmates (McDermott & Sokolov, 2009). Given the prevalence and limited resources available to corrections counselors, it is crucial that they are able to identify malingering behaviors as accurately as possible.

Malingering

The Diagnostic and Statistical Manual of Mental Disorders-IV-TR (DSM-IV-TR; 2000) reports Malingering as "...the intentional production of false or grossly exaggerated physical or psychological symptoms, motivated by external incentives such as avoiding military duty, avoiding work, obtaining financial compensation, evading criminal prosecution, or obtaining drugs for personal gain" (p. 726). The DSM-5 (2013) states malingering is, "...the intentional reporting of symptoms for personal gain (e.g., money, time off work)" (p. 326). Although these definitions are widely accepted by mental health professions they suggest a false and outdated dichotomy of either malingering or not. Additional research has advanced the malingering diagnosis. These research advances require malingering to be assessed via the presence of multiple risk factors that provide degrees of malingering exaggeration based on a continuous score (Berry & Nelson, 2010; Rogers, Bagby & Dickens, 1992; Walters, et al., 2009). Founded upon the DSM-5 malingering definition, existing research, and their combined corrections counseling and consulting experience that spans more than 37 years, the authors created the MO(o)D PIRATE Malingering Mnemonic Risk Assessment.

Currently, several screening assessments and comprehensive evaluations are available for use in detecting malingering in correctional settings. The Miller Forensic Assessment of Symptoms Test (M-FAST; Miller, 2001 [as cited in Vitacco & Rogers, 2005]) is a 25-question survey that consists of seven scales and an overall score. The benefits of this assessment are that it is brief and has good reliability and validity (Vitacco & Rogers, 2005). The Structured Inventory of Malingered Symptoms (SIMS; Smith & Burger, 1997 [as cited in Vitacco & Rogers, 2005]) is a 75-question survey with five overlapping scales. This measure is easy to read, useful in small groups and has shown effectiveness with small groups and adolescent offenders (Rogers, Hinds & Sewell, 1996; Vitacco & Rogers, 2005). The M Test (Beaber, et al., 1985 [as cited in Vitacco & Rogers, 2005]) is a 33-question survey that has a true-false format. This measure has extensively documented validity and utility (Smith, Borum

& Schinka, 1993; Vitacco & Rogers, 2005). More comprehensive inventories such as the Structured Interview of Reported Symptoms (SIRS), the Minnesota Multiphasic personality Inventory 2nd edition (MMPI-2), the Personality Assessment Inventory (PAI), and the Millon Clinical Multiaxial Inventory-III (MCMI-III). Of these more lengthy assessments, the SIRS is specifically intended to detect malingering (Vitacco & Rogers, 2005).

Existing American Counseling Association journals including the *Journal of Addictions & Offender Counseling* have never published a standardized, free, brief, face-to-face malingering risk assessment with corresponding malingering intervention guidelines. This article will provide such a malingering risk assessment. Specifically, the article will describe the MO(o)D PIRATE Malingering Mnemonic Risk Assessment with its corresponding guideline scale, and demonstrate how each can be used when corrections counselors are assessing clients for potential malingering.

Evidenced Informed

The MO(o)D PIRATE Malingering Mnemonic Risk Assessment is evidenced informed (Rogers, 1984; Vittacco & Rogers, 2005). It is founded upon malingering risk factors found within existing research literature and the authors' correctional counseling and consulting experiences that jointly spanned more than 37 years. Most of the risk factors were gleaned either directly or indirectly from the 13 scales of the SIRS developed by Rogers (1986), and the text on correctional mental health (Scott & Gerbasi, 2005). The SIRS is a 172 item structured interview with thirteen scales (direct appraisal, defensive symptoms, symptom management, rare symptoms, improbable and absurd symptoms, symptom combination, overly specified symptoms, symptom onset, blatant symptoms, severity of symptoms, selectivity of symptoms, inconsistency of symptoms and reported versus observed symptoms; Rogers, Gillis & Bagby, 1990). The SIRS has also been validated and shown to be effective with inmate populations and is also the most widely used assessment for detecting psychiatric symptom malingering (Rogers, Gillis & Bagby, 1990; McDermott & Sokolov, 2009). Many of the MO(o)D PIRATE malingering risk factors were used by the authors when assessing inmates for malingering within corrections settings. The author's found these risk factors extremely helpful in determining appropriate clinical interventions and assessing inmate reported symptomatology and suicide intent. The ten risk factors were also tested for face validity with groups of entry level counseling master's students, advanced level counseling students and doctoral level counselor educators and psychologists.

Why Use Mnemonics

Ten malingering risk factors are difficult to recall during an inmate's assessment, especially when the inmate is demonstrating or reporting severe mental health symptoms (e.g., hallucinations, mania, etc.) or suicidal intent. Mental health and other professionals, as well as physicians, police, and branches of the U.S. military have long used mnemonics to enhance memory of important assessment or intervention factors. For example, Patterson, Dohn, Bird, and Patterson's (1983) and Juhnke's (1994) research demonstrated the effectiveness of mental health trainees utilizing mnemonics within the suicide assessment process. Their findings indicated medical and counseling students who used mnemonic memory aids were statistically better able to recall important risk factors than those who simply learned multiple assessment factor lists. They further found that students who utilized mnemonics facilitated more thorough assessments and more accurately scored clinical vignettes. Similarly, most addictions counselors trained in the late 1980's and early 1990's were trained in the CAGE (Ewing, 1984), an acronym created to assess clients for the presence of alcoholism. The corresponding four CAGE risk factors included: (a) "Cut down" on drinking or alcohol use, (b) "Annoyed" by others' criticizing the client's drinking behaviors, (c) "Guilty" feelings engendered by the client's alcohol behaviors, and (d) "Eye-opener" or using alcohol first thing in the morning to reduce or eliminate hangovers or steady the client's nerves.

Today, mnemonics are broadly utilized as a means to recall important factors and sequences, and to remember relevant instructions. For example, the American Association for Suicidiology (2012) encourages counseling professionals to utilize the mnemonic, IS PATH WARM when assessing suicide risk. Medical professionals frequently use mnemonics such as, Every Little Boy Must Pray, to remind providers the specific order of drugs to be given when attempting to resuscitate patients' whose hearts have stopped (Epinephrine, Lidocaine, Bretylium, Magsulfate, Procainamide; C. Weiner, personal communication, February 6, 2012). Law enforcement professionals use mnemonics such as GO WISELY to help them thoroughly investigate a crime scene (Grounds, Object, Warrant, Identification, Station, Entitlement, Lawfully, Year; D. Macintosh, personal communication, February 7, 2012). The U.S. military commonly use mnemonics like the Four F's and BRASS to aid soldiers in their assigned charges and enhance memory recall (Find, Fix, Flank and Finish; Breath, Relax, Aim, Slack, Shoot; J. LoBrutto, personal communication, February 6, 2012). Given research demonstrating the benefits of mnemonics and the widespread application of mnemonics to aid factor recall and memory, the authors' believed creating a mnemonic malingering risk assessment would generate greater recall of the 9 risk factors.

Based upon these risk factors the authors created the Mnemonic MO(o)D PIRATE and believed the acronym would be easy to recall. The authors' perceptions that the Mnemonic MO(o)D PIRATE would be easy to recall was later confirmed by three samples of convenience. These samples of convenience included entry-level, counseling master's students advanced-level, counseling master's students, and doctoral counselor educators and psychologists with more than 10 years clinical experience.

Table 1
Convenience Sample of Students, Faculty and Practitioners who Provided Validity for MO(o)D PIRATE Mnemonic

Sample Group	Group Size	Mean Age	Mean number of years since degree was earned
Entry level Counseling Masters Students	29	30.74	N/A
Advanced level Counseling Masters Students	33	27	N/A
Doctoral level Counselor Educators and Psychologists	13	52	18

All but one of the 75 volunteer respondents, an entry-level counseling master's student, believed the mnemonic MO(o)D PIRATE and the corresponding risk factors in mnemonic sequence would be easy to recall.

As is the case with all assessments, potential error exists. Thus, to ensure selection of the most appropriate counseling intervention, corrections counselors should always convene a risk assessment committee comprised of experienced and licensed mental health providers (e.g., Licensed Professional Counselors, etc.) and utilize the "four out of five" rule (Juhnke, Granello, & Granello, 2010). The use of an assessment committee and utilizing the "four out of five" rule (a) increases the probability of appropriate interventions, (b) reflects a standard of care commensurate with the corrections counselor's degree level and professional practice scope, and (c) helps insulate from potential for liability. Specifically, regarding the "four out of five" rule, corrections counselors can utilize the MO(o)D PIRATE Malingering Mnemonic Risk Assessment to identify best interventions. Corrections counselors then consult with an assessment committee minimally composed of five, master's level or higher, licensed mental health professionals to determine if the proposed intervention is clinically, ethically, and legally appropriate. If four of five professionals believe the proposed interventions are appropriate, the intervention is initiated. As always, consultation with one's clinical supervisor(s), legal counsel, and professional liability insurance risk management division are warranted when assessing appropriate intervention with those who may be presenting with minimal to extreme degrees of malingering.

The Scale and Risk Factor Scoring

The MO(o)D PIRATE Malingering Mnemonic Risk Assessment is atheoretical in nature. The Assessment was created to serve corrections counselors as a front-line assessment tool when assessing inmates who are presenting with suspect behaviors or symptoms that may initially appear as malingering in nature and more time consuming pencil and paper or computer generated tests are inopportune or immediately unavailable. In most cases the assessment should take less than five minutes to complete. Thus, the assessment can be easily administered immediately upon suspect inmate self-report of exaggerated or severe psychological and emotional symptoms.

The Assessment is comprised of 9 risk factors identified within the literature (Vittacco & Rogers, 2005; Rogers, 1984) or based upon the authors' clinical corrections experiences. Except for the second "o" in the word "MO(o)D," each letter in the mnemonic "MO(o)D PIRATE" corresponds to a specific malingering risk factor. These malingering risk factors include:

Manipulation (Previous),

Only (Reports Significant and Disturbing Symptoms),

Details (Lack of),

Pending (Charges, penalties, or disciplinary actions),

Inconsistent (In observed verses reported psychological symptoms and stressors),

Rapid (Symptoms have rapid onset without precursors),

Answers (Inmate is focused on solutions other than mental health treatment),

Tick off (Or angers other inmates or guards), and

Extreme Symptoms.

Each factor receives an individual factor score of either "0" indicating the complete absence of the risk factor or "1" indicating the presence of the risk factor. Out of the 9 risk factors only Extreme Symptoms (e.g., hallucinations, mania, depression, anxiety, etc.), **Only** (Reports Significant and Disturbing Symptoms) and **Rapid** (symptoms have rapid onset without precursors) require immediate referral for medical evaluation. The possible total score range is between "0" and "9" (see Table 2). The individual mnemonic and corresponding succinct description are provided below.

Manipulation (Previous)

Here, corrections counselors assess the inmate and interview others to determine if the inmate has a history of manipulation with guards, other inmates, or mental health workers, or is perceived as manipulating for a specific purpose. For example, has the inmate been utilizing veiled suicide threats or manipulated or coerced others to gain desired secondary gains such as an observation cell away from the general inmate population or to be excused from physical exercise or work duties? If so, the inmate receives one point for manipulation; if not the inmate receives no point specific to this risk factor.

Only (Reports significant and disturbing symptoms)

This risk factor is specific to inmates who only report significant and disturbing symptoms such as vivid command hallucinations where the Devil tells the inmate to kill others while failing to report or describe minor negative symptoms such as a lack of concentration, an inability to focus, or minor feelings of anxiety. Failing to report more mundane and typical symptoms while focusing solely upon severe symptoms suggests one may be malingering and, therefore, results in one point.

Details

Inmates who have an inability to describe symptoms in detail (e.g., "Was the voice a female or male voice?," "What exactly did the voice say?," etc.) and too eagerly agree to counselor symptoms prompts (e.g., "Do you ever hear voices or see things that other people don't see?," "Did the voice sound angry?," etc.) are more likely to be malingering. It is as if they had not previously considered or experienced the counselor's more in-depth symptom description query and insincerely or too quickly agree to the symptom's presence despite being unable to fully describe what the symptom was like or having an inability to describe commonly associated symptom features. For the purposes of MO(o)D PIRATE scoring, inmates who are unable to provide adequate symptom descriptions and too eagerly agree to counselor symptom prompts receive one point.

Pending (Charges, penalties or disciplinary actions)

Malingering can occur when inmates are anticipating punishment or sanctions for inappropriate behaviors or rule violations. Thus, the authors have found that greater degrees of malingering are often associated with inmates seeking to avoid pending punishments or sanctions, or seeking escape from anticipated reprimands or sentencing. Therefore, inmates facing charges, penalties or disciplinary actions receive one point.

Inconsistent

Inmates whose observed behaviors are incongruent with their reported psychological or physical symptoms may also be malingering. Examples of such inconsistency might be inmates who report being overwhelmingly depressed, yet who frequently smile in a non-sarcastic manner, and appropriately joke, engage, and interact with others. Such inconsistency between inmate reported symptoms and presenting affect, behaviors, and interpersonal interactions with others results in one point.

Rapid (Symptom onset)

Most psychological symptoms typically do not have a rapid onset. Instead, symptoms typically escalate over time. Thus, inmates who experience a rapid onset of multiple severe symptoms without previously documented medical or psychological documentation are suspect and receive one point for the presence of Rapid Symptom Onset.

Answers

It has been the authors' experiences that inmates who readily provide "answers" or "remedies" for their presenting mental health concerns often have ulterior motives and are more interested in getting their desired "answer" or "remedy" than eliminating the reported symptoms. For example, inmates who fail to describe their depressive feelings and instead tell correction counselors what changes could be made to abruptly eliminate their "depression" (e.g., cell change or transfer to a different cell block or prison, etc.) are more likely to be malingering. Hence, one point is awarded to inmates who provide answers or remedies for their reported mental illness.

Tick off

A risk factor observed by both authors during their experience in corrections is associated with a personality type within inmate populations that "ticks off" (i.e., frequently angers) others. Sometimes these inmates can present as "whiney," self-centered, and exceedingly self-absorbed. These inmates often anger fellow inmates or guards, because they constantly seek special privileges or fail to share work duty responsibilities. They may malinger in an effort to eliminate responsibilities or receive special privileges. Mental health professionals may observe or receive reports from staff and inmates about annoyance and frustration that is directed at a specific inmate. One point is awarded to those who fulfill this risk criterion.

Extreme Symptoms

Inmates who report extreme symptoms that are overly severe (e.g., hallucinations, extreme mania, etc.) and rare within the general population may also be attempting to malinger. This risk factor is distinct from the Only and Inconsistent factors in that it focuses primarily on inmates reporting severe and rare symptoms rather than whether or not the inmate reports both severe and moderate symptoms (i.e., Only risk factor) or whether or not they report symptoms that are congruent with their observed behavior (i.e., Inconsistent risk factor). When such extreme and rare symptoms are reported by the inmate, they receive one point.

Total Scale Score Range

MO(o)D PIRATE offers general response guidelines based upon the Total Scale Score. Table 3 describes the general response guidelines for the range of possible total scores. These suggested responses are presented in a general template format that encourages correction counselors to adapt and mold the general response guidelines to the assessed inmate's specific needs. Unique situations and other idiosyncratic issues particular to the inmate such as previous physical or psychological diagnoses, suicide attempts, anniversary dates (e.g., wedding, sentencing, failed release or probation, etc.), gang affiliations, deaths of important family members, graduations of important family members, releases, deaths, injuries, or movement of close inmate friends, perceived reasons or lack of reasons for continuing to live, and substance abuse must be considered.

Vignettes

Earnest

Earnest presents as 24-year-old, Caucasian male. He has been incarcerated at a Level 4 Maximum Security Prison for the last two years. Earnest is serving a 5 to 12 year sentence for Aggravated Robbery. Yesterday, Earnest referred himself to the corrections counselor. Earnest reports he wants to be moved to an observation cell, "...because the Devil is telling me to kill myself." When asked what the Devil says, the Devil's exact words, and the loudness and tone of the Devil's voice, Earnest appears dumbfounded and flustered. Instead, of responding to these questions Earnest reports placement in the prison's medical ward or observations cells should make the hallucinations cease. Earnest denies other auditory, visual, olfactory, gustatory, tactile, or thermoceptive hallucinations: "No, no, no, just the Devil telling me to kill myself." Earnest is unable to recall previous hallucinations and does not remember when the hallucinations began, "I don't know. I guess, yesterday." Earnest is oriented to person, place, and time, his affect is normal, he interacts socially with other inmates and appropriately with guards, denies concentration problems, mood concerns, or any other psychological or physical problems. A brief conversation with guards suggests: (a) they have neither directly encountered nor do they perceive Earnest as more or less manipulative than others in the general prison population, and (b) Earnest has not reported hallucinations to them nor has he demonstrated behaviors that would suggest to them that he is actively hallucinating. Guards, however, reported that Earnest will have his television privileges suspended due to failing to adequately clean his cell and stow his bedding and towels.

Based upon Earnest's vignette his MO(o)D PIRATE Total Scale Score is "8." Earnest's MO(o)D PIRATE Malingering Mnemonic Risk Assessment factors include: **O**nly Reports Significant and Disturbing Symptoms, **D**etails (Lack of), **P**ending (Charges, penalties, or disciplinary actions), **I**nconsistent (in **O**bserved Verses Reported Psychological Symptoms and Stressors), **R**apid (Symptom Onset Without Precursors), **A**nswers (Inmate is Focused on Solutions Other Than Mental Health Treatment), and Extreme Symptoms. The corresponding general guidelines for Earnest's MO(o)D PIRATE score of "8" includes: Consulting with clinical supervisors, psychiatrists, legal staff, and administrators, monitoring of Earnest for a minimum 120 days, and consideration of moving Earnest to an observation or medical cell. Of course, these are only general guidelines that must be used in conjunction with input from the risk assessment committee, clinical supervisor and legal counsel consultation, and the correction counselor's clinical and professional judgment.

Maria

Maria presents as 24-year-old mother of two. She was incarcerated for three years at a Level 4 Maximum Security Prison. Last year Maria was moved to a Medium Security Prison that houses 190 female inmates. With good behavior, Maria will be moved to a Level 2 Minimum Security Prison in a year. She anticipates parole in two to three years. Upon arrival at Smithville, Maria was diagnosed with 296.22 Major Depressive Disorder Moderate Severity with Mixed Features. She was prescribed antidepressant medications. Maria's father was charged with physical abuse of Maria's oldest son. This happened two weeks ago. The abuse charge resulted in Maria's parents losing guardianship of Maria's children. Once this happened, Maria's depression became more severe and the consulting psychiatrist increased her antidepressant levels. Fellow inmates and prison guards and staff reported concerns about Maria's depression a week ago. She had stopped eating, was unable to sleep, and reported to others she wished to die. When the corrections counselor spoke with Maria, she reported her depression was "...a black cloud hanging over me and suffocating my life." Maria reported many physical and psychological symptoms (i.e., general body aches, inability to concentrate, anxious and depressed feelings, difficulty getting out of bed or working in the Smithville laundry, etc.). When asked if she had any suggestions on how to reduce her feelings of depression or eliminate her suicidal ideation she stated, "I have no idea. I am trapped in a nightmare and unable to help my kids." When interviewing guards and Maria's inmate friends, none believed Maria was manipulative or had pending charges, penalties, or disciplinary actions.

Maria's MO(o)D PIRATE Total Scale Score is "0." Maria has no strikingly evident malingering risk factors. Specifically, guards and fellow inmates do not perceive Maria as manipulative or as someone who ticks off or angers others. Guards are unaware of additional pending charges or sanctions. Maria reports a combination of significant symptoms (i.e., depression, suicidal ideation, anxiety) and less severe symptoms (i.e., concentration problems, body aches, etc.). Concomitantly, she can describe detailed aspects of how she feels. Additionally, consistency exists between her voiced depressive symptoms and observed behaviors such as her discontinuing eating. Her symptoms did not have a rapid onset, and although she reports both suicidal ideation and depressive feelings, she does not report these in combination with even more extreme symptoms such as hallucinations or mania. One final important final point should be noted. Maria does not continually provide "the answer" indicating what will eliminate her depression or suicidal thoughts. In other words, she does not present with an "answer" agenda. Contrary to Ernest above, who continually indicated transfer to the medical ward and observation cells would eliminate his hallucinations and suicidal ideation, Maria reports she is unaware of anything that will make her better.

The corresponding general guidelines for Maria's MO(o)D PIRATE score of "0" includes: Treating Maria for her reported depressive symptoms. Given her depressive symptoms and the strong correlation between depression and suicide and her current diagnosis and medications, consultation with one's clinical supervisor and the consulting psychiatrist are warranted. As well, one may wish to monitor Maria for suicidal ideation and behaviors to ensure her safety.

Limitations

Despite the many positives related to the MO(o)D PIRATE, the Assessment has limitations. MO(o)D PIRATE cannot precisely identify every inmate who is or is not malingering, nor can it precisely identify the exact degree of malingering presence. Furthermore, it cannot tell each corrections counselor how to respond to every potentially malingering inmate or every situation. Thus, MO(o)D PIRATE was instead designed to serve as a brief, triage assessment that should be just one component within an organized and thorough psychological and malingering assessment process that includes other components, such as psychological testing, clinical interviews with the inmate, guards, and other inmates and visitors who know and frequently interact with the inmate, as well as other components deemed necessary to make an informed and logical decision and responding intervention. The suggested responses should be viewed as general in nature and modified to meet the specific idiosyncratic needs of the inmate.

Additionally, the presence or perceived presence of any one malingering risk factor does not mean the inmate is malingering or will malinger. However, a significant clustering of high-risk malingering risk factors suggests increased probability of malingering that should be further investigated via interviews and other psychological instruments such as the SIRS (Rogers, 1984). Additionally, scores with single factors such as **O**nly Reports Positive Symptoms, **R**apid Symptom Onset and Extreme Symptoms indicate the need for further psychological assessment and counseling to address the noted risk factors. Concomitantly, whatever decisions made should be made in conjunction with input from one's supervisor, legal counsel, and a team of skilled, experienced, and licensed mental health professionals who are knowledgably in malingering risk assessment.

The malingering indicators presented in this scale are not intended to be the basis for determining crisis intervention responses. Crisis interventions should be based primarily on safety and counselors should understand that the threat of harm can be present in both malingering and non-malingering individuals (Cummings & Thompson, 2009). Other assessments specific to crisis intervention (Juhnke, et al., 2010; Myer & Conte, 2006; Patterson, et al, 1983) must be used for determining these types of interventions. Stated differently, MO(o)D PIRATE provides suggested templates that must be modified as necessary to address the specific needs of the inmate and ensure the inmate's safety and appropriate mental health treatment. The resulting intervention should be constructed in a manner that will provide the greatest degree of safety and protection. Finally, it is noted that MO(o)D PIRATE mnemonic warrants further research. Such investigation is currently in process and expected to begin within the year.

Conclusion

MO(o)D PIRATE is the only free, standardized, brief, face-to-face malingering mnemonic with corresponding general intervention suggestions published to date in existing corrections counselor literature. Mason, Cardell and Armstrong (2013) recently proposed three mnemonics for detecting malingered psychosis for auditory hallucinations (FACING IT), visual hallucinations (HELPS) and delusions (IDEA). Although these mnemonics may be useful in many psychiatric settings, they are primarily intended to detect the malingering of psychotic symptoms and do not address symptoms connected to other mental illnesses (e.g. depression and anxiety). The mnemonic described in this paper is intended to not only address a more broad range of reported symptoms, but also to be more specific to correctional and institutional settings.

The MO(o)D PIRATE mnemonic is founded upon the DSM-5 malingering definition, existing malingering research, and the author's combined corrections counseling and consulting experiences that have spanned 37 years. MO(o)D PIRATE demonstrates potential utility for front-line corrections counselors who wish to quickly conduct a brief maltreatment assessment. The mnemonic is easy to use, and reported by beginning and advanced counseling students, as well as senior counseling professionals with more than 10 years clinical experience as easy to remember. Administration and scoring time are minimal. MO(o)D PIRATE provides corrections counselors viable alternative to intuition-based, haphazard, random, and nonsystematic face-to-face malingering assessments.

References

American Association for Suicidology. (2012). *Know the warning signs: IS PATH WARM.* Retrieved from http://www.suicidology.org/web/guest/stats-and-tools/suicide-warning-signs

American Psychiatric Association. (2013). *Diagnostic and Statistical Manual of Mental Disorders* (5th ed.). Arlington, VA: Author.

American Psychiatric Association (2000). *Diagnostic and Statistical Manual of Mental Disorders* (4th ed., text rev.). Arlington, VA: Author.

Berry, D. T. R., & Nelson, N.W. (2010). DSM-5 and malingering: a modest proposal. *Psychology Inj. and the Law. 3*, 295–303.

Ewing, J. A. (1984). Detecting alcoholism: The CAGE Questionnaire. *Journal of the American Medical Association, 252*, 1905–1907.

Cummins, D. L., & Thompson, M. N. (2009). Suicidal or manipulative? The role of mental health counselors in overcoming a false dichotomy in identifying and treating self-harming inmates. *Journal of Mental Health Counseling, 31*(3), 201–212.

Glaze, L.E., & Parks, E. (2012). *Correctional populations in the United States, 2011(Bureau of Justice Statistics).* Washington, DC: U.S. Department of Justice.

Juhnke, G. A. (1994). Teaching suicide assessment to counselor education students. *Counselor Education and Supervision, 34*(1), 52–57.

Juhnke, G. A., Granello, D. H., & Granello, P. F. (2010). *Suicide, self-injury, and violence in the schools: Assessment, prevention, and intervention strategies.* Hoboken, NJ: John Wiley & Sons.

Mason, A.M., Cardell, R., & Armstrong, M. (2013). Malingering psychosis: Guidelines for assessment and management. *Perspectives in Psychiatric Care, 50*, 51–57 doi: 10.1111/ppc.12025

McDermott, B.E., Dualan, I.V., & Scott, C.L. (2013). Malingering in the correctional system: Does incentive affect prevalence? *International Journal of Law and Psychiatry, 36*, 287–292.

McDermott, B.E. & Sokolov, G. (2009). Malingering in a correctional setting: The use of the Structured Interview of Reported Symptoms in a jail sample. *Behavioral Science and the Law, 27*, 753–765.

Myer, R.A., & Conte, C. (2006). Assessment for crisis intervention. *Journal of Clinical Psychology, 62*(8), 959–970.

Patterson, W. M., Dohn, H. H., Bird, J., & Patterson, G. A. (1983). Evaluation of suicidal patients: The SAD PERSONS Scale. *Psychosomatics, 24*(4), 343–349.

Rogers, R. (1984). Towards an empirical model of malingering and deception. *Behavioral Sciences and the Law, 2*, 93–112.

Rogers, R. (1986). *Structured interview of reported symptoms (SIRS).* Unpublished scale, Clark Institute of Psychiatry, Toronto.

Rogers, R., Gillis, J. R., & Bagby, R. M. (1990). The SIRS as measure of malingering: A validation study with a correctional sample. *Behavioral Sciences and the Law, 8*, 85–92.

Rogers, R., Bagby, R. M., & Dickens, S.E. (1992). *Structured Interview of Reported Symptoms (SIRS) professional manual.* Odessa, FL: Psychological Assessment Resources.

Rogers, R., Hinds, J. D., & Sewell, K. W. (1996). Feigning psychopathology among adolescent offenders: Validation of the SIRS, MMPI-A, and SIMS. *Journal of Personality Assessment, 67*(2), 244–257.

Scott, C. L., & Gerbasi, J. B. (Eds.). (2005). *Handbook of Correctional Mental Health*. Washington, DC: American Psychiatric Publishing.

Smith, G. P., Borum, R., & Schinka, J. A. (1993). Rule-out and rule-in scales for the M Test for malingering: A cross-validation. *Journal of the American Academy of Psychiatry and the Law Online, 21*(1), 107–110

Torrey, E.F., Kennard, A.D., Eslinger, D., Lamb, R., & Pavle, J. (2010). More mentally ill persons are in jails and prisons than hospitals: A survey of the states. Treatment advocacy center, National sheriffs association. Retrieved from http://www.treatmentadvocacycenter.org/storage/documents/final_jails_v_hospitals_study.pdf

Vitacco, M.J., & Rogers. J. (2005). Assessment of malingering in correctional settings. In C.L. Scott, & J.B. Gerbasi (Eds.), *Handbook of correctional mental health* (pp. 133–153). Washington, DC: American Psychiatric Publishing, Inc.

Walmsley, R. (2011). World prison population list (9th edition). *International centre of prison studies*. Retrieved from http://www.prisonstudies.org/sites/prisonstudies.org/files/resources/downloads/wppl_9.pdf

Walters, G.D., Berry, D.T.R., Lanyon, R.I., & Murphy, M.P. (2009). Are exaggerated health complaints continuous or categorical? A taxometric analysis of the health problem overstatement scale. *Psychological Assessment, 21*(2), 219–226

Table 2

MO(o)D PIRATE Malingering Mnemonic Risk Assessment

Malingering Risk Factor	Risk Factor Absent	Risk Factor Present	
Manipulation	0	1	
Only (Reports Significant and Disturbing Symptoms)	0	1	
Details (Lack of)	0	1	
Pending (charges, penalties, or disciplinary actions)	0	1	
Inconsistent (in observed verses reported psychological symptoms and stressors)	0	1	
Rapid (symptoms have rapid onset without precursors)	0	1	
Answers (inmate is focused on solutions other than mental health treatment)	0	1	
Tick off (or angers other inmates or guards),	0	1	
Extreme Symptoms	0	1	
Subtotal Scores			Total Score Box

Instructions: Each risk factor has a value of either "0" or "1." Scores of "1" indicate malingering risk factor presence. Scores of "0" indicate malingering risk factor absence. Circle "1" for each present malingering risk factor. Sum the circled present risk factors and place the summed score in the Total Score box. Match the total score with Table 2's general implications and guidelines.

Table 3

MO(o)D PIRATE Malingering Mnemonic Risk Assessment General Malingering Implications and Guidelines.

Total Score	Generally Implications and Guidelines Depending Upon Identified Items
0 to 2	• Total Scores in this category typically suggest the inmate is likely lacking clear intent to malinger. • Although malingering may be present, the degree of the malingering is minimal and suggests the inmate may be unaware of purposeful intents to malinger. • Document assessment results in client's record. • Depending upon the risk factors noted (e.g., Extreme Symptoms [Suicidal intent with command hallucinations] vis-à-vis Self-Referring), consultation with one's clinical supervisor, psychiatric consult and risk assessment to determine imminent danger to self or others may be warranted. • Appropriate treatment and intervention for reported symptoms is recommended.
3 to 4	• Scores in this range suggest the presence of mild to moderate malingering and suggests the client may be aware of purposeful intent to malinger for secondary gains (e.g., release from mandatory duties or rules, movement to a less restrictive or perceived "safer" location, etc.). • Document assessment results in client record. • Identify common themes and concerns, and consult with one's clinical supervisor. • Should concerns be specific to reality testing (e.g., hallucinations, delusions, etc.) or harm to self or others, immediate assessment to determine imminent danger to self or others is warranted, as well as monitoring and psychiatric consult. • Appropriate treatment and intervention for reported symptoms is recommended.

5 to 6	• Scores of 5 to 6 indicate the inmate is endorsing over half of the MO(o)D PIRATE malingering risk factors. • This suggests significant probability of malingering and likely myopic focus on one or more specific secondary gain(s) and/or significant psychological distress. • Additional psychological and malingering assessment (i.e., MMPI & SIRS) may be warranted to determine the presenting degree of malingering and severe psychopathology. • Conduct risk assessment and necessary medical and safety interventions to address severe psychopathology or danger to self or others. • Given the tendency of such inmates to be perceived as being "high maintenance," it is imperative that the corrections counselor participate in frequent clinical supervision regarding this type of case and regularly monitor this inmate for a period of no less than 30 days for follow up re assessment.
7 to 9	• This is an extreme score category; Inmates scoring between 7 and 9 are minimally fulfilling all but 33% of the MO(o)D PIRATE's maligning risk factors. • Scores in this category indicate intentional malingering for secondary gains. • Additional comprehensive psychological and malingering assessment (i.e., MMPI & SIRS) is warranted. • If reports or concerns are related to threats of harm to self or others, appropriate suicide or crisis risk assessments should be utilized. • In addition to the guidelines for the preceding score ranges (i.e., supervisor and psychiatric consultation, inmate monitoring, frequent supervision for the corrections counselor, etc.), corrections counselors should consult agency legal counsel to ensure adequate care is provided to the inmate due to the high probability of litigation in cases like these. • This case should be continually monitored with supervisor, psychiatric, and legal counselor for a minimum of 120 or longer.

Note. These are general guidelines and not intended to supersede individual clinical judgment or client needs. Counselors are encouraged to follow all ethical and legal guidelines and to follow agency policies. Counselors are also encouraged to utilize treatment interventions that are grounded in theory and have empirical foundations.

**Extreme symptoms including but not limited to hallucinations, delusions, mania, veiled or direct threats of harm, suicidal or homicidal ideation, require immediate in-depth assessment and intervention, and on-going regular monitoring to ensure safety for the inmate and others.

12

Assessment of Treatment Fidelity to Moral Reconation Therapy
Are Treatment Providers Adrift?

JAMES S. KORCUSKA, DAVID HULAC, AND IRENE HARPER[1]

Moral Reconation Therapy (MRT; Little & Robinson, 1988) is a widely used treatment program for offenders. Treatment effect size is small (Ferguson & Wormith, 2012) and fidelity of implementation (FOI) of MRT unclear (Wilson, Bouffard, & Mackenzie, 2005). We examined FOI for a statewide offender program. Providers trained in MRT delivered it to participants in a pretrial sentencing program. No previous studies of MRT have employed a fidelity of implementation measure. Since no known Provider Quality Assessment (PQA) tool for MRT existed, we developed one. Our results from the MRT Integrity Check (MICk) suggest

---

1. James S. Korcuska, School of Education, College of Human Development and Education, North Dakota State University; David Hulac, Division of Counseling & Psychology in Education, The University of South Dakota; Irene Harper, School of Education, College of Human Development and Education, North Dakota State University. This investigation was a part of a contract from the U.S. Department of Justice. Material from this study appeared in the report by the authors, *An evaluation of the treatment fidelity of the Federal Probation and Pretrial Services' Moral Reconation Therapy and West River Camp.*(2011) published by the University of South Dakota Government Research Bureau. The views contained herein are our own and do not reflect any of the agencies or institutions affiliated with the report. Correspondence concerning this article should be addressed to James S. Korcuska, 1919 N. University Drive, SCG C118, P.O. Box 6050, Fargo, ND 58108–6050. Email: james.korcuska@ndsu.edu

that providers registered treatment with moderately high levels of fidelity, but that group facilitation skills as measured by the Group Psychotherapy Intervention Rating Scale (GPIRS; Burlingame, Fuhriman, & Johnson, 2002) were under-utilized.

Offender treatment is a high stakes venture with profound monetary and social implications. From a cost-benefit analysis, judicious investment in effective offender treatment programs yields favorable, even considerable, economic outcomes (Sedgley, Scott, Williams, & Derrick, 2010; Welsh, 2004). Meta-analytic reviews show cognitive behavioral treatment techniques to be effective with offenders, albeit with small to medium effect sizes (Hofmann, Asnaani, Vonk, Sawyer, & Fang, 2012). Because of the major economic and human costs of incarceration, even small improvements in the treatment efficacy of any program can make meaningful differences economically and socially (Ferguson & Wormith, 2012). This is particularly true for programs implemented on a large scale.

Moral Reconation Therapy (MRT) is a widely used cognitive behavioral-moral development treatment intervention for correctional and at-risk populations (Little & Robinson, 1988). MRT is used in 45 states in the U.S. and internationally. Several U.S. states implement MRT system wide (NREPP SAMHSA, 2008). MRT has produced outcomes similar to other cognitive behavioral therapy treatment programs for offenders with its small effect size of .16 (Ferguson & Wormith, 2012). Evaluating the efficacy of treatment programs such as MRT is complicated by at least two factors: (a) small sample sizes and (b) developer conducted research (Wright, Zhang, & Farabee, 2012). As discussed in detail later, the MRT literature has the second problem. The preponderance of developer conducted research calls into question whether or not non-developers can implement MRT with not only the same effectiveness and potency as its developers, but in the same manner. The purpose of this research is to explore the variable Fidelity of Intervention (FOI) as it relates to MRT. Accounting for FOI may subsequently address the issues related to developer-conducted research.

MRT

MRT is a proprietary program with training costs around $600 per person ("Correctional Counseling Inc. MRTTM Facilitator Training," n.d.). Little and Robinson (1988) developed MRT to make long-term personality and behavioral change with treatment resistant clients such as inmates. MRT is a "systematic treatment" (Little & Robinson, 1988, p. 135) that may be combined with other modalities such as behavioral management and groups. MRT treatment is manualized (i.e., trainers use manuals and clients use workbooks), portable (i.e., it may be used across treatment settings), hierarchical (i.e., clients move through progressive treatment steps), and pragmatic (e.g., it is cost effective). Little and Robinson designed MRT so providers with varied backgrounds and educational preparation could learn and implement it. The sections "Evaluating the Fidelity of MRT" and "Instrumentation" provide more detail about MRT's treatment protocol.

MRT, put into practice in 1985, is more than another cognitive behavioral therapy. Rather, it is a personality and moral development model. The heart of the model lies in the word "conation." Although Little and Robinson derive their understanding of "conation" from Descartes, its roots date back to Plato (Gerdes & Stromwall, 2008). Behavior is thought to arise out of a tripartite mind—cognitive, affective, and conative. The traditional cognitive-behavioral therapy cognitive (thoughts) and affective (feelings) elements are present in this model of the tripartite mind. There is no clean analog for the conative. It is more than motivation and goal setting. The conative is akin to a drive that keeps one moving toward a goal in spite of obstacles. Yet it is more than a drive as it is simultaneously conscious and instinctual, and includes desire, pleasure, and pain. The cognitive and affective elements of the tripartite mind work in unison with conation (Gerdes & Stromwall, 2008). Thus, individuals use conation to varying degrees to consciously direct their behavior, manage their impulses and emotions, and overcome obstacles to secure future goals.

Little and Robinson (1988) believe that the offender populations must undergo a "reconation" process whereby they learn and develop the conation aspect of the mind to make positive moral and relational choices, all the while constraining their impulses and negative emotions. In the view of Little and Robinson (1985), clients are unhappy and make antisocial decisions because, in part, their identity is ill defined or stunted, they possess a narcissistic world-view, and, most important, they have nascent moral development. Cognitively and morally egocentric, the individual at this point in development uses the environment to serve her or his ends (Adler, 1938). Thus, the aim of MRT is to mature the underlying personality structure. Rooted in Kohlberg's moral development model (Kohlberg, 1976), MRT works step-wise in hierarchal fashion to develop moral reasoning. Moral reasoning is linked to moral behavior. Van Vugt et al. (2011) conducted a meta-analysis of moral development studies that showed an inverse relationship with recidivism, with overall effect sizes ranging from small (r = .11) to medium (r = .19).

Reconation is the process of moving a client from impulsive to conscious choices. The aim is to direct behavior away from asocial or antisocial actions and goals toward those that are prosocial. Controlling impulses and directing behavior toward new goals, however, requires perseverance. This requires new behaviors, looking at alternatives, and taking risks (Kolbe, 2004). As individuals engage in prosocial behaviors and moral choices, enter into satisfying relationships, and contribute to the greater good, they become more satisfied, if not happier. These constructs are striking similar to Adler's idea of social interest, which has been linked to offender recidivism rates and post release employment (Daugherty, Murphy, & Paugh, 2001). Clients with narcissistic characteristics, antisocial behaviors, and poor impulse control, require more than behavioral interventions to spark this "reconation" (Little & Robinson, 1988).

Literature Review

Reviewers suggest MRT is effective (Allen, MacKenzie, & Hickman, 2001; Ferguson & Wormith, 2012; Wilson, Bouffard, & Mackenzie, 2005), although the level of effectiveness varies from small to moderate. The Substance Abuse and Mental Health Services Administration (SAMHSA) lists MRT on its National Registry of Evidence-based Programs and Practices (NREPP, 2008). NREPP (2008) estimates that over 1 million individuals have participated in MRT. The NREPP review of MRT included five MRT studies (i.e., Little & Robinson, 1989; Little, Robinson, & Burnette, 1990, 1991, 1993; Little, Robinson, Burnette, & Swan, 1999) and assigned various "quality of research ratings." Of the factors rated, fidelity, or adherence to the treatment protocol by providers, earned the lowest rating, a 1.0 out of 4.0. There was no explanation for the rating. None of the five studies, however, mentioned treatment fidelity. In addition to this review, there have been three non-MRT developer meta-analyses of the effectiveness of MRT published in peer-reviewed journals (Allen, et al., 2001; Wilson, et al, 2005; Ferguson & Wormith, 2012).

The first review appeared in 2001 authored by Allen and colleagues evaluated MRT in addition to other cognitive behavioral programs for offenders. Using the Maryland method that combines meta-analysis and literature review, Allen et al. ranked studies on a scale of 1 (weakest empirical evidence and methodology) to 5 (strongest empirical evidence and methodology). The MRT studies used in their analysis yield an overall rating of 2.71 out of 5.0. They concluded that (a) Little and Robinson conducted most of the studies used in the analysis, (b) MRT studies were weak methodologically, (c) studies produced consistent results, and (d) MRT showed some effectiveness in reducing recidivism. The designs of most of the MRT studies, according to these authors, were a concern.

In the second major review of MRT, Wilson, et al., (2005) determined effect sizes for various group-oriented cognitive-behavioral programs such as MRT. They used a quantitative synthesis method to examine the effectiveness of programs in reducing recidivism. These authors found that 45% of the MRT studies included in their sample were not published in peer-reviewed outlets, e.g., government reports. Using a scale similar to the Maryland scale, studies were rated on a scale from 1 (weak design) to 4 (true experiment). Only 16 out of 45 MRT studies received a ranking of 3, indicating a high quality design. Their final analysis of MRT was based on six studies. The mean effect size for MRT on recidivism was 0.36. Of the MRT studies with the strongest methodology ratings, Little and Robinson conducted three out of four. The authors concluded that Little and Robinson produced too much of the research supporting the effectiveness of MRT, thereby raising the question whether providers other than the developers can successfully implement MRT.

Ferguson and Wormith (2012) conducted the most recent meta-analysis of MRT, including 33 studies of MRT interventions. Focusing only on studies of MRT, they found a small effect size ($r = .16$). Based on these findings, they concluded that MRT is (a) effective and (b) "warrants serious consideration by any correctional agency that has designs to influence the antisocial and criminal attitudes, behavior, and lifestyle of its clientele" (2012, p. 25). However, they draw some of their conclusions from findings resulting from an analytic procedure controlling for publication bias, but not for program developer bias. Although not specifically referring to MRT, this is a concern raised by Wright et al., (2012) about treatments listed in the NREPP database. Although they raised the point in their discussion of the limitations, Ferguson and Wormith did not account for the quality of the research design of the studies used in their analysis.

Too few studies of MRT appear in peer-reviewed journals. Of the 33 studies used by Ferguson and Wormith, only eight (24%) appeared in peer-reviewed journals. Six of these were co-authored by Little and Robinson, MRT's developers. The majority (59%; n = 19) of the studies in this meta-analysis were published in Cognitive Behavioral Treatment Review, a publication of Correctional Counseling, Inc. (CCI), which is operated by Little. The remaining studies included one unpublished master's thesis and annual reports. Ferguson and Wormith's findings of a small effect (r = .16) on recidivism coincide with the conclusions reached by Allen, et al. (2001) a decade earlier. Ferguson and Wormith found that studies conducted after the year 2000 had a smaller effect size (r = .14; n = 13) than studies published in the 20th century (r = .19; n = 16). This unexpected finding runs contrary to the fact that most established interventions become more effective with time, as noted by Ferguson and Wormith.

Ferguson and Wormith (2012) found that studies published in venues not affiliated with CCI had a higher effect size than those published elsewhere. They conclude that this lack of publication bias indicates lack of "researcher bias" (p. 25). This does not tell the complete story, however. Although publication venues differ, the variability among authors publishing studies does not: six of the 12 studies in the non-CCI group were Little and Robinson. Closer inspection of the studies included in the Ferguson and Wormith analysis shows that Little and Robinson published five of the 13 pre-2000 studies, all of which appeared in peer-reviewed journals. Moreover, this same data show that Little and colleagues, usually with co-developer Robinson, were the primary authors on nearly 36% (n = 14) of 39 studies on MRT. Burnett, co-author of six of the Little studies, authored four more. These collaborators accounted for 46% (n = 18) MRT studies mentioned by Ferguson and Wormith in their meta-analysis.

In conclusion, MRT showed early, positive, modest effect sizes. Over time, the effect sizes diminished, contrary to what typically happens with a treatment technology. Research design may account for some of this loss in observed treatment effectiveness of MRT. A portion of this loss, however, may be due to implementation by providers differently skilled in MRT than its developers. In 2005, Wilson et al. averred that the treatment fidelity of MRT remained in question. These most recent findings lead us to suggest that the question of treatment fidelity to MRT remains open.

Treatment Fidelity

Treatment fidelity, at its most basic level, refers to whether or not a counselor or provider implements an intervention protocol as intended by its developer (Bellg et al. 2004; Noell, 2008; Sanetti & Kratochwill, 2009). Treatment fidelity is a multi-dimensional construct that includes exposure to the treatment (how frequently and for how long an individual receives treatment), quality of the treatment's implementation, and interventionist adherence to the treatment protocol (Sanetti & Kratochwill, 2007). Moreover, it encompasses three interrelated yet distinct treatment processes: (a) delivery, (b) receipt, and (c) enactment (Lichstein, Riedel, & Grieve, 1994). Thus, treatment fidelity not only refers to aspects related to the provider, but other elements that may be outside of his or her control, such as the quality of training she or he received. Providers deliver or implement treatment. On the other hand, clients receive (e.g., learn) and then enact (e.g., adhere to) treatment. For example, a client may not attend a session and miss a "dose" of treatment, or may refuse to cooperate and participate in the treatment (Jones, Clarke, & Power, 2008). FOI, the focus of this investigation, describes delivery, the provider component.

Consistent delivery of a treatment protocol is a critical step in evaluating the outcomes of an intervention (Alvarez-Jiminez et al., 2008; Barber, Foltz, Crits-Christoph, & Chittams, 2004; Bellg et al., 2004; Leventhal & Friedman, 2004; Lichstein et al., 1994; Miller & Binder, 2002; Miller, Sorensen, Selzer, & Brigham, 2006; Sanetti & Kratochwill, 2007; Witt, VanDerHeyden, & Gilbertson, 2004). Delivery involves provider adherence to the treatment protocol and her or his relative competence in its application (Barber et al., 2004; Bellg et al., 2004). Provider adherence and competence may affect clinical outcomes across various treatment modalities (Barber et al., 2004; Miller & Binder, 2002; Robbins, et al. 2011). One of the issues affecting FOI involves "'drift' in provider skills'" (Bellg et al. 2004), or the tendency for providers to deviate from the treatment protocol as time passes. We did not identify any literature that assessed the FOI of MRT on a large scale.

Evaluating the Fidelity of MRT

MRT's design has numerous strengths (Little & Robinson, 1988, 2009) that make it amenable to FOI: (a) conceptual integrity (i.e., MRT is user friendly) (Brooks, 1995); (b) the treatment is manualized; (c) training materials are available to providers for reference; (d) training of providers is standardized; (e) participants use copyrighted workbooks; and (f) delivery is designed for a specific population (e.g., offenders). Providers, whom all attend MRT training, follow multiple specific steps according to the facilitator's MRT manual. During the actual group, MRT participants mark progress through a paired workbook, assisted by their provider.

Those aspects of MRT that increase the likelihood of generalizability (e.g., manualization) may also make faithful implementation difficult. All cognitive behavioral interventions are complex, dynamic, and, ultimately, individualized. Group is the delivery medium (indeed, in a group where the membership is likely to change with each meeting), which provides a particularly dynamic environment, especially with a culturally diverse clientele (Pitner & Sakamoto, 2005). The audience for MRT adds additional confounds to FOI. Offenders are complex and challenging clients. They often resist change and may have learning problems (Rankin, 2005).

MRT clients progress according to their development. Individuals complete most steps and assignments within the group; however, some work is checked by the provider outside the group. Thus, effective providers need to be organized, manage time efficiently, track the individual progress of members, manage changing group membership, and, most importantly, have a ready and deep grasp of the MRT protocol so that they may implement it with fidelity. In addition to the usual individual delivery factors, MRT providers must account for the treatment fidelity factors of group facilitation. Groups may be as small as eight or as large as 15 (Little & Robinson, 2009). Members move in and out. Group may be the medium of treatment delivery, but the MRT manual and training does not emphasize group skill development.

In addition to member and intervention complexity, variations in training and education among trainers may challenge fidelity (Bellg et al, 2004). Typically, MRT training is five days. There are multiple training options, including advanced training ("Correctional Counseling Inc. Training Events," n.d.). When assessing treatment fidelity across multiple providers, there will be variation in when and where providers undertook training. Trainer effectiveness, provider receptivity to training, and provider competency in various related, relevant skills affect treatment fidelity (Bellg et al. 2004). Thus, the developers of MRT may be more likely to deliver it with fidelity than trained providers. Therefore, it is difficult to draw conclusions from outcome data when providers other than its developers deliver MRT because they may not follow the protocol as closely or they may not be as skilled in its delivery (Armstrong, 2003).

Purpose of the Study

Though MRT has wide-acceptance (NREPP, 2008), there have been questions about FOI. We could not find any studies addressing MRT treatment fidelity. Armstrong (2003) in a study on MRT's effectiveness in reducing recidivism in youth offenders, summarized the developer as researcher and its impact on treatment fidelity issue succinctly: "meta analytical evidence demonstrating the relationship between researcher involvement and program effect suggests the portability of programs needs to be carefully considered" (p. 669). This raises at least two questions regarding the portability of MRT. Do providers implement MRT according to the researcher's design? Do providers implement MRT with therapeutic skill, e.g., group counseling skills? The primary purpose of this study was to assess non-MRT developer provider adherence to those portions of MRT that are explicitly described (i.e., MRT steps), as well as those that are described by not explicitly taught (i.e., group counseling skills).

Methods

Participants

The appropriate Institutional Review Boards approved this study. This study included nine different MRT providers who contracted with a statewide federal probation agency presentencing program for offenders.

Since this study was a part of a program evaluation, the agency required participation of all of its providers. The agency agreed that all information would be used for program rather than individual evaluation. Providers received a confidential career development report worth approximately $50 for their time. Each participant had previously completed MRT training, though the period since the training ranged from 1 to 9 years. The providers' level of education ranged from a high school diploma (4 facilitators) to a Bachelor's degree (2 facilitators) to a Master's degree in counseling (3 facilitators). The three facilitators with Master's degrees also held state counseling licenses, e.g., LPC.

Data Collection Procedures

Data were collected from 10 different MRT meeting sites. There were nine providers; one provider led two MRT groups. Of the 10 sites included in the analysis, seven were visited and evaluated four times while three were visited and evaluated three times due to programming changes. MRT meeting locations included public meeting rooms, as well as two held within minimum-security facilities.

We gathered ratings data using in vivo observation and videotape review. At least one researcher collected data per MRT meeting. There were two raters attending meetings during most of the first round of meetings. Meetings were videotaped. The third author, an advanced doctoral student and licensed counselor completed all of the GPIRS assessments (Burlingame, et al., 2002). Two raters evaluated the MRT sessions using the MICk. Both raters completed MRT provider training as developed by its creators. The primary rater, a co-developer of the MICk, received a significant portion of the workshop training from Gregory Little, MRT's co-developer.

Instrumentation

We used direct and video observation to rate provider fidelity to MRT with two tools: the MICk and the GPIRS (Burlingame et al., 2002).

MICk. The MICk was an instrument created by the authors of this study. When creating a measure of FOI, practitioners most frequently rely on self-report, permanent product reviews, and direct observation (Sheridan, Swanger-Gagné, Welch, Kwon, & Garbacz, 2009). Unfortunately, relying on providers to estimate their own implementation often results in unreliable estimates (e.g., Jones, Wickstrom, & Friman, 1997). Therefore, we assessed FOI with outside observers using a standardized instrument. We developed the MICk as a provider quality assessment tool, since none existed for MRT. A brief checklist is included in the MRT training packet (NREPP, 2008). As a provider quality assessment tool for MRT, the checklist was neither sufficiently comprehensive nor behaviorally defined. Although best practices in treatment fidelity urge the use of an appropriate means of assessment (Bellg et al., 2004), the literature offers little guidance on tool development (Song, Happ, & Sandelowski, 2010).

We reviewed the MRT facilitator's manual to identify the multiple, critical steps of MRT. The team identified two separate types of activities or behaviors that would relate to FOI: (a) observable activities that needed to be followed in a particular order (e.g., MRT steps), and (b) those skills that were more inferential and needed to be in place throughout the MRT session (e.g., group facilitation skills). The MRT manual includes 12 steps (e.g., Step 1 or Step 8). These are sequential and redone until the participant completes them successfully. Within each of those steps, there are several sub components (e.g., Step 2 Shield & Life Integrity). Providers follow a series of tasks within each major component. These tasks are based upon the responses of the individual group member responses (e.g., "Ask the client if he or she has been using drugs"). We developed items from each of the 12 steps specified in the MRT participant workbook and the provider training manual, as well as the training session that one of the team members attended. Next, we revised the MICk after receiving input from the head of the statewide MRT program, a trained MRT facilitator. Before finalizing the instrument, we conducted a pilot study to evaluate the instrument's inter-rater reliability.

The final version of the MICk is a 15-page checklist, covering each of MRT's 12 steps and related items for each session (see Appendix A for the front page of the MICk). The checklist style format was easy to score. Higher order activities were subdivided into discrete behaviors. For example, providers during Step 2 enforce the rules for the activity called the "Life Wheel," which include four behavioral items (e.g., "client sits while presenting"). MRT requires providers to work in a sequential fashion with each participant. Raters select a page for each offender based upon their current MRT "step." We only rated offenders who presented. Thus, if the particular group included 11 offenders who presented, the raters would complete 11 pages of documentation, one per offender. Each page included a checked box next to each task a provider needed to follow. A checked boxed showed that the provider correctly followed the task. If the provider failed to follow the task, an "X" was marked in the box. If a task was not relevant to a particular offender, the rater left the box empty.

We conducted an inter-rater reliability analysis of the MICk to determine the relationship of agreement between raters. Given that the MICk is a new instrument, the inter-rater reliability and validity analysis was unknown. Early in the data collection, two raters completed the MICk while observing the same MRT group. An individual rater, however, collected most of the data. We calculated inter-rater reliability using consensus and consistency estimates. Data entered into Excel (Microsoft, 2007) spreadsheets were used to calculate consensus reliability. Overall, raters agreed on 78.5% of all observations (see Table 1). Consensus estimates above 70% are considered acceptable (Stemler, 2004). When correlating the number of tasks judged to be correct by each observer trained in MRT, the resulting agreement was a Pearson's r = 0.85, which is also considered acceptable for research purposes (Stemler), though not necessarily for high stakes decisions (Kottner, et al., 2011). These two estimates of reliability suggest that the raters showed acceptable levels of agreement on items and consistently applied the MICk within an acceptable range.

GPIRS. Group facilitation is fundamental to MRT (Anderson, Feimer, & McKeown, 2009; Little & Robinson, 2009). Little and Robinson (2009), the manual authors, assume that group skills require minimal training. There is no mention of specific qualifications (e.g., training) needed to run a successful MRT group. Thus, we assessed provider group facilitation skills with a standardized, existing instrument.

The GPIRS (Burlingame, Fuhriman, & Johnson, 2002) is an observer-rated measure of group leadership. The GPIRS appears to have concurrent validity with the Hill Interaction Matrix and the Group Climate Questionnaire, two standard measures of group leadership (Chapman, Baker, Porter, Thayer, & Burlingame, 2010). Chapman et al (2010) conducted a validation study of the 48 items assessing three domains of group leadership: group structuring (7 items; Cronbach's alpha internal consistency 0.75), verbal interaction (21 items; Cronbach's alpha internal consistency 0.89), and emotional climate (20 items; Cronbach's alpha internal consistency 0.81). Overall, the internal consistency is 0.93. Each domain is defined and has operational aspects. Group structuring is defined, for example, as developing boundaries and norms and contains the operational aspects of "identification," "explanation," and "facilitation." Raters assess leadership skills along a 5-point Likert-type scale (did not occur = 0; poor = 1; adequate = 2; well-done = 3; excellent = 4). For the present study, we used the GPIRS to measure group leadership skills related to MRT, as well as the extent to which the providers were using basic group facilitation skills. The third author completed the GPIRS during each observed group session.

Results

MRT Adherences by Component and Provider (MICk)

We entered data from the MICk into an Excel spreadsheet to calculate descriptive statistics. Overall, we observed nearly 1,100 MRT tasks (see Table 1, "MRT Adherence by Component"). MRT tasks were treated as nominal data. For the purposes of data analysis, we chose to utilize descriptive statistics to help understand how frequently providers were following the steps as recommended. In the intervention integrity research, percentage of steps reported correct is the most common metric (e.g., Sanetti & Fallon, 2011). In all, providers (n = 9) correctly completed 78.9% of the tasks on the MICk. Based on guidelines recommended in 2005 by Perepletchikova and Kazdin (less than 50% reflects low levels of integrity while greater than 80% reflects high levels of integrity), this approaches the threshold of "high" levels of treatment integrity. The lowest level of accuracy was for Step 3 Acceptance at 64.6% (82 steps observed). Providers completed five steps with 100% accuracy. The frequency count for total number of tasks observed for these components (range of 6 to 23 observations) ranked in the bottom 8 of 21. We observed some components infrequently or not at all, (e.g. "Step 9"). Of the 21 possible components, "Step 1 Testimony," "Step 3 Worries," "Step 4 Things in Life," and "Step 5 Best/Worst" accounted for nearly 40% of the tasks observed. The components with the lowest percentage of tasks performed correctly included "Step 3 Acceptance," "Step 4 Major Life Events," "Step 10 Trading," and "Step 11 Best/Worst." Table 2 shows the preceding data disaggregated by location of MRT delivery site, (i.e., provider). The range for steps that were followed by individual providers correctly was 71.1% to 85.3%.

Provider use of Group Therapy Skills (GPIRS)

We compiled data from GPIRS score sheets into an Excel spreadsheet. The rater assessed leadership skills along a 5-point Likert-type scale (did not occur = 0; poor = 1; adequate = 2; well-done = 3; excellent = 4). Zero scores were not calculated. The average score on the GPIRS was 1.45 (see Table 2). Provider GPIRS scores ranged from 1.0 to 1.93. The overall scores on the GPIRS fell between the "poor" (level 1) and "adequate" (level 2), with no provider receiving an aggregate score at "adequate" or higher. In a somewhat unexpected finding, individuals with master's degrees in counseling did not obtain the highest GPIRS scores and there appeared to be little relationship between educational level and observed group therapy skills.

Discussion

The providers of MRT evaluated in this study displayed high levels of following behavioral steps accurately, but low levels of group counseling skills. FOI was deemed to be a necessary construct to evaluate to understand a possible reason for the mixed outcomes produced by non-developers of MRT. For example, Anderson and colleagues (2009) found that MRT had a limited effect on functional outcomes for a statewide implementation of MRT with an offender population. Although MRT produces outcomes similar to other cognitive behavioral therapy treatment programs for offenders, the overall effect size for MRT, is small (r = .16) (Ferguson & Wormith, 2012). None of the studies we found accounted for FOI. Therefore, we sought to explore whether trained MRT providers implemented MRT in settings removed from the program's developers.

MRT purportedly can be learned and implemented by anyone completing training, regardless of prior educational background (Little & Robinson, 2009; "Correctional Counseling Inc., MRTTM Facilitator Training," n.d.). The results of our study suggest that the providers trained in MRT followed the steps with reasonable, though not perfect accuracy (m = 78%; range = 71%-85%). These data refer to procedural adherence.

Providers correctly follow four out of five of the manualized components as measured by the MICk. During the observations, some steps were implemented more frequently than others. Based on the data represented in Tables 2, providers implemented MRT steps 1 ("Pyramid"), 2 ("Testimony"), and 5 ("Circle"). They administered relatively high percentage of Steps 4 and 5, however, in the wrong order, incorrectly, or simply skipped them. These error rates also continued into steps 6, 8, 10, and 11. Some of these errors may be due to a drifting phenomenon (Bellg et al., 2004) whereby individual providers fall away from protocols over time.

The relationship between FOI rates and treatment effectiveness is unclear (Dane & Schneider, 1998; Sanetti & Kratochwill, 2009). As such, there is no "acceptable threshold" for FOI. Rigid adherence to manualized steps, which may occur in an effort to achieve 100% FOI, may impede a treatment's therapeutic effect (Hagermoser, Sanetti, & Kratochwill, 2009; Perpletchikova & Kazdin, 2006). For example, Barber et al. (2006) found a U-shaped relationship between FOI and outcomes, with extremely high rates of FOI corresponding to lower rates of treatment effectiveness. For example, the treatment effects of therapeutic alliance may make issues such as FOI moot (Barber et al., 2006; Webb, DeRubeis, & Barber, 2010). This suggests that delivery factors may be as important as the treatment itself.

One delivery factor is group leadership and intervention skills. The overall scores on the GPIRS fell between the "poor" and "adequate" levels, with no provider scoring at the "adequate" level or higher. This may suggest that this component of MRT, which is more difficult to operationalize than simply following "steps" of an intervention, may be overlooked in training. These results suggest that MRT trainees may not come with or can readily acquire group facilitation skills as suggested by Little and Robinson (2009). Alternately, MRT may not use group dynamics and processes in ways measured by the GPIRS. Finally, it is possible that the scripted and sequential nature of MRT makes using group therapy skills difficult.

Limitations and Implications

We did not focus on MRT treatment outcomes; rather we focused on FOI for MRT. Although we examined a statewide program, our sample size of providers was small and geographically constrained. The structure of MRT lends itself to the development of an instrument such as the MICk to assess FOI. As a newly developed tool, the reliability of the MICk is not established. The reliability scores from the current study suggest, however, that it might be used to make low-stakes (i.e., reversible) decisions, such as identifying steps of the MICk that can be improved, and not for high-stakes (i.e., permanent) decisions, such as assessing research outcomes, dramatic program changes, or personnel decisions (Kottner et al., 2011). We suggest further refinement of the MICk to ensure that providers and raters find it useful for formative and summative evaluations and that it functions as a resource for researchers and providers (e.g., during MRT meetings). Only those steps that occurred in the group sessions were observed as many steps occur within a private meeting between the provider and an offender.

We encourage future effectiveness research on MRT and other CBT programs to include measures of treatment fidelity to check consistency of delivery. This is an important aspect in evaluating research outcomes (Alvarez-Jiminez et al., 2008; Barber et al., 2004; Bellg et al., 2004; Leventhal & Friedman, 2004; Lichstein et al., 1994; Miller & Binder, 2002; Miller, Sorensen, Selzer, & Brigham, 2006; Sanetti & Kratochwill, 2007; Witt & VanDerHeyden, & Gilbertson, 2004). Moreover, repeated use of measures of treatment fidelity may assist in establishing effective therapeutic base rates for MRT. This would have a practical, clinical application, as well. Although FOI of MRT by our providers was acceptable (range = 71.1 to 85.3 percent), a target adherence rate of 90 percent or higher may be desirable (e.g., Sheridan et al., 2009). We are mindful, however, that too much adherence might have a negative treatment effect (Barber et al., 2006). In addition, since MRT occurs in a group milieu, our results from the GPIRIS suggest researchers may wish to investigate the nature of MRT groups and how group factors and leadership skills operate within this context.

Treatment fidelity is an issue that, if not addressed, reflects a threat to the internal validity of effectiveness studies (Sanetti & Allen, 2011). Intervention fidelity hardly appears in the MRT research base and there has been even less effort to understand it. The latest meta-analysis suggest that MRT's effect size is small, $r = 0.16$ (Ferguson and Wormith, 2012). Little and Robinson, MRT's developers, have conducted nearly all of the peer-reviewed studies on MRT and have demonstrated the highest levels of success (Wilson et al., 2005). This raises concerns of portability (e.g., Wright, et al, 2012). One such factor might be FOI, which has not been addressed by previous researchers. This study was the first to explore a portion of treatment fidelity known as FOI of MRT by a small group of providers trained in MRT. Our results suggest that these providers trained in MRT implemented it with moderate to high accuracy. However, it must be noted that merely following the steps of a protocol should not be confused with competence (Perepletchikova & Kazdin, 2005). In fact, the constructs may not be strongly related (Miller & Binder, 2002). Group therapy skills for the sample fell well below acceptable levels. Future research might establish reliable and valid instruments for assessing FOI (e.g., the MICk).

References

Adler, A. (1938). *Social interest, a challenge to mankind*. London, UK: Faber and Faber.
Allen, L. C., MacKenzie, D. L., & Hickman, L. J. (2001). The effectiveness of cognitive behavioral treatment for adult offenders: A methodological, quality-based review. *International Journal of Offender Therapy & Comparative Criminology, 45*(4), 498–514.
Alvarez-Jimenez, M., Wade, D., Cotton, S., Gee, D.; Pearce, T., Crisp, K., & Gleeson, J. F. (2008). Enhancing treatment fidelity in psychotherapy research: Novel approach to measure the components of cognitive behavioural therapy for relapse prevention in first-episode psychosis. *Australian & New Zealand Journal of Psychiatry, 42*(12), 1013–1020.
Anderson, W. D., Feimer, S., & McKeown, S. (2009). *An evaluation of Federal Probation and Pretrial Services' Moral Recognition Therapy (MRT) program*. Vermillion, SD: The University of South Dakota Government Research Bureau.
Armstrong, T. A. (2003). The effect of Moral Reconation Therapy on the recidivism of youthful offenders: A randomized experiment. *Criminal Justice and Behavior, 30*(6), 668–687.
Barber, J. P., Foltz, C., Crits-Christoph, P., & Chittams, J. (2004). Therapists' adherence and competence and treatment discrimination in the NIDA Collaborative Cocaine Treatment Study. *Journal of Clinical Psychology, 60*(1), 29–41.
Barber, J. P., Gallop, R., Crits-Critoph, P. Frank, A., Thase, M. E., & Weiss, R. D. (2006). The role of therapist adherence, therapist competence, and alliance in predicting outcome on individual drug counseling: Results from the National Institute Drug Abuse Collaborative Cocaine Treatment Study. *Psychotherapy Research, 16*, 229–240.
Bellg, A. J., Borrelli, B., Resnick, B., Hecht, J., Minicucci, D. S., Ory, M., Czajkowski, S. (2004). Enhancing treatment fidelity in health behavior change studies: Best practices and recommendations from the NIH Behavior Change Consortium. *Health Psychology, 23*(5), 443–451.
Brooks, F. P. (1995). *The mythical man-month: Essays on software engineering* (2nd ed). Boston, MA: Addison-Welsley.
Burlingame, G. M., Fuhriman, A., & Johnson, J. E. (2002). Cohesion in group psychotherapy. In J. C. Norcross (Ed.), *Psychotherapy relationships that work: Therapist contributions and responsiveness to patients* (pp. 71–87). New York, NY: Oxford University Press
Chapman, C. L., Baker, E. L., Porter, G., Thayer, S. D., & Burlingame, G. M. (2010). Rating group therapist interventions: The validation of the Group Psychotherapy Intervention Rating Scale. *Group Dynamics: Theory, Research, and Practice, 14*(1), 15–31. doi: 10.1037/a0016628
Correctional Counseling Inc. MRTTM facilitator training. (n.d.). Retrieved from https://www.ccimrt.com/training/mrt-facilitator-training
Correctional Counseling Inc. training events. (n.d.). Retrieved from https://www.ccimrt.com/training/trainings
Dane, A. V. & Schneider, B. H. (1998). Program integrity in primary and early secondary prevention: Are implementation effects out of control? *Clinical Psychology Review, 18*(1), 23–45.
Daugherty, D. A., Murphy, M. J., & Paugh, J. (2001). An examination of the Adlerian construct of social interest with criminal offenders. *Journal of Counseling & Development, 79*(4), 465–471.

Ferguson, L. M., & Wormith, J. S. (2012). A meta-analysis of moral reconation therapy. *International Journal of Offender Therapy and Comparative Criminology.* doi:10.1177/0306624x12447771

Gerdes, K. E., & Stromwall, L. K. (2008). Conation: A missing link in the strengths perspective. *Social work, 53*(3), 233–242.

Hofmann, S. G., Asnaani, A., Vonk, I. J. J., Sawyer, A. T., & Fang, A. (2012). The efficacy of cognitive behavioral therapy: A review of meta-analyses. *Cognitive Therapy and Research, 36*(5), 427–440.

Jones, H. A., Clarke, A. T., & Power, T. J. (2008). Expanding the concept of intervention integrity: A multidimensional model of participant engagement. *In Balance, 23*, 4–5.

Jones, K. M., Wickstrom, K. F., & Friman, P. C. (1997). The effects of observational feedback on treatment integrity in school-based behavioral consultation. *School Psychology Quarterly, 12*, 316–326.

Kohlberg, L. (1976). Moral stages and moralization: the cognitive-behavioral model approach. In T. Lickona (Ed.), *Moral development and behavior: theory, research, and social issues.* New York: Holt, Rinehart and Winston.

Kolbe, K. (2004). *Powered by instinct.* Phoenix, AZ: Momentus Press.

Kottner, J., Audige, L., Brorson, S., Donner, A., Gajewski, B. J., Hróbjartsson, A., & Streiner, D. L. (2011). Guidelines for reporting reliability and agreement studies (GRRAS) were proposed. *International Journal of Nursing Studies, 48*(6), 661–671.

Leventhal, H., & Friedman, M. A. (2004). Does establishing fidelity of treatment help in understanding treatment efficacy? Comment on Bellg et al. *Health Psychology, 23*(5), 452–456.

Lichstein, K. L., Riedel, B. W., & Grieve, R. (1994). Fair tests of clinical trials: A treatment implementation model. *Advances in Behaviour Research & Therapy, 16*(1), 1–29.

Little, G. L., & Robinson, K. D. (1988). Moral Reconation Therapy: A systematic step-by-step treatment system for treatment resistant clients. *Psychological Reports, 62*(1), 135–151.

Little, G. L., & Robinson, K. D. (1989). Treating drunk drivers with Moral Reconation Therapy: A one-year recidivism report. *Psychological Reports, 64*, 960–962.

Little, G. L., & Robinson, K. D. (1996). *How to escape your prison: A Moral Reconation workbook.* Memphis, TN: Eagle Wing Books.

Little, G. L., & Robinson, K. D. (2009). *MRT facilitator's handbook.* Memphis, TN: Eagle Wing Books, Inc.

Little, G. L., Robinson, K. D., & Burnette, K. D. (1990). Treating drunk drivers with Moral Reconation Therapy: A two-year recidivism study. *Psychological Reports, 66*, 1379–1387.

Little, G. L., Robinson, K. D., & Burnette, K.D. (1991). Treating drug offenders with Moral Reconation therapy: A three-year recidivism report. *Psychological Reports, 69*, 1151–1154.

Little, G. L., Robinson, K. D., & Burnette, K.D. (1993). Cognitive behavioral treatment of felony drug offenders: A five-year recidivism report. *Psychological Reports, 73*, 1089–1090.

Little, G. L., Robinson, K. D., Burnette, K. D., & Swan, E.S. (1999). Successful ten-year outcome data on MRT-treated felony offenders: Treated offenders show significantly lower reincarceration in each year. *Correctional Counseling, Inc., 8*(1), 1–24.

Microsoft. (2007). Microsoft Excel [computer software]. Redmond, Washington: Microsoft.

Miller, S. J., & Binder, J. L. (2002). The effects of manual-based training on treatment fidelity and outcome: A review of the literature on adult individual psychotherapy. *Psychotherapy: Theory, Research, Practice, Training, 39*(2), 184–198.

Miller, W. R., Sorensen, J. L., Selzer, J. A., & Brigham, G. S. (2006). Disseminating evidence-based practices in substance abuse treatment: A review with suggestions. *Journal of Substance Abuse Treatment, 31*(1), 25–39.

Noell, G. H. (2008). Research examining the relationships among consultation process, treatment integrity, and outcomes. In W. P. E. S. M. Sheridan (Ed.), *Handbook of research in school consultation: Empirical foundations for the field* (pp. 315-334). Mahwah, NJ: Erlbaum.

NREPP, SAMSHA. (2008). *Intervention summary*. SAMSHA's National Registry of Evidence-based Programs and Practices. Retrieved from http://www.nrepp.samhsa.gov/ViewIntervention.aspx?id=34.

Perpletchikova, F., & Kazdin, A. E. (2005). Treatment integrity and therapeutic change: Issues and research recommendations. *Clinical Psychology: Science and Practice, 12*(4), 365–383.

Pitner, R. O., & Sakamoto, I. (2005). The role of critical consciousness in multicultural practice: Examining how its strength becomes its limitation. *American Journal of Orthopsychiatry, 75*(4), 684–694. doi: Doi 10.1037/0002-9432.75.4.684

Rankin, C. E. (2005). Illiterate prisoners? Myths and empirical realities. Journal of Offender *Rehabilitation, 41*(2), 43–55. doi: 10.1300/J076v41n02_03

Robbins, M. S., Feaster, D. J., Horigian, V. E., Puccinelli, M. J., Henderson, C., & Szapocznik, J. (2011). Therapist adherence in brief strategic family therapy for adolescent drug abusers. *Journal of Consulting and Clinical Psychology, 79*(1), 43–53.

Salvia, J., Ysseldyke, J. E., & Bolt, S. (2007). *Assessment: In special education and inclusive education (10th ed.)*. New York: Houghton Mifflin.

Sanetti, L. M. H., & Kratochwill, T. R. (2007). Treatment integrity in behavioral consultation: Measurement, promotion, and outcomes. International Journal of Behavioral *Consultation and Therapy, 4*(1), 95–114.

Sanetti, L. M. H., & Kratochwill, T. R. (2009). Toward developing a science of treatment integrity: Introduction to the special series. *School Psychology Review, 38*(4), 445–459.

Sanetti, L. M. H., & Fallon, L. M. (2011). Treatment integrity assessment: How estimates of adherence, quality, and exposure influence interpretation of implementation. Journal of *Educational and Psychological Consultation, 21*, 209–232.

Sedgley, N. H., Scott, C. E., Williams, N. A., & Derrick, F. W. (2010). Prison's dilemma: do education and jobs programmes affect recidivism? *Economica, 77*(307), 497–517. doi: 10.1111/j.1468-0335.2008.00751.x

Sheridan, S. M., Swanger-Gagne´, M., Welch, G. W., Kwon, K., & Garbacz, S. A. (2009). Fidelity measurement in consultation: Psychometric issues and preliminary investigation. *School Psychology Review, 38*, 476–495.

Song, M. K., Happ, M. B., & Sandelowski, M. (2010). Development of a tool to assess fidelity to a psycho-educational intervention. *Journal of Advanced Nursing, 66*(3), 673–682. doi: 10.1111/j.1365-2648.2009.05216.x

Stemler, Steven E. (2004). A comparison of consensus, consistency, and measurement approaches to estimating interrater reliability. *Practical Assessment, Research & Evaluation, 9*(4). Retrieved from http://PAREonline.net/getvn.asp?v=9&n=4

Van Vugt, E., Gibbs, J., Stams, G. J., Bijleveld, C., Hendriks, J., & van der Laan, P. (2011). Moral development and recidivism: A meta-analysis. *International Journal of Offender Therapy and Comparative Criminology, 55*(8), 1234–1250. doi:10.1177/0306624X11396441

Webb, C. A., DeRubeis, R. J., & Barber, J. P. (2010). Therapist adherence/competence and treatment outcome: A meta-analytic review. *Journal of Consulting and Clinical Psychology, 78*(2), 200–211.

Welsh, B. C. (2004). Monetary Costs and Benefits of Correctional Treatment Programs: Implications for Offender Reentry. *Federal Probation, 68*(2), 9–13.

Wilson, D. B., Bouffard, L. A., & Mackenzie, D. L. (2005). A quantitative review of structured, group-oriented, cognitive-behavioral programs for offenders. *Criminal Justice and Behavior, 32*(2), 172–204.

Witt, J. C., VanDerHeyden, A. M., & Gilbertson, D. (2004). Troubleshooting behavioral interventions: A systematic process for finding and eliminating problems. *School Psychology Review, 33*(3), 363–383.

Wright, B. J., Zhang, S. X., & Farabee, D. (2012). A squandered opportunity?: A review of SAMHSA'S National Registry of Evidence-based Programs and Practices for offenders. *Crime & Delinquency, 58*(6), 954–972

Table 1
Percent of tasks performed correctly MRT Adherence by Component
—Entire Sample

		# not correct	# correct	total # observed	Percent Performed Correctly	Descriptive Label[a]
Step 1	Pyramid	1	54	55	98.2%	High integrity
	Testimony	22	86	108	79.6%	
	Shield & Life	0	23	23	100.0%	High integrity
Step 2	Life Wheel	0	14	14	100.0%	High integrity
	Testimony	1	34	35	97.1%	High integrity
Step 3	Worries	42	98	140	70.0%	
	Acceptance	29	53	82	64.6%	
Step 4	Things in Life	19	92	111	82.9%	High integrity
	Major Life	6	12	18	66.7%	
	Best/Worst	27	66	93	71.0%	
Step 5	Circle	4	47	51	92.2%	High integrity
	Important Relationships	5	12	17	70.6%	
Step 6	How I Helped	0	17	17	100.0%	High integrity
	Trading	18	52	70	74.3%	
Step 7	Years to Live	0	6	6	100.0%	High integrity
	Master	0	6	6	100.0%	High integrity
Step 8	Action Plan	3	8	11	72.7%	
Step 9						
Step 10	Trading	10	21	31	67.7%	
	Best/Worst	29	47	76	61.8%	
Step 11	Circle	5	45	50	90.0%	High integrity
	Testimony	11	72	83	86.7%	High integrity
Step 12						
Total		232	865	1097	78.9%	

Note. There were no items in steps 9 and 12 that could be directly observed during a group session. a—Based on guidelines established by Perepletichikova & Kazdin (2005).

Table 2
MICk & GPIRS Scores by Location

Location	Steps Performed Correctly	Steps Not Performed Correctly	Steps Observed	% Performed Correctly	GPIRS average score (Scale out of 4)
1	51	11	62	82.3%	(NA)
2	64	11	75	85.3%	1.15
3	63	13	76	82.9%	(NA)
4	87	15	102	85.3%	1.03
5	95	31	126	75.4%	1.58
6	208	40	248	83.9%	1.58
7	113	46	159	71.1%	1.13
8	54	15	69	78.3%	1.65
9	88	18	106	83.0%	1.93
10	94	36	130	72.3%	1.55

Appendix A

MICk front page
MRT Integrity Check (MICk)—version
Group Name:
Date:
Front page (Completed Every Session)—General group information

General group information	Observation	Provider Report
How many times a week does MRT group meet?	‹	‹
Is there a processing group separate from the MRT group?	‹	‹
Does the group have a list of written rules?	‹	‹
Are they enforced?	‹	‹
How many members are in the group? (8–15 is ideal).	‹	‹
How many clients are scheduled to testify?	‹	‹
How many clients actually testified?		
How many clients did NOT testify because there was not enough time?		
How many clients did NOT testify because they (the clients) were not prepared?		

Each Session	
New member introductions.	Yes No NA
Did this happen first?	Yes No
Facilitator checked homework. (Create new step appropriate page for each client)	Yes No
Followed through if homework was not completed before group.	Yes No NA
Number of members who completed homework/total.	_____/_____
Number of members who have their workbook/total	_____/_____
Did facilitator check homework at the start of session (after introductions if appropriate)	Yes No
Is the facilitator part of the circle?	Yes No
Preparation for next group.	
A. Did the facilitator ask the members to prepare a step or exercise for the next group at the end of group session?	Yes No
B. Did they get a commitment from the member of what they will have prepared for the next group meeting?	Yes No

Power struggles	Yes No
Is MRT kept separate from other treatments?	Yes No
Was group task oriented?	Yes No

www.ingramcontent.com/pod-product-compliance
Lightning Source LLC
Chambersburg PA
CBHW071443150426
43191CB00008B/1218